THE IMPOSITION OF METHOD

THE IMPOSITION
OF METHOD

═══

A Study of Descartes
and Locke

═══

BY

PETER A. SCHOULS

CLARENDON PRESS · OXFORD
1980

Oxford University Press. Walton Street, Oxford OX2 6DP

OXFORD   LONDON   GLASGOW
NEW YORK   TORONTO   MELBOURNE   WELLINGTON
KUALA LUMPUR   SINGAPORE   JAKARTA   HONG KONG   TOKYO
DELHI   BOMBAY   CALCUTTA   MADRAS   KARACHI
NAIROBI   DAR ES SALAAM   CAPE TOWN

Published in the United States
by Oxford University Press
New York

British Library Cataloguing in Publication Data

Schouls, Peter A
    The imposition of method.
    1. Descartes, René–Knowledge, Theory of
    2. Locke, John–Knowledge, Theory of
    3. Knowledge, Theory of
    I. Title
    121'.092'2   B1878.K6   79–41041

    ISBN 0–19–824613–7

*Set, printed and bound in Great Britain
by Billing and Sons Limited,
Guildford, London, Oxford and Worcester*

To
Jeanette,
Tim, Lynn, and Michelle

ACKNOWLEDGEMENTS

Several parts of this study are based on work already in print. Chapter II incorporates a good deal of 'Descartes and the Autonomy of Reason', published in the *Journal of the History of Philosophy*, X (1972), 307–22. Sections 1 and 2 of the third chapter incorporate parts of 'Reason, Method and Science in the Philosophy of Descartes'; this article was published in the *Australasian Journal of Philosophy*, 50 (1972), 30–9. Some parts of 'The Extent of Doubt in Descartes' *Meditations*', from Volume III (1973) of the *Canadian Journal of Philosophy*, pp. 51–8, have found their way into the first two sections of Chapter IV. Chapter VI presents an extensively rewritten version of 'The Cartesian Method of Locke's *An Essay Concerning Human Understanding*'; its original appeared in Volume IV (1975) of the *Canadian Journal of Philosophy*, pp. 579–601. Some of the paragraphs of section 4, Chapter III, are to appear in a *Festschrift* for T. A. Goudge, edited by members of the Philosophy Department of the University of Toronto and to be published by the University of Toronto Press; they appear there in the essay 'Peirce and Descartes: Doubt and the Logic of Discovery'. I wish to thank the editors and publishers in question for their permission to make use of these various items.

I am grateful to the University of Alberta for study leave granted for the entire academic year of 1972–3, and again for the first term of 1976–7. It was during these periods that this study was conceived and much of it was written. Thanks are due also to the Canada Council for support through a Leave Fellowship during the first of these periods. The second term of 1976–7 was spent as a Visiting Professor at the Free University of Amsterdam. A series of lectures to members of the staff and graduate students of its Department of Philosophy have helped much to give my ideas on Descartes's and Locke's methodology a coherent form. A special boon was the presence at the Free University of Dr. E. D. Fackerell, Senior Lecturer in the Department of Applied Mathematics at the University of Sydney, Australia; he generously gave of his sabbatical time to help me with the third section of Chapter III.

Many students and colleagues have contributed to this study through their encouragement and criticism. Persistent probing from Richard I. Aaron (Aberystwyth) forced me to rewrite several parts of Chapter VI. Equally persistent criticism from Hendrik Hart (Institute of Christian Studies, Toronto) led me to become clearer about both the nature of methodology and the status of scientific knowledge in Descartes's work. John W. Yolton (who, to the grief of Canadian philosophers, has left Toronto's York University to return to Rutgers) has helped me clarify the argument of especially Chapter VII.

My debt to friends and colleagues at the University of Alberta's Department of Philosophy is very great indeed. Patricia Brunel provided excellent manuscript typists through the services of Shari Berge and Anne Nield. My colleagues Richard Bosley and John King-Farlow generously gave me of their time; I am especially grateful to them for their willingness to read the entire penultimate typescript. Their very many suggestions concerning both style and content have made this a far better book than it would have been without their assistance.

I dedicate this book to my wife, and to our children. They cheerfully made it possible for me to spend my days in the seclusion I needed to be able to write.

Edmonton   P. A. S.
December 1978

CONTENTS

I

THE NEW METHOD
AND THE MODERN MIND

1. A rationale

There is no dearth of comprehensive studies on the philosophy of Descartes, nor on that of Locke. In several scores of recently published articles there is an even greater abundance of writing on many details of their positions. I do not propose to set another book alongside those dealing quite generally and comprehensively with either Descartes or Locke; neither do I intend to deal with some more or less isolated details of their positions. I propose rather to consider one pervasive aspect which, I hold, is insufficiently explored: that of methodology.

With respect to Descartes, scholars have devoted a great deal of attention to his 'method'. There nevertheless remains much to be said about the relationship between Cartesian method and reason, about the nature of method itself, and about how Descartes's method is related, for example, to the argument of his *Meditations*.[1] With respect to Locke relatively little has been said about his views on method and their illuminating relation to

[1] Three books which appeared after this study was completed aptly illustrate the point that more reflection on the nature and role of Descartes' method is in order. Margaret Dauler Wilson's *Descartes* (London, 1978) pays a good deal of attention to the notion of 'general doubt', but does not explore its methodological nature. Considerations of methodology are, in fact, almost entirely absent from this book. Since, by Descartes's own admission, the argument of the *Meditations* is structured by his method, Wilson's discussion of the *Meditations* apart from methodological considerations often leads to misinterpretation. In his *Descartes against the Skeptics* (Oxford, 1978) E. M. Curley misinterprets Descartes's position when he argues that there are two distinct methods in Descartes's work, one presented in the *Regulae* and one in the *Discourse*. Only the latter, according to Curley, includes the principle of doubt. Curley then further misinterprets Descartes by limiting the method which functions in most of Descartes's works to 'the method of doubt'. Bernard Williams, in *Descartes: The Project of Pure Enquiry* (Hassocks, Sussex, 1978), presents a good though limited account of Descartes's method. But also in his discussion of the *Meditations* his arguments sometimes stop short of providing an adequate exposition because of occasional insensitivity to the relevance of matters of a methodological nature. (For a more detailed discussion of these three books, see my review in *Philosophical Books*, Vol. 20, No. 2, May 1979.)

Descartes's. Perhaps this is because it has often been assumed that the most important issues of Lockean methodology are to be seen as related to his 'historical, plain method'; it is further assumed that there is little to be said about that method. There are, however, much more important methodological aspects of Locke's work. Once these aspects, revealed in his *Essay concerning Human Understanding*, are brought into focus, we shall find a striking similarity between Descartes's and Locke's methodology. In contemporary scholarship this similarity has been inadequately examined, with even those findings discussed by very few. Moreover, if these methodological aspects are kept in mind when one reads some of Locke's other writings, it becomes clear that they are of considerable help in forming sound interpretations of these works. For to a large extent they structure their arguments and determine their concepts. As far as I know there has been no important contemporary literature on the relation between the *Essay*'s methodology and the argument of the *Second Treatise of Government*, nor on that between his methodology in the *Essay* and its application in *A Paraphrase and Notes on the Epistles of St. Paul*. This study therefore deals with some of these insufficiently explored areas in the works of Descartes and Locke. One part of my task is to bring into focus the relationship between their positions, especially in terms of methodological similarity.

In the course of this study there will be many points of contact with related issues in contemporary scholarship. At times this contact will consist in providing support for my argument by indicating that others have reached conclusions similar to mine on certain points. At other times it will lead to the settling of problems left unresolved by others. And at times it will reveal the inadequacy of attempts to deal with such problems, or of existing statements about certain features of Descartes's or Locke's position. For reasons like these I take this study to be capable of illuminating several basic issues for the student of Descartes and Locke.

In the light of contemporary evaluations of Locke it is somewhat surprising that scholars have not paid greater attention to the area of methodology in his writings. For it is not as if the importance of Locke with respect to methodology has remained unnoticed. Let me mention just two instances. Maurice Cranston's concluding sentence of *John Locke, A Biography* is 'Locke did not merely

enlarge men's knowledge, he changed their ways of thinking'.[2]
More picturesquely, Gilbert Ryle wrote that:

It is not much of an exaggeration to say that one cannot pick up a sermon,
a novel, a pamphlet or a treatise and be in any doubt, after reading a
few lines, whether it was published before or after the publication of
Locke's *Essay concerning Human Understanding*, which was in 1690.
The intellectual atmosphere since Locke has had quite a different
smell from what it had before Locke. If we could fly back in a time-
rocket to England in 1700, we could already breathe its air, and we
could already converse with our new acquaintances there without
feeling lost. In the England of, say, 1600, we should gasp like fishes
out of water.[3]

To 'change . . . ways of thinking' would, one might say, involve
an approach to subject-matter different from that taken in previous
centuries. And one might assume that it is this different method
of approach which accounts at least to a considerable extent for
the difference in 'intellectual atmosphere' in the England of the
year 1700 as compared to that of the previous age. One might
infer that, if twentieth-century man feels himself a stranger in
the England of 1600 but feels at home in that of 1700, the change
in ways of thinking presented in Locke's *Essay* at least in part
accounts for the fact that he can converse with his late seventeenth-century 'acquaintances'; and if that inference is correct, it
may well indicate that twentieth-century man still shares with
Locke these changed ways of thinking.

Grant the correctness of the statement that Locke changed
man's ways of thinking. Grant that Western man still possesses
this changed manner of thinking. It can then be said that although
the seventeenth century's exuberant confidence in reason has by
and large disappeared, the stance of that earlier century, taken up
with respect to any matter of which one seeks knowledge, is still
very influential in the present. Because this stance is known to
have grave shortcomings, not least of these being the fragmenta-
tion to which it led in the politics of individualism and nationalism,
and its attendant inequities in capitalist economics, it may well
deserve to be recognized as outmoded. To show what, precisely,
this stance or method of approach really is, to make clear why this
method of approach is bound up with a particular view of reason

[2] Maurice Cranston, *John Locke, A Biography* (London, 1957).
[3] Gilbert Ryle, 'John Locke', *Critica*, Vol. 1, No. 2, 1967, p. 3.

and a particular view of man, to explain how it presupposes a particular nature of the object to be known, or how it imposes such a nature on the object—these are tasks I have set myself in this study. The first elaborate articulation and implementation of this stance or method of approach was given by Descartes. A less elaborate articulation though equally thorough implementation of it is to be found in Locke. Therefore this study is about these seventeenth-century thinkers. But to the extent that twentieth-century thought and practice is still cast in a seventeenth-century mould, this study is meant to be of relevance to the twentieth century. Questions as to what extent contemporary thought and practice fits this mould I will have to leave here largely to the reader's judgement. Nevertheless, it is important to be critical with respect to the principles which underlie our thought and practice. To the extent that this stance involves presuppositions about the nature of reason and man, and about the nature of the object of knowledge, it is also important to examine these pre-suppositions and either adopt them as one's own or reject them. If they are rejected, retention of this stance will call for a justification different from that given by Descartes. Personally I do not believe that its retention is a viable option. Neither do I believe that a justification of it substantially different from that provided by Descartes can be found. Elaboration of these comments is not, however, part of the task I have set myself in this study. Instead, this study may be seen as a preliminary step necessary for such an elaboration. For it is an exposition of the 'changed way of think-ing' in its first important articulations and in some of its first consistent implementations.[4]

⁴ There are several reasons why I select Descartes and Locke rather than, for example, Hobbes and Descartes, or Hobbes and Locke. First, whether in the seventeenth or in succeeding centuries, Hobbes's influence never approached that of Descartes or Locke. Secondly, to the extent that Hobbes's method in-volved a genuinely universalized method, this was expressed especially in his *Leviathan* (1651) and *De Corpore* (1655). Both of these works saw the light more than a decade after Descartes's *Discourse on Method* (1637) was well known in England. (An English translation of the *Discourse* appeared as early as 1649, with a preface by the influential Cambridge Platonist Henry More.) Finally, a work which argues that the characteristic contents of Hobbes's political philosophy is 'determined by and, as it were, implied in the method of resolution and com-position' has already been written by J. W. N. Watkins (*Hobbes's System of Ideas*, London 1965). The quotation in the previous sentence is from p. 16 of Watkins's book. Watkins, in turn, quotes it from Leo Strauss, *The Political Philosophy of Hobbes* (Oxford, 1936), p. 2.

2. The break with tradition

That in important respects there is much continuity in terms of central doctrines and attitudes from the medieval to the modern mind is a view which is becoming generally accepted among historians and philosophers. The work of John Herman Randall Jr. is possibly the most important single factor which has led to this view during the past two decades.[5] I do not want to deny the importance of Randall's scholarship. Nevertheless, it remains true that, in spite of such a degree of continuity, there are profound differences between the modern and medieval mind. And perhaps the major difference between the two arises from matters of methodology. In brief, that can be stated as follows. An individual approach to particular kinds of subject-matter (which, for instance, in physics culminated in its clear expression in Galileo's science) was replaced in the seventeenth century by a general method through which, it was held, any kind of subject-matter must be approached, if knowledge of that subject was to be attained. Owing to the efforts of Descartes more than anyone, the fundamental principles of a single methodology came to be applied to mathematics, physics, medicine, and metaphysics. Through the writings of Locke, this same methodology was applied to political theory and theology. This universalization of method, this single approach to all objects of knowledge, is a crucial element in the constitution of the new mentality, and appears as a new element in history. It makes legitimate the application of the phrase 'modern man' as a term quite distinct from 'sixteenth-century man' or 'medieval man'.

Giacomo Zabarella (1532–89) formulated the classic version of the teaching of the influential school of Padua on method 'in the terms and with the distinctions later so fruitfully employed and consciously expressed by Galileo'.[6] For Zabarella, logic and method

---

[5] Especially important is Randall's 'The Development of Scientific Method in the School of Padua', first published in the *Journal of the History of Ideas*, Vol. 1, No. 2, Apr. 1940, pp. 177–206. This article is reprinted in *Renaissance Essays*, eds. Paul O. Kristeller and Philip P. Wiener (New York, 1968), pp. 217–51. In the rest of this chapter I shall refer to this article as 'The Development . . .', and shall identify quotations in terms of the pagination of the original place of publication. Equally important is Randall's *The Career of Philosophy*, Vol. I (New York, 1962). I shall refer to this work as *The Career* . . ..

[6] Randall, 'The Development . . .', p. 196.

become interchangeable terms. He identifies method with logic, and also gives great prominence to the ancient concepts 'resolution' and 'composition', which occur in Aristotle and, for example, in Galen (c.130–c.200) and Boethius (c.475–c.525). In these two respects Zabarella is notably close to the modern attitude. There are, however, several elements which distinguish his position from that of the seventeenth century. Especially important is his characterization of logic or method as an 'instrumental discipline, created by philosophers from the practice of philosophy'.[7] Method is not yet fully seen as the exemplification of the procedure of reason; and even if it is partially seen as such an exemplification, it is treated as pertaining to the procedure of certain forms of reasoning, of reasoning syllogistically. This limitation of method in terms of the procedure of a single specific discipline, or of only a limited number of disciplines, is what makes Zabarella a transitional figure.

The universalization of method, its identification with logic (though not with syllogistic logic) is characteristic of modern man. This characteristic is not accidental, but definitive. For Descartes, man is essentially a rational being.[8] Moreover, as I shall show in Chapter III, for Descartes 'methodic reasoning' means the same as 'correct reasoning', and both of these expressions he would take to be pleonasms. Going about one's intellectual pursuits methodically is going about one's intellectual pursuits rationally. But the connotation of 'rational' now is broader than that of 'successful at reasoning syllogistically'. A new content, a content different from that given by Aristotle and his medieval followers, has therefore been given to the concept 'rational'. Since reason, both before and during the seventeenth century, is taken to be definitive of man; and since in the seventeenth century the connotation of 'rational' differs from that in earlier centuries, the seventeenth century presents us with a new definition of man. When we come to Locke it is not possible to speak of a new definition of man

---

[7] As quoted by Randall, 'The Development . . .', p. 196.

[8] See e.g. the *Discourse on Method* (HR1, 82; AT6, 2; and HR1, 117; AT6, 58), the *Meditations on First Philosophy* (HR1, 190; AT7, 78), and the Author's Letter prefaced to the *Principles of Philosophy* (HR1, 205; AT9–2, 4). Wherever possible the quotations from Descartes's writings are from the translation of Haldane and Ross, *The Philosophical Works of Descartes*, Vols. I and II (Cambridge, 1911), abbreviated as HR1 and HR2. The second reference in each case is to the Adam and Tannery, *Œuvres de Descartes* (Paris, 1965–75).

without qualification. For Locke, man is a substance, and in our ideas of substances we must distinguish between real and nominal essences, and we can only be said to know man's nominal essence. In practice, however, this does not present a picture different from that provided by Descartes. Locke holds that the 'proper difference' wherein man and beast are 'wholly separated' is to be found in the 'power of Abstracting', a power possessed by man but not by beasts, a power which therefore 'puts a perfect distinction betwixt Man and Brutes' (2.11.10–11).[9] This 'power of Abstracting', which I shall discuss in a later chapter as related to one of the two characteristic aspects of the new method, is also identified by Locke as one of the two fundamental aspects of reasoning. For most practical and theoretical purposes man is a 'corporeal rational creature' (3.11.16), that is, a corporeal reasoning creature. It is not his somewhat different corporeal features but his power of reasoning which distinguishes him from beasts. Reasoning, therefore, at least as far as man's nominal essence is concerned, is definitive of man. And, as will become clear in a later chapter, reasoning is tied up with method just as much for Locke as reason is tied up with method for Descartes. Since the concept of method will be seen not to differ essentially from Descartes to Locke there is, then, also for Locke a new definition of reasoning, and hence a new definition of man.

To say that a new definition of reason, a new concept of method, distinguishes modern from medieval man is too sweeping a historical generalization if it is left to stand without qualification. For, although it is valid with respect to many, probably most, influential thinkers and movements, it must first be recognized that (A) to advance this generalization is not to say that there are no additional aspects characteristic of modern man and which are not found in his predecessors. Next it should be emphasized that (B) not every major thinker since the sixteenth century can be characterized in terms of this distinction. (As will be seen in the next part of this chapter, this characterization does not hold without qualification even for some of the truly influential thinkers in the early part of the seventeenth century.) A few remarks on both these points are in order.

[9] Quotations from the *Essay concerning Human Understanding* will give Book, Chapter, and paragraph in Peter H. Nidditch's edition (Oxford, 1975). In all quotations I have omitted the italicization of this edition.

Point A. The application of the new method will, as Descartes states, lead to knowledge in mathematics, metaphysics (which 'contains the principles of knowledge, among which is the explanation of the principal attributes of God'), physics ('in which having found the true principles of material things, we examine generally how the whole universe is composed'), and the 'branches' of physics ('medicine, mechanics, and morals') (HR1, 211; AT9-2, 14). The new method will therefore make it possible for man to attain a kind of 'wisdom' which consists in 'a perfect knowledge of all things that man can know, both for the conduct of his life and for the conservation of his health and the invention of all the arts' (HR1, 203-4; AT9-2, 2). In short, the principles of the new method, once we 'employ them in all those uses to which they are adapted', will make it possible for us to 'render ourselves the masters and possessors of nature' (HR1, 119; AT6, 62). An important additional characteristic of modern man is thus his unlimited trust in natural reason, his expectation of deliverance from drudgery, evil, and sickness through consistent application of the new method. It is therefore in the context of a passage in which Descartes expresses his trust in the new method that we also find the statement about man's anticipated mastery over nature. Statements to be made in a moment may well give grounds for the position that the ideal of mastery over nature is a characteristic more generally descriptive of modern man than is the methodological stance articulated by Descartes. In Descartes's works, however, the ideal of mastery appears as a concomitant notion: it accompanies the new stance taken up towards all subject matter.

In connection with *Point A,* it should be stressed that there are further concomitant aspects which are distinctive of modern man. His trust in natural reason alone signals a decisive break with other earlier attitudes. For this kind of trust excludes an interpretation of man which would place him in a framework which transcends his natural existence and natural context; or if it does not totally exclude such an interpretation, it at least does so for all practical purposes. Modern man's stance therefore makes irrelevant a Platonic relation of man to the Good, or an Augustinian–Thomistic relation of man to God.[10]

[10] David Gauthier has written that 'To characterize a person as rational is not to relate him to any order, or system, or framework, which would constrain his

Point B. When one speaks in this manner about modern man and modern man's stance, some qualifications are in order to the extent that this stance is further characterized in terms of a view of logic or methodology which, basically, involves reference to concepts like *resolution* and *composition*. For it cannot be claimed that all Western thinkers have accepted terms which express those concepts as descriptive of what is essential in human reasoning. The views on logic of Hegel and Marx present us with clear exceptions. In spite of these exceptions, however, some of the concomitant aspects remain present even in the case of these thinkers. Especially, it is the motif of mastery over nature which is present in Hegel and Marx—a motif from which some contemporary neo-Marxists struggle to escape. They see it as a presupposition which Western man inherited from the Enlightenment, as a presupposition which underlies Western man's theory and practice, as a presupposition which is symptomatic of an outmoded stance.[11] Is the ideal of mastery over nature more fundamentally and generally descriptive of modern man than is the methodological stance articulated by Descartes? That is a question I must here leave unresolved.

3. Resolution and composition

In the previous section I introduced the terms 'resolution' and 'composition' as characteristic aspects of the new method. These terms, as I indicated, already had a long history behind them when they were adopted by Zabarella. The details of this history, the various shifts in their meaning and their importance within dis-

---

activities. It is not, as Plato thought, to relate man to the Good. It is not, as St. Thomas thought, to relate man to God.' This new (negative) content of 'rational' Gauthier calls 'the modern Western view of man', a 'presupposition' which 'underlies our scientific theories and our social practices'. Cf. Gauthier's 'Reason and Maximization', *Canadian Journal of Philosophy*, Vol. IV, No. 3, Mar. 1975 pp. 411–33; esp. pp. 412–13.

[11] See e.g. M. Horkheimer and T. W. Adorno, *Dialectik der Aufklärung: Philosophische Fragmente* (Frankfurt am Main, 1947; S. Fischer Verlag, 1969, pp. 47–8). Also H. Marcuse, *One Dimensional Man: Studies in the Ideology of Advanced Industrial Society* (London, 1964), pp. 153–5. And J. Habermas, *Technik und Wissenschaft als Ideologie* (Frankfurt am Main, 1968; and Suhrkamp Verlag, 1971, pp. 80–4). See further the discussion of this aspect of neo-Marxism in Jacob Klapwijk's *Dialektiek der Verlichting* (Amsterdam, 1976).

cussions of methodology especially at the University of Padua, I need not go into. On this subject I do not find that Randall's scholarship (in the two works mentioned before) stands in need of either correction or augmentation.

The use of the terms 'resolution' and 'composition' became almost commonplace during the period between Zabarella's death (1589) and the publication of Descartes's *Discourse on Method* (1637). In discussions on method during these years, the Greek terms ἀναλυτική and συνθετική came to be used as synonymous with the Latin *resolutiva* and *compositiva*, and by the year 1600 the former had carried over into Latin as *analytica* and *synthetica*.[12]

In Galileo's 'new science', the joint use of the *metodo risolutivo* and the *metodo compositivo* is well known.[13] In their as yet non-universalized form, that is, as borrowed from the mathematical or physical sciences rather than as an expression of reason's universal procedure, they came to be used in many other disciplines during the years following the publication of Galileo's works. They came to be adopted, for example, by some of that period's most influential theologians, such as Arminius, and jurists, such as Grotius.

Arminius, in the second of his Private Disputations ('On the Method in which Theology must be Taught', 1610), writes:

It has long been a maxim with those philosophers who are the masters of method and order, that the theoretical sciences ought to be delivered in a synthetical order [*ordine compositivo*], but the practical in an analytical order [*vero resolutivo*], on which account, and because theology is a practical science, it follows that it must be treated according to the analytical method [*methodo resolutiva*].[14]

Even more than those of Arminius, the writings of Grotius were of influence in the seventeenth century. His *De Jure Belli ac*

---

[12] The synonymity of 'resolution' and 'composition' with 'analysis' and 'synthesis', although not commonplace before this time, was present in some medieval works. It is already found in the twelfth century in the writings of Grosseteste. Cf. A. C. Crombie, *Robert Grosseteste and the Origins of Experimental Science* (Oxford, 1953), p. 63 ff.

[13] For an account, see Randall's *The Career . . .*, pp. 339–60.

[14] *The Works of James Arminius*, Vol. II, translated by James Nichols, Auburn and Buffalo, 1853, p. 10. Note how in his translation Nichols has no qualms about rendering *compositivo* as 'synthetical' and *resolutivo* as 'analytical'. The fact that these sets of terms had become interchangeable by the time of Arminius's writing provides justification for this translation.

Pacis Libri Tres (1625) was perhaps his most influential work. During Locke's lifetime alone it went through twenty-six editions in Latin and three editions in the English translation (not to mention translations into most of the other major European languages). In it, these concepts of the new method (but a method adapted from mathematics or physics, thus still in its non-generalized form) clearly present themselves. Grotius writes that 'With all truthfulness I aver that, just as mathematicians treat their figures as abstracted from bodies, so in treating law I have withdrawn my mind from every particular fact.'[15] The methodological principle of resolution or analysis is explicitly introduced, for instance in his statement that 'The moral goodness or badness of an action, especially in matters related to the state, is not suited to a division into parts; such qualities frequently are obscure, and difficult to analyse.'[16] By this statement Grotius does not mean that the concept 'moral goodness of an action' cannot be subject to a process of resolution; for this concept is not 'atomic' or 'basic' for him. The point is, rather, that since this concept contains various other concepts or ideas, and since it is not at all easy to see at first glance or even after a less superficial examination which these are, such a concept is *'difficult* to analyse' and does not easily lend itself to a 'division into parts'. It is not that, in this statement, Grotius indicates an inadequacy in this method. What he does point out is that even if one adopts the method employed by the mathematicians, its use does not obviate sustained and careful work. In the pages following those of *De Jure*'s Prolegomena, Grotius uses this method when, in Book I, he finds it necessary to explain the nature of sovereignty. He then makes it quite clear that the rights of the ruler of a nation can only be explained in terms of arguments which deduce these rights from the rights possessed by the individual persons who constitute the nation. In other words, the question of whether rulers are to be obeyed or may be legitimately disobeyed is to be answered by an argument which takes its point of departure from the irreducible 'simplest elements' of 'individuals'. It is no longer the Platonic or Aristotelian *polis* which is the explanatory principle of a ruler's rights;

[15] Hugo Grotius, *De Jure Belli ac Pacis Libri Tres*, Prolegomena, para. 58. The parallel Grotius draws between the method of mathematics and the method of the science of the law of nature is especially clear in *De Jure*, Book II, ch. 20, section 43, sub. 1.
[16] *De Jure*, Book I, ch. 3, section 9, sub. 2.

the concept of the autonomous individual takes over this role. In this argument, the concept of the state, of the politically organized community, is taken to be that of an 'effect' which needs to be explained. This 'effect' is explained through a 'division into parts'. The 'part' beyond which no division is possible, and which thus becomes the 'cause' or explanation of the 'effect', is the 'individual'. It is then to the individual, rather than to the *polis,* to which the notion of rights is made to apply fundamentally; and hence the ruler's rights are explained in terms of those of the individual.[17] Because of the non-universalization of method, one also finds many passages in this work which still present a medieval or a Greek picture. In the early parts of *De Jure*'s Prolegomena, for example, one reads that 'among the traits characteristic of man is an impelling desire for society, that is, for the social life—not for any and every sort, but peaceful, and organized to the measure of his intelligence, with those who are of his own kind; this social trend the Stoics called "sociableness" ' (para. 6). It is the mainte- nance of this peaceful, intelligently organized social life, of this 'social order', which he there considers 'the source of law properly so called' (para. 8). If one emphasizes the presence of the second of these two strands in Grotius's work, this makes him more of a transitional figure than a modern figure. Nevertheless, the concepts of the new method, though still borrowed from science, were present. They did help structure his political theory, to such an extent that some of the starting-points for Grotius's arguments as well as some of his arguments' conclusions, are in many respects close to those of Locke's *Second Treatise of Government.*

To speak about Grotius as a 'transitional figure' is useful because it can help us to see a point about the method of resolution and composition which should be noted at the outset. (i) If the method of resolution and composition is taken to be the method of a parti- cular science (say, of mathematics, or of physics) so that other sciences (like political theory, or theology) need a different approach, then the method of resolution and composition is one method among others. Its applicability is limited to a specific discipline, or to a few specific disciplines. It is not taken to be the universal method. Thinkers who, in the late sixteenth or early seventeenth century, considered the method of resolution and

[17] *De Jure,* Book I, ch. 3, section 8, sub. 1, 2; section 10, sub. 5; ch. 4, section 2, sub. 1, 2, 6.

composition limited in its application in this way may be said to be 'pre-modern'. (ii) Grotius did not consider this method to be limited in its application to specific disciplines. On the other hand, neither did he take the method of the mathematicians to be a particular application of the general method. Because he was impressed with the results achieved through the application of this method in mathematics, he began to apply it in a discipline other than mathematics, namely, in political theory. But because he did not take the method of mathematics to be a particular application of the general method, he applies it in political theory alongside, or supplementary to, another method. Thus when Grotius explains the rights of a ruler over his subjects in terms of an argument which is based on a 'simplest element', on the concept of 'autonomous individual', he may be said to be applying the general method. When, however, in the same work, he bases 'law' on a different kind of concept, on that of 'society'—a concept different in kind from that of 'individual', because 'society' may be said to 'contain' the concept 'individual', and may be said to need to be explained in terms which involve the concept 'individual'—he may be considered to be using a different method. One could say that, in *De Jure*, there is both a 'reductionistic' and a 'holistic' approach to the subject-matter. Each of these two approaches is given a limited application within one and the same discipline. Because there is this limited application within the confines of a specific discipline, I call Grotius a 'transitional figure'. (iii) If the method of resolution and composition is taken to be the general method, that is to say, if this method is taken to be the only method which one can apply with respect to any subject-matter if one is to gain systematic knowledge of that subject matter, the limitation of neither (i) nor (ii) above is present. This attitude is characteristic of the modern mind. It does not, however, imply that there may be no limitations to the application of the process of resolution within a specific discipline. This point can be illustrated easily in terms of doctrines held by Descartes. Descartes holds that, in a discipline like arithmetic, fundamental concepts like 'unity' or 'equality' may well come before the mind in a cluster of other concepts. One may well become aware of 'unity' through being confronted with a statement like 'two and three are equal to five'. If one understands this statement one must know what is meant by 'two', 'three, and 'five'. But to be able to handle these concepts correctly, one must possess the concept 'unity'. To have the latter concept before the mind clearly and distinctly in this case calls for resolution of the cluster of concepts presented in 'two and three are equal to five'. But once, through resolution of this proposition, one has the concept 'unity' before the mind clearly and distinctly, no further resolution of this concept is possible. For the concept 'unity' is an epistemic atom, utterly 'simple', in no way complex. More interesting illustrations can be drawn from Descartes's metaphysics. In metaphysics, it is not just 'simple' concepts like 'unity' and 'equality' (or, more to the point, concepts like 'thought' and 'existence') which play a fundamental role. There are also certain fundamental principles which serve to link these concepts. Such principles are, according to Descartes, known *per se*, and also in this doctrine of 'knowledge *per se*' a limitation of the process of reduction is implied. Take the principle: 'The cause is as great as or greater than the effect.' If one cannot 'see' this principle to be self-evident, reduction into its simple or simpler parts ('cause', 'greater than', 'effect') will not lead to knowledge of this principle. One may well become aware of this principle for the first time by means of resolution to its simple(r) parts of an argument in which this principle plays a role. However, once this principle has been separated from that context, it will either be known *per se* or not known at all. In the latter case, further resolution will not lead to knowledge of it. Thus, even though the causal principle 'contains' several concepts and therefore cannot be said to be 'simple', application of the process of resolution to the causal principle itself is not a step in the process of getting to know this principle; for the smallest unit of knowledge that can be a unit of knowledge in this case is this principle as a whole. Thus, within any specific discipline, there are limits to the application of the principle of resolution. This does not mean that, once one has reached these limits, further knowledge may be gained through the application of a different method: there is no different method available. Instead, it means that once resolution must stop, one has reached the foundational elements of the discipline in question. These foundational elements may differ from one subject-matter to the next. For Descartes, they are concepts like 'unity' and 'equality' in arithmetic; and in metaphysics they are concepts like 'thought' and 'existence' and principles like the causal principle.

In the years between Zabarella's death and the publication of the *Discourse*, references to mathematics (rather than to medicine or physics) begin to appear frequently in discussions of method. Grotius, as we have just seen, explicitly related his procedure in political theory to that of the mathematicians in their disciplines. The emergence of mathematics into prominence, as Randall states, was 'due to its cultivation by a small group of men working on the periphery of the main intellectual movement of the sixteenth century'. Its importance must not be underestimated. For, in Randall's words:

The mathematical methods of analysis and synthesis of Archimedes . . . were the one element which neither the fourteenth-century Ockhamites nor the sixteenth-century Paduans possessed. From them, the mathematicians took their start, and carried the day for the quantitative side of the Paduan discussion. . . . With this mathematical emphasis added to the logical methodology of Zabarella, there stands complete the 'new method'. . . . By the analysis of the mathematical relations involved in a typical 'effect' or phenomenon we arrive at its formal structure or 'principle'. From that principle we deduce further consequences, which we find illustrated and confirmed in experience. Science is a body of mathematical demonstrations, the principles of which are discovered by the resolution of selected instances in experience. This is the method called by Euclid and Archimedes a combination of 'analysis' and 'synthesis', and by the Paduans and Galileo, 'resolution' and 'composition'.[18]

In one important respect too much is claimed for mathematics in this statement. All of science is said to be 'a body of mathematical demonstrations'. This may imply that it is after all the mathematical method which comes to be elevated to universal method. This implication seems present also when Randall writes that what 'the Italian mathematicians down through Galileo . . . found in the ancients and what they worked upon themselves was no mathematical vision of the world, but effective techniques and practical problems of procedure and discovery'; that it 'remained for Descartes' to present this 'mathematical vision of the world', to show that 'science is a body of mathematical demonstrations'.[19] Too much is claimed for mathematics for—to use Robert McRae's words—'method was not derived from mathematics but applied

[18] Randall, 'The Development . . .', pp. 204–6.
[19] Loc. cit.

to mathematics' by Descartes.[20] That this identification of 'the mathematical method' with 'the new method' is incorrect will become clear in the next chapter.

When we come to Descartes we can adopt the terms 'analysis' and 'synthesis', as well as the terms 'resolution' and 'composition', as descriptive of the two major characteristics of the new, now universalized, method.

Descartes's method has two aspects to it. First, there is the deriving and isolating from one another of 'simple entities'. This procedure has been called one of 'analysis', 'reduction', 'resolution', or 'division'. It is to result in an intuitive grasp of the end-products of this process. However—as is clear from what he writes, notably under the Third point of his *Reply to Objections II* (HR2, 38; AT7, 140)—Descartes does not call knowledge of these end-products 'science'. To gain systematic, that is, scientific, knowledge, a process which has been described as 'synthesis', 'composition', or 'combination' also has to take place. This process of synthesis is the second aspect of the Cartesian method. Without such composition there is no extension of knowledge; no science is generated.

The terms 'analysis' and 'synthesis' are used by Descartes himself in the context of discussions of method. But the term 'method' is not univocal for him; and this makes for a difference in connotation of 'analytic' and 'synthetic', a difference depending on the meaning of 'method'. A brief explication of this point will suffice at this stage.

When philosophers convey the results of their thinking to others they can, says Descartes, make use of either the analytic method or the synthetic method. When Descartes speaks this way (cf. HR2, 48–9; AT7, 155–6) he considers both of these as *methods of exposition*. The former is used by Descartes himself as the method of exposition in the *Meditations*. It involves first, resolution (or 'analysis') to 'simples' or to 'truths known *per se*' and second, (re)composition (or 'synthesis') to intelligible complexity. Of the synthetic method of exposition Descartes gives an illustration in the Appendix to his Reply to the second set of Objections brought against his *Meditations*. In this Appendix (HR2, 52–9; AT7,

[20] Robert McRae, *The Problem of the Unity of the Sciences: Bacon to Kant* (Toronto, 1961), p. 63.

160–70) he presents the *Meditations'* 'arguments demonstrating the existence of God and the distinction between soul and body' in 'geometrical fashion', that is, in the synthetic rather than in the analytic manner. As in geometry, the starting-points for the demonstrations consist of definitions, postulates, and axioms; and as in geometry, it is not shown how one obtains these definitions, postulates, and axioms. Because it does not show how the starting points are obtained, because the synthetic method of exposition omits the process of resolution to 'simples' or to 'truths known *per se*', it is not really suitable for philosophic or scientific exposition. (There is no *cogito* statement in the 'arguments . . . drawn up in geometrical fashion'; one does not work one's way to an 'Archimedean point' from which composition takes place.) On the other hand, the analytic method of exposition includes both analysis or resolution and synthesis or composition. This analytic method of exposition is therefore the method to be used in philosophy and in the sciences, and not just in their exposition but also in their development. Hence it is the analytic method which is also the method of discovery. This is because it embodies the two fundamental aspects of the procedure of reason: resolution or analysis (resolving complex items to their simpler or simplest constitutents), and composition or synthesis (combining simpler or simplest items into intelligible complex wholes). It is this procedure of reason which will be my central concern in this study.

The terminology of analysis or resolution, and of composition, though used more sparingly by Descartes himself than by contemporary commentators on his work, does appear in several passages. In the *Rules for the Direction of the Mind* we read that 'the ancient Geometricians made use of a certain analysis (*analysi*) which they extended to the resolution (*resolutionem*) of all problems'. In this context 'analysis' is identified as one of the 'inborn principles of the discipline here in question', one of the principles of the method whose 'province ought to extend to the eliciting of true results in every subject' (HR1, 10–11; AT10, 373). In a later passage of the *Rules* we read that 'there can be no falsity save in the . . . class . . . of the compounds made by the understanding' (*ab intellectu componuntur*) (HR1, 27; AT10, 399). And in the 'Dedication' of the *Meditations on First Philosophy* he writes that 'I had cultivated a certain Method for the resolution of difficulties of every kind in the Sciences' (*ad quaslibet difficultates in scientiis resolvendas*) (HR1, 134–5; AT7, 3).

Locke also, in passages relevant to a discussion of method, uses the terms 'resolution' and 'composition'. The specific activities which these terms are meant to describe for Locke are ones which, in important respects, are like or analogous to the activities which they describe for Descartes. In a later chapter I shall give grounds for the correctness of this assertion. My concern at present is simply to introduce terms which will be needed for my exposition, and to indicate the meaning of these terms in a preliminary fashion.

The terms 'resolution' and 'composition' occur in several important sections of Locke's *Essay concerning Human Understanding*. He writes that ' 'Tis not easie for the Mind to put off those confused Notions and Prejudices it has imbibed from Custom, Inadvertancy, and common Conversation: it requires pains and assiduity to examine its Ideas, till it resolves them into those clear and distinct simple ones, out of which they are compounded' (2.13.27). Also, to mention just one other passage, 'Justice is a Word in every Man's Mouth, but most commonly with a very undetermined loose signification: Which will always be so, unless a Man has in his Mind a distinct comprehension of the component parts, that complex Idea consists of; and if it be decompounded, must be able to resolve it still on, till he at last comes to the simple Ideas, that make it up. (3.11.9). In other passages he uses as terms apparently interchangeable with 'resolution' or 'decomposition' the words 'abstraction', 'separation', and 'definition'. Whether or not these terms all refer to the same activity will be examined in a later chapter.

Since there are contexts relevant to my argument where the terms 'resolution' and 'composition' occur in both Descartes and Locke I shall, in my discussion, make use of these terms unless the particular context makes advisable the use of terms which are interchangeable with them.

Without giving much further content to these concepts, it will be useful to make two further points about them. The first (i) concerns terminology used in discussions of methodology in the context of contemporary writings on Descartes. The second (ii) concerns the difference in meaning which some of these terms have in contemporary writings as compared with those of Descartes and Locke.

(i) Commentators on Descartes's method speak of the method (or rules) of analysis and synthesis, of the method of resolution and composition, or even use a phrase which combines a term from each of these two sets. Thus, L. J. Beck speaks of 'The rules of analysis and synthesis'.[21] Gerd Buchdahl identifies 'analysis' and 'resolution' in Descartes's methodology.[22] And Robert McRae writes of Descartes's method of 'analysis and combination'.[23] Although all these uses of such expressions are unobjectionable some others are problematic. John W. Yolton, for example, refers to Descartes's 'method of intuition or deduction'.[24] But whereas terms like 'analysis' and 'synthesis' belong under the heading 'method', terms like 'intuition' and 'deduction' belong under that of 'reason'. Although there is such an intimate connection between these sets of terms that there need be no fundamental objection to the identification, prima facie at least it involves a conflation of categories. An objection of a fundamental nature would have to be made if commentators were to describe Descartes's method as 'the mathematical method', for that might imply that the universal method had come about through a generalization of the method of mathematics . This phrase, although it occurs infrequently in contemporary writings, does occasionally present itself. Its most conspicuous occurrence is in the Haldane and Ross collection of Descartes's works.[25] In the (unsigned) foreword to this collection one reads that 'Clearly expressed are all Descartes' key ideas, as . . . the astonishingly fruitful concept that all phenomena of the universe (except mind) could by application of mathematical method be reduced to clear and readily formulated laws.' When this phrase occurs in writings on either Descartes or Locke it is often in a context of comments on passages like 'Those long chains of reasoning, simple and easy as they are, of which

[21] L. J. Beck, *The Method of Descartes* (Oxford, 1952). The phrase in question is the title of Chapter XI.

[22] Gerd Buchdahl, 'Descartes' Anticipation of a "Logic of Scientific Discovery" ', in A. C. Crombie, ed., *Scientific Change* (London, 1963), p. 406.

[23] McRae, *op. cit.*, p. 56.

[24] John W. Yolton, 'Philosophy of Science from Descartes to Kant', *History of Science*, Vol. 10, 1971, p. 108.

[25] Here it occurs on the inside of the front covers of the 1955 Dover edition. The phrase also occurs on pp. 5 and 7 of W. von Leyden's *Seventeenth-Century Metaphysics* (London, 1968); the context seems to indicate that von Leyden's phrase 'the mathematical method' is there to be taken as synonymous with 'the Cartesian method'.

geometricians make use in order to arrive at the most difficult demonstrations, had caused me to imagine that all those things which fall under the cognizance of man might very likely be mutually related in the same fashion' (*Discourse;* HR1, 92; AT6, 19); or 'General and certain Truths, are only founded in the Habitudes and Relations of Abstract Ideas. A sagacious and methodical application of our Thoughts, for the finding out these Relations, is the only way to discover all, that can be put, with Truth and Certainty concerning them, into general Propositions. By what steps we are to proceed in these, is to be learned in the Schools of the Mathematicians, who from very plain and easy beginnings, by gentle degrees, and a continued Chain of Reasonings, proceed to the discovery and demonstration of Truths, that appear at first sight beyond humane Capacity' (*Essay*: 4.12.7). These passages do not state that the method of approach to any subject-matter of which we may expect to obtain knowledge is the mathematical method. Instead, for a number of reasons, the method of the mathematical sciences is held up as a model, as an ideal. How the method of a particular science can be considered an ideal without this presupposing or leading to its generalization will be made clear in a later chapter.

(ii) The word 'analysis' is much in use in contemporary philosophy. It is not however a univocal concept. Some of its meanings are like those or at least related to those that would be given to it by Descartes or Locke. But some are quite different from what either of them would have had in mind when they used the term. For instance, a contemporary philosopher may be engaged in giving a conceptual analysis of something. Such an analysis would involve an attempt to be clear and precise about the concepts involved (and in this respect there are certainly affinities between the contemporary and Cartesian sense of 'analysis'); but it would also involve tracing connections between concepts—not necessarily analytic connections, but connections of various sorts. However, such tracing of connections places the concepts between or among which these connections are traced in a system; it places them in a system of contingent or necessary relations. Speaking here of 'analysis' would be misleading if we used the word in a Cartesian sense. For in the latter sense 'analysis' is 'resolution' or 'decomposition', while in the former it may involve 'construction' or even 'demonstration'. Only when a contemporary writer uses 'analysis' in a context of concepts being separated from more complex wholes or entities, is there anything like a close relationship to Cartesian 'analysis'.[26]

4. Rationalism and empiricism

Although Descartes never called himself a Rationalist, and Locke never called himself an Empiricist, and the 'two-party system of Rationalism versus Empiricism just did not exist' (as Ryle has put it),[27] there are nevertheless profound differences between these two, differences which could be couched in terms of labels like 'rationalism' and 'empiricism'. For it remains true that in Descartes's work sense perception has no foundational role, while in Locke's it has. It will therefore be helpful at this point to indicate how, without reading Locke through Cartesian spectacles, it is none the less possible to speak about 'the method' in both Descartes and Locke.

To do so implies the ascription of at least a high degree of methodological likeness to their respective works, and whether I am right to ascribe such a high degree of methodological likeness is a question to be settled by careful reconsideration of their relevant writings. Even if it is found that a fundamental method of Locke is also that of Descartes, there will remain important differences which clearly distinguish the two positions from one another; and perhaps the most important distinction which will remain is that of what one might call the difference in the status of the human mind's reasoning power. One might say that for Descartes, on the one hand, reason is thoroughly *autonomous* in a crucial sense which will be explicated in the next chapter. Locke, on the other hand, places restrictions on man's power of reasoning, which are incompatible with Descartes's view of such autonomy. Reason, for Locke, does of course remain autonomous in the sense that, for example, it is independent of faith: faith does not direct reason, but reason directs faith (4.17.24; 4.19.14). But he also

[26] The use of 'analysis' as 'separation' does of course appear in contemporary philosophical writing. D. W. Hamlyn, for example, writes about the 'temptation' of providing an 'analysis of the notion of knowledge' in terms of 'breaking down or reducing the notion of knowledge to something different'. D. W. Hamlyn, *The Theory of Knowledge* (London, 1970), p. 78.

[27] Ryle, op. cit., pp. 3–19.

writes: 'Unless the ideas of objects penetrate the mind there will be no subject-matter of reasoning, nor could the mind do more to the construction of knowledge than an architect can towards the building of houses if he falls short of stones, timber, sand, and the rest of building material.' As early as 1663 Locke held that in any example of human knowledge there is always something 'presupposed and taken for granted and derived from the senses by way of borrowing'.[28] The first Book of the *Essay* can be taken as a statement of this same position in terms of an attack upon and dismissal of the rival position of innate ideas.[29] Also in the *Essay* 'reason' is described in terms of its fundamental dependence on sense experience (as at 4.18.2). Locke therefore believes that a philosopher like Descartes who, prior to an examination of the particulars derived from sensation, proceeds to 'establish maxims . . . about the operations of nature' merely succeeds in making 'a world to himself, framed and governed by his own intelligence'.[30] If one wants to adopt the terminology of 'rationalism' and 'empiricism' it is not a matter of, say, both Locke's and Descartes's being thoroughgoing rationalists. It is rather a case where both an empiricist and a rationalist adopt the same methodological stance. This stance is based on a doctrine about the process of reason, and leads to a doctrine about the nature of the object which can become an object of knowledge. It is the affinity in doctrine about reason's process which accounts for the high degree of similarity in their methodology. It is, also, the affinity in doctrine about that process which leads them to a similar view of the nature of the object of knowledge.

To place the discussion about methodology in the context of rationalism and empiricism at this point is useful because it helps us to see how there remains an area for what was possibly a common methodology, without making us ignore the fact that some elements play a more extensive or very different role in one position from

---

[28] *John Locke, Essays on the Law of Nature,* translated and edited by W. von Leyden (Oxford, 1954), p. 149.

[29] This does not of course mean that the first Book of the *Essay* is directed primarily against Descartes's position. On this point, see John W. Yolton, *John Locke and the Way of Ideas* (Oxford, 1956).

[30] These statements are from Locke's *De Arte Medica,* 1668; the fragment from which they are taken can be found in Maurice Mandelbaum's *Philosophy Science, and Sense Perception: Historical and Critical Studies* (Baltimore, 1964), pp. 47–8. For a similar comment in the *Essay,* also possibly directed against Descartes, see 4.12.13.

that played in the other. It is also profitable because it at once makes clear that the terms 'rationalism' and 'empiricism' cannot be used, in this case, as indicative of elements present in the one position but quite absent from the other. Somewhat schematically, it can be put as follows, first with respect to Descartes and second with respect to Locke.

First: (i) If we assume Descartes's rationalism to be of a strictly innatist kind, we could say that the materials of knowledge are given to the mind by the mind; we could call this the rationalist principle. (ii) How (some or all of) these materials are given (as in systems of occasionalism) is part of a metaphysical discussion, which is of no relevance to the methodological issues I want to discuss. (iii) But what is meant by "mind" in (i) above? The use of 'mind' in that statement is not univocal. The 'mind' to which the materials of knowledge are given is reason, the understanding, or the natural light. (For the time being we may take these as interchangeable expressions.) The 'mind' which gives these materials of knowledge is the understanding, imagination, memory, and 'sense'. (iv) What is given by the understanding is clear and distinct and, if the things given are items at the foundation of science, they are simple or known *per se*. Once, on this foundation, a science is being constructed, imagination and memory come to play a role, but nothing given by 'sense' is needed in addition for the construction of the 'pure' sciences like mathematics, metaphysics, theoretical physics. What is given by the imagination and memory need not be clear and distinct, and generally is complex. To the extent that these items given by the imagination and memory are neither clear and distinct nor simple, a methodological procedure is called for to make these given things clear and distinct; this procedure is that of 'resolution' of complexity into simplicity. (v) In the proper construction of an applied science—as with a form of mechanics which is about the world in which we live—the things presented or given by the senses cannot be ignored. What is given by sense is neither clear and distinct, nor simple. Hence resolution of also these givens is called for. (vi) The construction of a scientific system, whether of a pure science [as in (iv)] or of an applied science [as in (v)] involves the methodological principle of composition. (vii) Items (iv) and (v) are in part about the construction of a system of knowledge. Such construction involves knowledge of the clear and distinct foundational elements, as well as of their combination or composition, and of the resulting system. Both the grasping and combining of foundational elements, as well as the grasping and combining of elements further removed from but still related to the foundational elements, are activities of reason. (viii) Furthermore, items (iv) and (v) show us something about the nature of the objects of knowledge, in terms of their simplicity at the foundation of a science, their complexity in the body of a science, and their clarity and distinctness in either case. (ix) Items (iii) to (viii) present a picture of an intimate relation between epistemological and methodological aspects of Descartes's position. (x) It will be seen that these epistemological and methodological aspects can be discussed apart from the metaphysical aspects implicit in items (i) and (ii).

Second: (i) According to Locke, ideas, which are the 'materials of knowledge', are 'given' to the mind by objects through the senses. We could call this the empiricist principle. It involves a causal theory of knowledge which rules out complete scepticism without having earlier reverted to Cartesian arguments against such scepticism. (ii) An account of how these ideas enter the mind through the senses would be part of a discussion which is of no relevance to the methodological issues I want to explore. (iii) Sensory experience provides sentient states. It will be shown that any sentient state is held by Locke to involve complexity, that is, that the form which one's experience initially takes is always characterized by the complexity of ideas experienced as coexisting. (iv) It will also be shown that Locke holds that the foundations of general knowledge are general ideas, basically, simple general ideas. (v) If one asks the methodological question of how one obtains simple general ideas, the answer is in terms of 'abstraction', 'decomposition', or 'resolution' of the complexity which characterizes the contents of one's sentient states. (vi) And if one asks the methodological question of how, once one has obtained these simple general ideas one proceeds to construct a body of knowledge, the answer introduces the term 'composition'. (vii) If it is asked why the complexity of ideas experienced as coexisting —compare item (iii)—cannot serve as the immediate foundation of knowledge, this introduces a discussion of the nature of reasoning. (viii) Items (iv) and (vi) tell something about the nature of the objects of knowledge, in terms of their simplicity or irreducibility at the foundation of a science and in terms of their complexity within a scientific system. (ix) Items (iii) to (viii) reveal an intimate connection between the epistemological and methodological aspects of Locke's position. (x) It will be seen that these epistemological and methodological aspects can be discussed apart from metaphysical aspects implicit in items (i) and (ii).

The two last items in these schematic statements about the positions of Descartes and Locke are similar. More important is that this similarity points back to a similarity present in some of the earlier items of both outlines: for example, 'resolution' plays a role in both item (iv) of the first and item (v) of the second outline; also, 'composition' is present in item (vi) of both the first and second outline. A conclusion to be drawn is that it is quite possible to discuss some central epistemological and methodological issues of both Descartes's and Locke's positions without the introduction of those metaphysical aspects which make their positions very different from one another. It will in fact become clear that one can speak of a high degree of methodological similarity without doing violence to the rationalist principle of the one or the empiricist principle of the other. And one can do this because—as will be shown in subsequent chapters—the terms 'resolution' and 'composition' stand for comparable activities in the works of Descartes and Locke.

The use of 'rationalist' and 'empiricist' in the previous paragraph (the first with respect to Descartes, the second with respect to Locke) should not be taken as an indication that 'empiricist' elements play no role in a discussion of Descartes' position, or that 'empiricist' elements play no role in the discussion of the methodology of both Descartes and Locke. That 'empiricist' elements must be considered at certain points in a discussion of Descartes's methodology is clear, for example, from the role 'sense' plays in the construction of an 'applied' science. (See item (v) of my first outline.) And that 'empiricist' elements regularly enter into a discussion of Locke's methodology is clear enough from items (iii) and (v) of the second outline. A similar statement could be made about the use of 'rationalist'. The point to be stressed is that the metaphysical aspects which make the two positions distinct need not be overlooked, but neither do they preclude a good deal of similarity in terms of methodological posture.

5. Scope of this study

As I stated in the opening paragraph of this chapter, I do not intend to provide a systematic exposition of all the important aspects of either Descartes's or Locke's works; instead, I will focus on a discussion of the method which, according to Descartes and Locke, is to be used if one is to be successful in obtaining (systematic) knowledge. Concentration on this general method does not exclude mention of other 'methods' or other 'methodological principles' which may be present in their writings. These other methods, or these other principles, will be introduced only to the extent that they help clarify the nature and function of the general method.

In preceding sections of this chapter the nature of method has been related to the nature of reason or to the nature of the reasoning process. For both Descartes and Locke the theory of method is intimately connected with a theory of knowledge, with a view of what is involved in reasoning. Descartes, in the *Rules for the Direction of the Mind,* writes that at least once during our lifetime we should undertake the kind of inquiry 'which seeks to determine the nature and scope of human knowledge', for 'in pursuing it the true instruments of knowledge and the whole method of inquiry come to light' (HR1, 26; AT10, 397–8). And whereas 'nothing can be known prior to the understanding, since the knowledge of all things else depends upon this and not conversely' (HR1, 24–5; AT10, 395), the inquiry into the nature and scope of human knowledge becomes one into the nature of reason. This inquiry involves two intricately related questions: (i) what is the nature of reason? and (ii) under what conditions can it function unhindered? (To pose question (ii) is to ask: under what conditions can it attain knowledge?) Similar statements could be made with respect to Locke's position. The question about the conditions under which knowledge can be obtained will turn out to be a question about methodology. The relevant conditions depend upon the nature of reason or, for Locke, upon the nature of reasoning; ultimately, for Descartes and Locke, they depend upon the nature of man (even though for Locke this is in terms of a nominal definition of man). A discussion of method, whether with respect to Descartes or Locke, will therefore have to be preceded by a discussion of reason(ing).

After a discussion of the nature of reason(ing) the ground is clear for an exposition of the nature of method. This exposition will lead to the conclusions that the nature of method determines the general nature of the argument of a system of knowledge, as well as to a large extent the nature of the concepts used in such an argument and the nature of the objects named by these concepts. In other words, the discussion of the nature of method will bring us to the conclusion that the nature of the body of knowledge which results from the application of the method, no less than the nature of the object of knowledge, is itself in part determined by the nature of method.

These abstract statements about methodology will in subsequent chapters be illustrated in terms of some arguments presented by Descartes and Locke. For Descartes this illustration will be provided in terms of parts of his work on geometry, and in terms of the first three of his *Meditations*. The discussion of these initial *Meditations* will also enable us to make explicit Descartes's justification for the general imposition of his method. For Locke, this illustration will be given in terms of his political theory as this is presented in the *Second Treatise of Government*, as well as in terms of certain aspects of his theology as these are presented in the *Letters Concerning Toleration, The Reasonableness of Christianity* and its *Vindications*, and especially in the *Paraphrase and Notes on the Epistles of St. Paul*.

Although this study is not meant to be a vindication of either Descartes's or Locke's position, some of the conclusions which may be drawn as the argument develops will reveal an internal strength in these positions at some points where many have argued for or assumed the existence of weaknesses. For example, contrary to Peirce's criticism of Descartes's principle of doubt, that principle will be shown not to be 'an idle and self-deceptive pretence'.[31] And contrary to the opinion of many contemporary critics, it will be shown that the argument of the first three of the *Meditations* is not viciously circular, at least not at the point where it has traditionally been supposed to be. Contrary to Laslett's view that there is only 'an accidental symmetry, an aesthetic coherence, between [Locke's] atomic view of matter and his atomic view of society', and that there is no 'formal consistency' between

[31] *Collected Papers of Charles Sanders Peirce*, eds. C. Hartshorne and P. Weiss (Cambridge, Mass., 1934), Vol. 4, para. 71.

or among Locke's various works,[32] it will be seen that such symmetry can be accounted for, and that a good deal of essential consistency is present and far from obscure. It will be shown that some of the central doctrines of Locke's *Second Treatise of Government*, as well as some aspects of his 'theological' works, are very much related to the methodology presented in his *Essay concerning Human Understanding*.

The main task which I have set myself is to give grounds for the following assertion: *in the seventeenth century, thinkers believed that if we apply one and the same method to the subject-matter of any discipline in which we can expect to gain knowledge, we shall be successful in that discipline*. Thus I shall give grounds for this assertion in the course of examining the writings of two of that century's most influential figures. My related tasks will be to demonstrate that, fundamentally, Descartes and Locke took up a similar methodological stance when they approached any subject-matter of which they believed they could attain knowledge; to explain how this stance structures their theory about this subject-matter; to show what that methodological stance is; and to make clear how it is related to their view of reason(ing).

In those parts of the following chapters in which I attempt to illustrate that Descartes and Locke actually did take up a similar methodological stance when they approached a subject-matter of which they believed they could obtain knowledge, my emphasis will be on the *resolution* rather than on the composition aspect of the method. There is a good reason for this limitation. To illustrate the presence of resolution in terms of some of the works of Descartes and Locke will call for the introduction of a good deal of the materials presented by them in these works. Illustrating in some detail the presence of both resolution and composition would call for the introduction of an even greater amount of these materials. In fact, following the latter course would lead to a presentation of complete commentaries on all those works, or at least very large parts of those works, which I have selected as materials and in terms of which I shall demonstrate the presence of the method. If such projects are at all of interest and of importance, they are best taken up in independent studies dealing with each of these

---

[32] Peter Laslett, Introduction to *John Locke, Two Treatises of Government* (Mentor Book, New York, 1965, first published by the Cambridge University Press, 1960), p. 102.

works in turn. The limitation I have thus imposed does not, of course, prevent me from making clear from the relevant writings of Descartes and Locke *that* they advocated the adoption of both resolution and composition. It is only in the illustrations of *how* these methodological principles actually function in their works that I will focus my discussion on *resolution* rather than on *composition*.

II

DESCARTES'S
CONCEPT OF REASON

Descartes's methodological stance is intimately related to his
view of reason; indeed, his theory of method cannot be understood
apart from his view of what is involved in reasoning. In this chapter
I shall therefore give an account of what Descartes takes to be
involved in reasoning.

After a distinction has been drawn between 'mind' and 'reason'
in the first section of this chapter, the second section is devoted to
an explication of 'reason' in terms of 'intuition' and 'deduction'.
This explication constitutes the first step in providing an account
of Descartes's methodology. In terms of concepts which belong
under the heading of 'reason', rather than under that of 'method',
this explication gives part of the answer to the question: how
does reason function in its pursuit of knowledge? Once this
partial answer has been given, we are meant immediately to find
ourselves in possession of the materials which allow us to bring
into focus an additional relevant characteristic of reason, namely,
that of its 'autonomy'. Discussion of reason's autonomy will take
up the third part of this chapter. During this discussion it will
begin to become clear what direction an argument would have to
take if it is to lead us to a validation of reason in the face of the
sceptic's attack upon its trustworthiness. Because of the relationship between reason and method, it will be seen that such a validation implies a justification for the universal application of method.

Thus the present chapter provides the groundwork for important
aspects of the arguments to be presented in Chapters III, IV, and
V. Specifically, I shall lay the groundwork first for explicating the
relationship between reason and method in the third chapter;
and second, for showing in Chapters IV and V what form Descartes's validation of reason takes, and how that validation implies
a justification for the universal application of method.

1. 'Reason' and 'mind'

References to 'reason' are plentiful in Descartes's writings. Often he uses the term 'reason' without a qualifying word or phrase. Just as often the term is accompanied by one. So he speaks of 'human reason', 'natural reason', 'the pure light of reason'. No suggestions about multivocality seem to be expressed in his use of such qualifying or otherwise associated terms. Descartes also frequently uses phrases intended to be interchangeable with 'reason'. He speaks, for example, of 'the light of nature', of the 'faculty of knowledge', and of 'Good sense'. Regardless of whether the word 'reason' appears in them or not, Descartes employs many expressions to refer to what he takes to be the capacity of man through which he can get at the truth. Given such employment, these expressions are all used interchangeably. In the *Principles of Philosophy*, for example, we read that 'the light of nature, or the faculty of knowledge . . . can never disclose to us any object which is not true, inasmuch as it comprehends it, that is, inasmuch as it apprehends it clearly and distinctly' (HR1, 231; AT8-1, 16). Also, 'we shall never take the false as the true if we only give our assent to things that we perceive clearly and distinctly. Because . . . the faculty of knowledge . . . cannot be fallacious . . .' (HR1, 236; AT8-1, 21). In the opening paragraph of Part I of the *Discourse* he writes that 'the power of forming a good judgment and of distinguishing the true from the false . . . is properly speaking what is called Good sense or Reason . . .'. Descartes writes to Father Dinet that 'I did not desire to mix myself up with any theological controversies; as inasmuch as I only treat in my philosophy of things clearly known by the light of nature. They cannot be contrary to the theology of anyone, unless this theology is manifestly opposed to the light of reason . . .' (HR2, 372; AT7, 598).

The terms 'mind' and 'understanding' are related to 'reason' as well; but whereas 'understanding' is intended to be synonymous with 'reason', 'mind', strictly speaking, is not, even though Descartes does use 'mind' and 'reason' interchangeably at times. Note how he replies to one of Bourdin's objections that 'I did not say that I was a soul but merely a thinking thing. To this thinking thing I gave the name of mind, or understanding, or reason . . .' (HR2, 290; AT7, 491). An indication of the distinction which

Descartes usually draws between 'mind' on the one hand and 'understanding' or 'reason' on the other is presented in his polemic against Regius:

He [Regius] teaches that, so far as nature shows, it is doubtful whether any material things are really perceived by us, and submits as his reason the statement that 'the mind can be affected in the same degree by things imaginary as by things real'. If this theory is to be received as true, it must be granted that we have use of no understanding properly so called, but only of the faculty which is usually termed the 'common sense' whereby impressions are received of things imaginary as much as of things real, so that they affect the mind. . . . But surely those who have understanding . . . even although they are affected not only by images of real things but also by those which occur in the brain from other causes (as happens in sleep), can distinguish the one kind of image from the other with the utmost clearness, by the light of reason. (HR1, 441; AT8-2, 356-7.)

This doctrine is affirmed throughout Descartes's writings. Mind includes understanding, imagination, memory, sense. As he says in the *Rules for the Direction of the Mind* 'it is the same faculty that . . . is called either pure understanding, or imagination, or memory, or sense' (HR1, 39; AT10, 416). But of these four 'it is the understanding alone which is capable of knowing', and in the understanding's attempts to perceive the truth it can be helped but also hindered by imagination, memory, and sense (HR1, 27; AT10, 398).

2. Intuition and deduction

If we grant for argument's sake that it is reason, the understanding, or the natural light which enables man to know, we can go on to ask how reason actually functions in its pursuit of knowledge or in its attempt to perceive the truth. Part of the answer to this question calls for the introduction of terms which come under the heading of methodology. Discussion of that part must be left for the following chapter. At the moment all that needs to be done is to give a further explication of the nature of reason. This calls for the introduction of the terms 'intuition' and 'deduction'. An examination of their use will lay the groundwork for a more complete answer to the question of how reason actually functions in its pursuit of knowledge, and so for an explicit treatment of the relevant methodological aspects.

In the *Rules* there are a number of passages which describe intuition and deduction. In Rule 3, for example, we read:

> By intuition I understand, not the fluctuating testimony of the senses, nor the misleading judgment that proceeds from the blundering constructions of the imagination, but the conception which an unclouded and attentive mind gives us so readily and distinctly that we are wholly freed from doubt about that which we understand. Or, what comes to the same thing, intuition is the undoubting conception of an unclouded and attentive mind, and springs from the light of reason alone; it is more certain than deduction itself, in that it is simpler, though deduction, as we have noted above, cannot by us be erroneously conducted. (HR1, 7; AT10, 368.)

The reference to deduction pertains to a passage in Rule 2, where we read that 'deduction . . . cannot be erroneous when performed by an understanding that is in the least degree rational' (HR1, 5; AT10, 365). In Rule 3 he calls deduction a 'supplementary method (*modum*) of knowing . . . by which we understand all necessary inference from other facts that are known with certainty' (HR1, 8; AT10, 369).

We shall first have to examine what is the relationship between 'intuition' and 'deduction' on the one hand, and reason on the other. On this point Descartes is quite clear. In the *Rules* he states that 'our method rightly explains how our mental vision (*mentis intuitu*) should be used, so as not to fall into the contrary error, and how deduction should be discovered in order that we may arrive at the knowledge of all things' (HR1, 9; AT10, 372). 'No science', he continues, 'is acquired except by mental intuition or deduction'. We cannot be taught a set of rules telling us how to intuit or how to deduce, for unless the understanding functions intuitively and deductively, it cannot comprehend anything whatsoever, and hence no set of rules either. To say that the understanding can acquire knowledge in a way other than through intuition and deduction would be false, for 'nothing can be added to the pure light of reason which does not in some way obscure it' (HR1, 10; AT10, 372-3). Thus it is these 'two operations of our understanding, intuition and deduction, on which alone . . . we must rely in the acquisition of our knowledge' (HR1, 28; AT10, 400). Intuition and deduction express the very nature of reason.

This means that we cannot say that intuition alone, or deduction alone, is the same as reason. Intuition and deduction *together* express the essence of reason. This point I want to emphasize for, elementary though it is, some commentators have overlooked it. One cause of this oversight is, perhaps, the fact that when Descartes uses the word 'deduction' to refer to one of the ways in which reason characteristically operates, he is using a word which is intimately connected with some traditional forms of formal logic. It may be that commentators then take his use of 'deduction' to be no different from that which was then popular in texts on (neo-) Aristotelian syllogistic. Descartes's intention not to follow such a use should be clear from his rejection of the syllogism as a paradigm of useful argument: he considers the current notions of syllogistic to be of no value in the discovery of truth. He explicitly opposes his own use of 'deduction' to that in such texts. His view of the nature of deduction, and of its difference from the (neo-) Aristotelian view, is indicated in the *Rules* when Descartes writes that since 'the syllogistic forms are of no aid in perceiving the truth' we should 'reject them altogether'. He urges that we 'conceive that all knowledge whatsoever, other than that which consists in the simple and naked intuition of single independent objects, is a matter of the comparison of two things or more, with each other' (HR1, 55; AT10, 440). When, for whatever reason, Descartes's use of 'deduction' is identified with Aristotle's or his followers' such identification inevitably leads to misinterpretation of many important passages in Descartes's work. Once Cartesian and Aristotelian deduction have been identified then, given Descartes's dismissal of the syllogism as a means for discovery of truth, only intuition remains as the expression of the nature of reason. However, it is this identification of reason with intuition alone, together with attention to just one sense of 'intuition' in Descartes, which leads to further misinterpretation.[1] If reason were identical with intuition alone, Descartes would be

---

[1] A clear example of the identification of Aristotelian and Cartesian deduction can be found in Bernard Williams's paper 'The Certainty of the Cogito' when he discusses the well-known passage from HR2, 38. This paper, which first appeared in French in *Cahiers de Royaumont, Philosophie No. IV: La Philosophie analytique* (Paris, 1962), pp. 40–57, is printed in translation in Willis Doney's *Descartes, A Collection of Critical Essays* (Garden City, N.Y., 1967), pp. 88–107. The discussion to which I refer is on p. 90 of Doney's volume.
    The error of the identification of 'reason' with 'intuition' alone invalidates, e.g. part of Harry G. Frankfurt's 'Descartes' Validation of Reason'. See Willis Doney, op. cit., pp. 209–26; first published in *American Philosophical Quarterly*, Vol. II, No. 2, 1965. Cf. esp. pp. 218 ff. in Doney's volume.

unable to account for systematic knowledge. Furthermore, if reason were identical with intuition, the problem of the validation of reason would never have arisen for Descartes. Indeed, he would have had additional reasons for considering the hypothesis of the evil genius of *Meditation I* to be meaningless. Substantiation for these points will be provided in the next part of this chapter.

A further distinction still has to be made, namely, that between two distinctly different types of intuition. This distinction is usually overlooked in contemporary literature on Descartes.[2] But unless it is made, an important element in the account of 'reason' is missing. Moreover, drawing this distinction clears the ground for the solution of a number of problems which have generally been assumed to exist in the *Meditations*. Since the distinction between these two kinds of intuition can be made only after an account has been given of the difference between intuition and deduction, I will turn to that first. Fortunately, the latter difference is so well known that not much need be said about it.

An act of intuition is taken to occur instantaneously, so that what is intuited 'must be grasped . . . at the same time and not successively'. By contrast, deduction is construed as a process which 'appears not to occur all at the same time, but involves a sort of movement on the part of our mind when it infers one thing from another' (HR1, 33; AT10, 407). Because of the presence of duration and movement, a further characteristic distinguishing intuition from deduction is the presence of memory in deduction (HR1, 8; AT10, 369-70; also HR1, 33; AT10, 407). Whereas the work of intuition consists in the grasping of (sometimes self-evident) data, that of deduction consists in connecting these various data by means of links. Deduction is dependent on intuition for the

[2] Once this distinction was overlooked, many commentators interpreted Descartes's position as one which introduced total scepticism with respect to *all* of man's faculties and all of man's knowledge. This interpretation is common to both English and French commentators. It is, for example, found in Alan Gewirth's 'The Cartesian Circle Reconsidered' (*Journal of Philosophy*, Vol. LXVII, No. 19, 1970, pp. 668–85); as well as in Henri Gouhier's *Essais sur Descartes* (Paris, 1949); and in F. Alquié's *La Découverte métaphysique de l'homme chez Descartes* (Paris, 1950), see especially Part III of this work. In part, this distinction *is* made in terms of the different *objects* of the two distinct kinds of intuition, by G. Nakhnikian (in his 'The Cartesian Circle Revisited', *American Philosophical Quarterly*, Vol. 4, No. 3, 1967, pp. 251–5; as well as by John Morris, in his 'Cartesian Certainty', *Australasian Journal of Philosophy*, Vol. 47, No. 2, 1969, pp. 161–8.

items to be connected; that is, it is impossible for deduction to link two data if one or both of them cannot be grasped intuitively. 'If', says Descartes, 'in the matters to be examined we come to a step in the series of which our understanding is not sufficiently well able to have an intuitive cognition, we must stop short there. We must make no attempt to examine what follows' (HR1, 22; AT10, 392). Deduction is also dependent on intuition for establishing the links between the data it is to connect (HR1, 7–8; AT10, 368–70). In the pursuit of knowledge intuition and deduction are both necessary: 'these two operations aid and complement each other. In doing so they seem to grow into a single process by virtue of a sort of motion of thought which has an attentive and vision-like knowledge of one fact and yet can pass at the very same moment to another' (HR1, 34; AT10, 408). Apart from the memory-aspect involved in deduction, one could characterize deduction as intuition-on-the-move.[3]

Intuition and deduction are further distinguished in terms of their respective objects. One can intuit that one exists, that one thinks, that the triangle is bounded by three lines only, that the sphere is bounded by a single superficies (HR1, 7; AT10, 368). One can intuit what is the meaning of 'cause', 'simple', 'universal', 'one', 'equal', 'like', 'straight' (HR1, 15; AT10, 381–2); what the act of knowing is, what doubt is, what ignorance is, as well as what is figure, extension, motion, existence, unity, or duration (HR1, 41; AT10, 419). Again, one can intuit that what has once been done cannot ever be undone (HR1, 193; AT7, 82–3; also HR1, 239; AT8–1, 24); that it is impossible that anything can be formed of nothing; that it is impossible that the same thing can be and not be at the same time; that he who thinks must exist

---

[3] Support for the characterization of 'deduction' as 'intuition-on-the-move' I find on p. 55 of Robert McRae's *The Problem of the Unity of the Sciences: Bacon to Kant*. McRae writes: 'The first kind of object appropriate to intuition is something so simple that it cannot be analyzed into anything more distinctly known. Once having apprehended these simples the mind can then extend the same vision to any necessary connections between them, and in that way come to know compounds of simple natures. Beyond that it cannot go. "No knowledge is at any time possible beyond those simple natures and what may be called their intermixture or combination with each other" [HR1, 43; AT10, 422]. Although the act of compounding is referred to deduction, it is, however, "quite clear", says Descartes, "that this mental vision extends both to all those simple natures and to the knowledge of necessary connections between them" [HR1, 45; AT10, 425].'

while he thinks (HR1, 239; AT8-1, 24). As a specific example of
what one can deduce Descartes gives: that two and two is the
same as three and one (HR1, 7; AT10, 369). In general, as we
read earlier, by deduction 'we understand all necessary inference
from other facts that are known with certainty'.

When we consider what characterizes the objects of intuition
mentioned so far, it is clear that they are all either what Descartes
calls simple ideas, or else what he calls propositions known *per se*.
Whatever is deduced is compounded from other, simple(r)
elements; hence whatever is deduced can be divided or analysed
into, or defined in terms of, its simple(r) components. These
objects of intuition, however, cannot themselves become known
through a further process of division or analysis. Of the simple
ideas it is said that 'no definitions are to be used in explaining
things of this kind lest we should take what is complex in place
of what is simple' (HR1, 46; AT10, 426); they are therefore 'known
per se' (HR1, 42; AT10, 420). And also of course the propositions
known *per se* (sometimes these are called first principles) are
'intelligible *per se*' (HR2, 54; AT7, 162); if one were to find one
of these not intelligible *per se*, its division into parts would not
lead to knowledge of it. Implicit in this doctrine is the view that
we can only get to know a simple idea all at once, that successive
apprehension of it is impossible.[4] Hence, if we know any simple
idea at all, we know it completely (HR1, 42; AT10, 420). Something
similar holds for propositions known *per se*, for 'we cannot fail
to recognize them when the occasion presents itself for us to do
so, and if we have no prejudices to blind us' (HR1, 239; AT8-1,
24). However, none of this holds for the object of deduction, for
here division, analysis, definition, is always possible. For example,
for us to know that two and two is equal to three and one we must

---

[4] It is clear that Descartes uses 'simple' to mean 'absolutely', rather than
'relatively', simple. Since the time of Wittgenstein's statements on 'absolute
simplicity' and 'absolute exactness' in the *Philosophical Investigations* (cf. I,
46–7, 88 f.) this notion of 'absolute simplicity' is by and large rejected by contemporary philosophers. Rejection of this notion has come to play a role in some
contemporary discussions of rationalist philosophies. As an example of such an
interpretation one could refer to Norman Malcolm's cautionary remarks —
remarks with which I am in agreement —made with respect to Leibniz, when the
latter uses 'simple' in a way similar to Descartes's use. Cf. Malcolm's 'Anselm's
Ontological Arguments' in *Knowledge and Certainty* (Englewood Cliffs, N.J.,
1963), pp. 141–62, 159. This material was first published in the *Philosophical
Review*, Vol LXIX, No. 1, 1960.

first know that two and two as well as three and one is four, and
that two things equal to a third thing are equal to one another.
We must know as well what 'unity' and 'equality' are. There are,
thus, criteria which can be used to distinguish an object of intuition from an object of deduction. The criterion of importance in
the present context involves the notion of indivisibility. Objects
of intuition, when they are single ideas, are simple or indivisible
or unanalysable. When the objects of intuition are propositions,
they are of the kind that are known *per se*; that is, because they
have not been derived from what is simple, their division or analysis
does not lead to knowledge of them. With respect to both these
ideas and these propositions, the smallest unit that can be known
is such an idea, and is such a proposition.

The kind of intuition described so far I shall call intuition$_1$.
There is another kind of intuition which I shall call intuition$_2$.
Intuition$_1$ and intuition$_2$ have in common that the act of intuition
occurs instantaneously and hence excludes successive movement
and memory. They differ in that whereas the object of intuition$_1$,
qua object of intuition$_1$, is not subject to division or analysis, the
object of intuition$_2$ can be divided or analysed. Intuition$_2$ is
therefore more closely related to deduction than is intuition$_1$. In
fact, whereas intuition$_1$ is in no way dependent on deduction,
intuition$_2$ can occur only after deduction has taken place.

Although the distinction between the two kinds of intuition is
not brought into sharp focus by Descartes and has usually been
overlooked by commentators, several passages, especially from the
Rules, provide good grounds for drawing it. And although I will
now limit myself to the *Rules*, in Chapters IV and V it will be
seen that the distinction introduced in the *Rules* is present in later
works as well. In the *Rules* Descartes calls for special attention
to the simple objects of intuition. Nevertheless, there is sufficient
evidence in this work to support also my interpretation concerning
the propositions known *per se*. Of the simple objects of intuition
he writes, for instance, that 'we are in error if we judge that any
one of these . . . is not completely known by us'. As reason for this
he gives that 'if our mind attains to the least acquaintance with it
. . . this fact alone makes us infer that we know it completely'. If
this were not so, it could not be said to be simple, but must be
complex—a compound of that which is present in our perception
of it, and that of which we think we are ignorant' (HR1, 42; AT10,

420–1). The doctrine contained in this passage is not abandoned in the later works. We will see that it plays an important role in the argument of the *Meditations*.

Descartes refers to what I call intuition$_2$ in the following passages. He writes that 'propositions . . . which are immediately deduced from first principles are known now by intuition, now by deduction, i.e. in a way which differs according to our point of view. But the first principles themselves are given by intuition alone' (HR1, 8; AT10, 370). He holds that the first principles cannot be reached through a chain of deduction, because such principles are indivisible *qua* objects of intuition. Here the intuition through which we know them is intuition$_1$. But, as is clear for instance from the opening paragraphs of Rule 11, Descartes also wants to say that propositions which are in any way deduced from first principles or from simple ideas, cannot themselves be indivisible, or cannot themselves be simple, even if they become objects of intuition. These propositions will vary in complexity, depending on how far they are removed from the items from which they are ultimately derived. It is possible, especially with short deductions, to come to see the different steps involved in the deductive process at a single glance. When propositions are 'immediately derived from first principles' the deductive process involves one step only. Hence in such an instance it will not be difficult to grasp the entire deductive process in a single intuition. Intuition then has as its object something complex and divisible. Here we have intuition$_2$. Since a piece of deduction, when it is not encompassed within a case of intuition$_2$, involves memory; and since such encompassing, given the limitations of the human mind, is relatively rare; and since Descartes holds that any particular memory may be erroneous; he holds that most deduction is less certain than intuition (HR1, 7, 8; AT10, 368, 370). If we eliminate memory from deduction, deduction will have the certainty of intuition$_2$, a certainty which, in the *Rules*, is equal to that of intuition$_1$. For, prior to the introduction of the first *Meditation's* metaphysical doubt, Descartes held that deduction 'cannot be erroneous when performed by an understanding that is in the least degree rational'. The elimination of memory is accomplished by a kind of 'enumeration', namely, the kind of enumeration which is a 'continuous movement of thought' by which we run through the different steps of the argument as quickly as possible 'in such a way that while it is intuitively perceiving each fact it simultaneously passes on to the next' until one learns 'to pass from the first to the last so quickly, that no stage of the process [is] left to the care of memory', and one can 'have the whole in intuition' before one 'at the same time' (HR1, 19; AT10, 388). 'The whole' thus held in a single intuitive grasp is, again, the kind of compound which, *qua* object of intuition, is divisible, and intuition is intuition$_2$. Again, we read that 'if we wish to consider deduction as an accomplished fact . . . then it no longer designates a movement, but rather the completion of a movement, and therefore we suppose that it is presented to us by intuition when it is simple and clear, but not when it is complex and involved' (HR1, 33; AT10, 407-8). As the context makes clear, the use of 'simple' in this passage does not allow us to infer that the object of intuition is non-compound and non-divisible. Rather, we are being told that the material is sufficiently non-complex for it to be apprehended in one intuition. The material may be thought of as lying somewhere in the middle region between 'first principles' and 'remote conclusions'. Here also, the sense of intuition is that of intuition$_2$.

If we call the instantaneous nature of intuition, the exclusion of successive apprehension and memory, a psychological characteristic; and if we refer to the characteristics of the item intuited, namely its being either simple and non-divisible *qua* object of intuition, or complex and divisible, as logical characteristics; we can say that intuition$_1$ and intuition$_2$ are identical in their psychological, but different in their logical nature. Both intuition$_1$ and intuition$_2$ differ from deduction in respect of their psychological nature, but only intuition$_1$ differs from deduction as to its logical nature. Although, except for the limitation of the human mind, all objects of deduction can become objects of intuition, this does not make deduction identical with intuition. For, first, the objects of deduction that become objects of intuition become objects of intuition$_2$ only. And, second, the objects of intuition$_1$, the simple ideas and non-derivable propositions, can never be objects of deduction, can never be obtained through deduction.

It must be emphasized that intuition$_2$ comes about only after deduction is an accomplished fact. Also 'the first principles themselves are given by intuition$_{[1]}$ alone, while, on the contrary, the remote conclusions are furnished only by deduction' (HR1, 8;

AT10, 370); that is (as the context of this sentence clearly indicates), 'remote conclusions' cannot, given the limitations of the human mind, be reduced to intuition$_2$. One task of reason is to give man systematic knowledge. Simple ideas or propositions known *per se* are not themselves systematic knowledge; rather, systematic knowledge is to be built on them as its basis. This building activity is the work of deduction. It culminates either in intuition$_2$ or in 'remote conclusions' which we remember to have been deduced step by step from simple or simpler ideas and propositions. All of this indicates, again, that deduction as well as intuition expresses the essence of reason. It also justifies my earlier statement that if reason were identical with intuition alone, systematic knowledge would be impossible to attain. For intuition$_1$ does not give us systematic knowledge, but only the foundational elements for it. And since a necessary condition for intuition$_2$ is that deduction be an 'accomplished fact', we would never reach the stage of intuition$_2$ if deduction were not characteristic of reason as well. Hence, unless also deduction expresses the essential nature of reason, we will have to identify reason with intuition$_1$ and then systematic knowledge becomes impossible.

3. The autonomy of reason

The account so far given provides the basis for making explicit an additional characteristic of reason. This characteristic may be called that of reason's autonomy, where 'autonomy' has the connotation of what is 'ultimate' or 'absolute'. The subject of reason's autonomy can be approached in two ways.

First: We can say that reason is autonomous in the sense that its own trustworthiness, no less than the trustworthiness of the results obtained through its use, is not established through the introduction of elements which, themselves, are not 'rational'; that, for example, it is not elements furnished by faith which allow one to trust reason. There is support for putting the matter this way in Descartes's works, for example, in terms of a statement like that from the *Principles of Philosophy*: the 'sovereign good' is 'the knowledge of truth through its first causes, i.e. the wisdom whose study is philosophy'; this 'sovereign good' we obtain 'by the natural reason without the light of faith' (HR1, 205; AT9–2, 4).

Second: A more fruitful approach to the subject of reason's autonomy goes along the following lines. If we consider the statement quoted from the *Principles* in the previous paragraph, it may appear to us prima facie that Descartes contradicts the position expressed there when he makes other statements in several of his works, statements which appear to assert that reason is non-autonomous. For example, in the *Discourse* we read 'that which I have just taken as a rule . . . that all the things which we very clearly and very distinctly conceive of are true, is certain only because God is or exists . . .' (HR1, 105; AT6, 38). In the penultimate sentence of *Meditation V* we read that 'the certainty and truth of all knowledge depends alone on the knowledge of the true God, in so much that, before I knew Him, I could not have a perfect knowledge of any other thing'. And in the *Reply to Objections VI* Descartes argues that since the atheist has 'reason for doubting whether he may not be of such an imperfect nature as to be deceived in matters which appear most evident to him' the atheist's knowledge 'is not immutable and certain'; it cannot become certain 'unless he first acknowledges that he has been created by the true God, a God who has no intention to deceive' (HR2, 245; AT7, 428). This appearance of contradiction disappears if, first, 'all' in 'the certainty and truth of all knowledge' refers to all knowledge *of a certain kind* only, e.g. to all knowledge of a derived nature; and, second, if the knowledge of God is not reached through faith but through reason, so that the trustworthiness of one function of reason (namely, that which gives us knowledge of a derived kind) is established through the use of another function of reason (namely, that which gives us knowledge of an intuitive or non-derived kind). If the certainty and truth of *all* knowledge depends on the knowledge of God reason might, indeed, be non-autonomous. However, Descartes constantly reiterates that the knowledge of God is not reached through faith, but that it is reason which leads us to it. Hence his position is that the trustworthiness of reason is established through the use of reason. Many critics have maintained that, at this point, Descartes' argument becomes hopelessly circular. But if one takes careful notice of certain distinctions which Descartes introduces during his discussion of the nature of reason, it becomes much more difficult to endorse or uphold this charge of circularity, if not completely impossible. For if Descartes gives clear indications that the function of reason which leads to knowledge of the existence of God does not stand in need of validation, or, if it does, that it can be shown to be valid without reference to the existence of God, he has done nothing to warrant a charge of circularity. Or at least he is innocent of the sort of charge which is usually presented. The form which this charge takes is basically Arnauld's:

the only secure reason we have for believing that what we clearly and distinctly perceive is true, is the fact that God exists. But we can be sure that God exists, only because we clearly and evidently perceive that; therefore prior to being certain that God exists, we should be certain that whatever we clearly and evidently perceive is true. (HR2, 92; AT7, 214.)

If attention is paid to the proper distinctions, such a charge may be seen to be groundless. This has major repercussions for the interpretation of the arguments in the first three *Meditations*. One implication is that we will have to find grounds there for saying that Descartes puts limits to the successful applicability of 'universal doubt'. For if it were to be found in the *Meditations* that Descartes allows nothing to withstand the test of doubt, this would indeed call for a divine guarantee of the validity of all of reason. The notion of the autonomy of reason, or of the autonomy of a function of reason, would become inapplicable and the charge of circularity would be inescapable. A further implication would then be that the whole case for the universal applicability of the new method would have to rest on a divine guarantee for such applicability. Because an adequate examination of the argument of the first three of the *Meditations* requires prior clarity about Descartes's *concept of method* as well as his concept of reason, I must postpone this examination until Chapter IV. However, the relevant distinctions in 'reason' can be introduced at this point, for they are both founded on and, indeed, implicit in the material I have provided in the first two sections of the present chapter.

The statements quoted in the previous paragraph, statements which may seem to point to reason's non-autonomous status, are counterbalanced by statements which seem to imply quite the opposite. And one finds examples of this latter kind of statement throughout Descartes's works. In a passage from the *Discourse* some pages preceding that from which I have just quoted Descartes writes that 'this truth "I think, therefore I am" was so certain and so assured that all the most extravagant suppositions brought forward by the sceptics were incapable of shaking it'. From such a ground he concludes that he 'could receive it without scruple as the first principle' of his system. He then immediately proceeds to say that from this principle, which he knows to be 'true and certain', he can establish 'as a general rule, that the things which we conceive very clearly and distinctly are all true' (HR1, 101–2; AT6, 33). In *Meditation II* he searches for what he calls an Archimedean point, a point which he finds when he realizes that 'I am, I exist, is necessarily true each time that I pronounce it, or that I mentally conceive it' (HR1, 150; AT7, 25). It is, apparently, possible to reach his Archimedean point before he comes to the existence of God; in fact, the point seems to be reached in spite of the supposition of the non-existence of God and the presence of 'some evil genius not less powerful than deceitful' who employs 'his whole energies in deceiving me' (HR1, 148; AT7, 22). In *The Search After Truth* Descartes seems to attain certainty and truth even before he comes to the *Cogito*. He there seems to identify his Archimedean point with universal doubt itself in speaking of 'universal doubt which is like a fixed and unchangeable point'. Here too, however, 'the fixed and unchangeable point' is immediately connected with the *Cogito*, for 'you cannot deny that you doubt' which means that it is 'certain that you doubt', and 'it is likewise true that you are, you who doubt', 'for if I did not exist I could not doubt' (HR1, 316; AT10, 515). Again, the existence of the 'I' is known to be certain, and the certainty coincides with truth, before we know anything of the existence of God. These passages suggest that, prior to our ever having considered the existence of God at all, we have found our Archimedean point, as well as a general criterion for truth.

In the first two parts of this chapter it was made clear that whereas Descartes did use 'reason' and 'natural light' interchangeably, he did not so use 'intuition', 'reason', and 'natural light'. 'Reason' or 'natural light' gives us systematic knowledge, a philosophic or scientific system, and cannot therefore be limited to the function which gives us knowledge of 'simples' or of 'truths known *per se*'. For, as we have seen, such awareness only provides necessary (foundational) elements for systematic knowledge. 'Intuition' is the technical term which, we saw, Descartes uses to describe the capacity to know 'simples' or any items 'known *per se*'. Since it has been shown that 'intuition' is a term not used univocally, 'intuition' in the previous sentence has to be replaced by 'intuition₁'. The objects of intuition₁ comprise the class of objects of knowledge which are known with certainty even before the proof of the existence of God. Intuition₁ is therefore held to be autonomous. It is the autonomy of intuition₁ which we have to presuppose in order to defend Descartes against the charge of circularity.

It is now possible to justify some of the statements made in the previous section of this chapter, namely, if reason were identical with intuition the problem of the validation of reason would never have arisen for Descartes, and he would have had additional reasons for considering the hypothesis of the evil genius of *Meditation I* to be meaningless. In support of these statements I want to draw attention to the following two passages and their implications.

(i) In *Reply to Objections II* we read that:

when I said that we could know nothing with certainty[5] unless we were first aware that God existed, I announced in express terms that I referred only to the science apprehending such conclusions as can recur in memory without attending further to the proofs which led me to make them. Further, knowledge of first principles is not usually called science by dialecticians. (HR2, 38; AT7, 140.)

This passage, and the sentences immediately following it, have been variously interpreted. But what is at least clear is that 'first principles', which are among the objects of intuition₁, can be known with certainty before we know that God exists and is veracious. This passage, then, states intuition₁ to be autonomous. The specific 'first principle' Descartes is discussing in what follows the lines just quoted is 'I think, hence I am, or exist.' Hence Descartes's

⁵ The phrase 'knowing with certainty' is significant, and is not interchangeable with phrases like 'to feel certain that . . .' or 'to be certain of . . . or 'to take as certain'. Thus, to attain certainty is not necessarily the same as to attain truth. An item may be indubitable, i.e. experienced as certain, says Descartes, but it may still be that what we can only take as certain is, nevertheless, not true. The argument for the validation of reason in Descartes has, in fact, been put in these terms: Descartes needs to prove that a veracious God exists in order to be able to show that what one cannot help feeling certain about, what one can only experience as indubitable, is in fact true. See e.g. Alan Gewirth, op. cit. This way of putting the problem is not, of course, limited to Gewirth, or to commentators writing in English. Henri Gouhier, for example, makes the same distinction in his *Essais sur Descartes*, pp. 143–54. The distinction between 'knowing with certainty' and 'feeling certain of' will become important in the fourth chapter.

position in this passage is that the Archimedean point of his philosophy has been reached through the exercise of autonomous reason.

(ii) In the same *Reply* from which the material in the preceding paragraph is taken there is further substantiation for my interpretation. Descartes writes:

If, then, any certitude does exist, it remains that it must be found only in the clear perceptions of the intellect.

But of these there are some so evident and at the same time so simple, that in their case we never doubt about believing them true: e.g. that I, while I think, exist; that what is once done cannot be undone, and other similar truths, about which we clearly can possess this certainty. For we cannot doubt them unless we think of them; but we cannot think of them without at the same time believing them to be true; i.e. we can never doubt them. (HR2, 42; AT7, 145.)

In the sentences following this material Descartes contrast the certainty of these 'clear perceptions' with that attaching to conclusions deductively derived. That is, the 'clear perceptions' are intuitions. Since Descartes draws special attention to the 'evidence' and 'simplicity' of the objects of these intuitions it seems safe to conclude that these are objects of intuition$_1$. The specific examples introduced support this conclusion, for as we saw, he elsewhere calls these objects 'intelligible *per se*', hence not derivative or derivable. Of the conclusions which are deduced Descartes says that their certainty is dependent on the knowledge of God. In contrast, the certainty of what is known through intuition$_1$ is not dependent on the knowledge of God. There is a line of possible doubt which should be mentioned here. If we are unable to doubt these perceptions because of the 'evidence' and 'simplicity' of their objects 'without at the same time believing them to be true', does it follow that they must necessarily be true? What if, as Descartes himself here asks, that which we thus believe to be true appears 'false to God or to an Angel', and so is false 'absolutely speaking'? Although Descartes raises this possibility, he does not consider it seriously: 'what heed do we pay to that absolute falsity, when we by no means believe that it exists or even suspect its existence? We have assumed a conviction so strong that nothing can remove it, and this persuasion is clearly the same as perfect certitude' (HR2, 41; AT7, 145). If the supposition 'the truth of which we are so firmly persuaded, appears false to God or to an Angel' is a variant of the evil genius hypothesis of *Meditation I*, Descartes here excludes intuition$_1$ from being affected by that hypothesis.

That my interpretation of these passages makes good sense can be shown in the following way. If Descartes were to hold that the hypothesis about the evil genius does apply to intuition$_1$ and its objects, so that the knowledge obtained by means of intuition$_1$ is not certain and true, the 'Cartesian circle' results. A defence against circularity may be formulated in two ways. (a) If the hypothesis applies to all exercises of reason the hypothesis is, first, meaningless because untestable and therefore, second, cannot be rejected. Descartes believed he could reject the hypothesis. The rejection consists in, first, finding an Archimedean point and, second, in proving from it the existence of a veracious God. We can only come to a veracious God through the use of reason. If every use of reason is untrustworthy, its use in the proof of the existence of a veracious God and in the attendant rejection of the hypothesis about the evil genius is untrustworthy as well. But Descartes was quite convinced that he had provided an unshakeable proof for the existence of a veracious God and that he had been able to show that the hypothesis about the evil genius is untenable. Therefore he cannot have held that every use of reason is untrustworthy. (b) Descartes wants to show that reason is reliable. Unless one is blind to a glaring instance of question-begging, one would not be tempted to use reason in order to show reason to be reliable. One can, however, attempt to show the reliability of certain functions of reason by means of other functions of reason which are already held to be reliable. Therefore, again, since we may assume that Descartes was quite capable of discerning circular from non-circular argumentation, or at least could discern such circularity once a person like Arnauld had drawn attention to it, he cannot have held that every use of reason is untrustworthy. Specifically, he must have held at least intuition$_1$ to be trustworthy, and he must have considered at most deduction and intuition$_2$ to stand in need of a justification.

The case for insisting that Descartes's use of reason to validate reason does not provide room for the charge of circularity which has traditionally been laid against the argument of the *Meditations*, has also been partly supported by some other commentators, such as Alan Gewirth. However, because Gewirth fails to draw the distinction between two types of intuition[6] he is forced to impute *some* kind of circularity to Descartes after all. Gewirth writes that Descartes's 'metaphysics consists of a critical examination *of* reason *by* reason' and that this results in the kind of circularity which 'is implicit in all epistemologies insofar as they inquire into the cognitive powers of the mind in general, for one or more of these powers must themselves be used in the enquiry'.[7] Whether it is correct to speak of 'circularity' at this point is doubtful. Instead, I would hold that when we come to the cognitive power which is used to 'inquire into the cognitive powers of the mind in general' we have reached the presuppositional base on which the entire philosophical position rests. For although it may be argued that philosophers cannot present *arguments for such presuppositions* without entangling themselves in a *petitio,* such a view does not imply that therefore the philosophical position itself involves circularity. Instead it indicates that philosophical positions, at their very bases, must involve non-philosophical elements.[8] For Descartes, these non-philosophical elements are related to his acceptance of the autonomy of that function of reason which expresses itself as intuition$_1$. I say 'related to' because, as I shall argue in Chapter IV, it may be held that Descartes *shows* that intuition$_1$ is autonomous, and to the extent that there is such a 'showing' it cannot be said that Descartes merely 'accepts' the 'autonomy of that function of reason which expresses itself as

[6] See especially pp. 671–3 of Gewirth's article cited above. On these pages he contrasts 'intuitional' with 'metaphysical' certainty. This contrast does, indeed, hold for all cases where whatever is intuited is complex. However, in instances where whatever is intuited is genuinely simple or known *per se*, intuitional and metaphysical certainty coincide. Gewirth's failure to recognize this point also prevents him from giving a complete analysis of the metaphysical doubt about mathematics in *Meditation I* (cf. pp. 671–9); his argument there concerns itself only with mathematical *propositions* (to which metaphysical doubt does indeed attach) and not with those simple elements which make mathematical propositions possible in the first place (and which are not subject to metaphysical doubt). Even apart from these considerations, it is doubtful whether Gewirth's distinction between intuitional (or psychological) and metaphysical certainty is valid in the way he has drawn it; for reasons advanced by Kenny, I do not think it is. (Cf. Anthony Kenny, 'The Cartesian Circle and the Eternal Truths', *Journal of Philosophy*, Vol. LXVII, No. 19, 1970, pp. 685–700; esp. pp. 686–8.

[7] Gewirth, op. cit., p. 682.

[8] That philosophers cannot present non-circular arguments for such presuppositions I have argued elsewhere. Cf. my 'Communication, Argumentation, and Presupposition in Philosophy', *Philosophy and Rhetoric,* Vol. II, No. 4, 1969, pp. 183–99.

intuition₁'. What is accepted by Descartes is that the distinction between absolutely simple and complex knowledge can be maintained, and hence that there are truths known *per se*. It seems to me that the acceptance of the possibility of knowing each of many items in isolation (items which are, according to Descartes, known through intuition₁) constitutes at least one profoundly important non-philosophical element at the basis of the Cartesian position.

In summing up, I can say that Descartes makes it quite explicit that reason stands in need of validation; that as long as we can entertain the possibility of an omnipotent deceiver not 'all that we perceive clearly' is known to be true; that reason or the natural light is not to be trusted without qualification. The qualification is that reason is to be trusted to the extent that it reveals to us things like 'if I am doubting it follows that I exist'. Descartes consistently holds that, in its intuitive function of grasping truths known *per se*, reason is autonomous. He just as consistently maintains that in its deductive function, in its construction of any scientific system, reason stands in need of validation. The argument which is to provide this validation of that function of reason is given in the *Meditations*. How, given the autonomy of reason in its intuitive function, this argument is not subject to the charge of circularity, is an issue that remains to be discussed in Chapter V.⁹

At this point one might ask the question: if reason, or an aspect of it, is autonomous, why would there be so much talk about God in the *Meditations*? It is entirely in keeping with my interpretation to say that it becomes important to prove the existence of God in order to show that the hypothesis about the evil genius is self-contradictory. All that Descartes would need to argue then is that there are no grounds for supposing that there is an external power capable of interfering with reason's deductive function. Once that point has been established—and it would be established as soon as it is recognized that *if* an omnipotent being exists, that being cannot be evil—there would be no further gain in showing that a divine being *actually* exists, and that there is a divine guarantee for the trustworthiness of reason's deductive function. Since, however, Descartes does continue the argument beyond the point of showing

⁹ For further substantiation for the position I have sketched, see John Morris's article mentioned in n. 2 above. In addition, see my 'Cartesian Certainty and the "Natural Light" ', *Australasian Journal of Philosophy*, Vol. 48, No. 1 1970, pp. 116–19.

that there can be no omnipotent evil being, we may assume that there is more to the argument for God's existence than merely making the point that no omnipotent evil being can exist. Hence a second line of argument, also in keeping with my interpretation, would be that the role of God consists in extricating Descartes from a solipsistic position when he arrives at the *Cogito* as the first principle of his philosophy. Another way of putting that is that since intuition₁ may have nothing to do with the existence of anything beyond the I and its ideas, we get beyond this stage by making God the guarantor of the truth of a certain class of complex ideas, namely, of those that are clear and distinct. In this class are also the adventitious ideas, and God's guarantee makes it possible for us to know that, to some extent at least, they represent the essences of things. (Cf. HR1, 185; AT7, 71; and HR1, 191; AT7, 79–80.) This line of interpretation is supported by what Descartes wrote to Clerselier: '. . . it is very useful indeed to convince oneself first of the existence of God, *and then of the existence of all creatures*, through the consideration of one's own existence' (my italics).[10]

It may be suggested that if an aspect of reason is autonomous, it should be possible to validate all of reason in terms of it in such a way that God need not enter the discussion at all. What of those passages in which Descartes makes, or seems to make, the validity of any aspect of reason depend on God (or at the least on an argument which shows that if an omnipotent being exists, such a being cannot be evil)? Might one not then call these expressions of Descartes's 'aberrant view'?[11] It is, however, not necessary to call them that, for an examination of these passages will make it clear that at least many of them do not conflict with the autonomy of reason of the sort for which I have argued in this chapter. If, for example, we look again at the three passages from Descartes's works in the third paragraph of this section, it will be seen that they support, rather than conflict with my interpretation. The context of the passage from the *Discourse* makes it very clear that since Descartes is there speaking of 'body', 'stars', and 'earth' he is referring to things which are composite (HR1, 104; AT6, 37).

---

[10] See Descartes's letter of June 1646 (AT4, 442 ff., esp. pp. 444–5). The translation is from A. J. P. Kenny's *Descartes, Philosophical Letters* (Oxford, 1970), p. 197, hereafter referred to as Kenny, *Letters*. A similar statement is to be found in *The Search After Truth* (HR1, 316; AT10, 515).

[11] This is a phrase from G. Nakhnikian's 'The Cartesian Circle Revisited', (cited in n. 2, above). The phrase occurs throughout the article.

THE AUTONOMY OF REASON

The passage from *Meditation V* is written in the context of a discussion of mathematical demonstration. Demonstration always involves the use of deduction, and hence involves complexity. The last of the passages I there introduced, that of the atheist's knowledge, again involves demonstration. For one of the specific examples used by Descartes's objectors is: 'the three angles of a rectilinear triangle are equal to two right angles' (HR2, 235; AT7, 414). In the *Principles* Descartes states explicitly that we know this through demonstration (HR1, 224; AT8–1, 9–10); hence, again, the object of knowledge is complex. Our way of gaining knowledge of what is complex stands in need of validation. This validation introduces the talk about God. But I have argued that such validation is possible only if intuition₁ is autonomous. Rather than refer to the above passages as Descartes's aberrant view, we could say that Descartes's talk about God basically amounts to little more than saying that reason is divine or absolute (Descartes, in the *Rules*, says that 'the human mind has in it something that we may call divine'; cf. HR1, 10; AT10, 373). The divine guarantee of reason then simply becomes reason's self-guarantee. Saying this does, of course, go beyond the argument I have presented in this chapter. The argument may well, however, point in this direction.

A third line of argument will be presented in Chapter V. Also this line of argument will include the notion of the autonomy of that function of reason expressed through intuition₁; and it will not conflict with the role assigned to God in the preceding paragraphs, namely, that knowledge of God's existence allows Descartes to extricate himself from a solipsistic position when he arrives at the *Cogito* as the first principle of his philosophy. This third line of argument will, however, contradict the statement that 'intuition₁ may have nothing to do with the existence of anything beyond the I and its ideas'. For it will become clear that, according to Descartes, what we are aware of through the intuition of the *Cogito* is not just the I and its ideas—intuition of the *Cogito* will be shown to involve also knowledge of the existence of God. This line of argument will allow us to remove an ambiguity which is present in Descartes's statement to Clerselier ('. . . it is very useful indeed to convince oneself first of the existence of God, and then of the existence of all creatures, through the consideration of one's own existence'). The logical order in this statement will be seen *not* to be: 'through the consideration of one's own existence' one convinces 'oneself first of the existence of God, and then of the existence of all creatures'. Instead, the order intended by Descartes is: one convinces 'oneself first of the existence of God, and then'—'through the consideration of one's own existence'—'of the the existence of all creatures'. This order coincides with that presented in *The Search After Truth*: 'For it is really from this universal doubt which is like a fixed and unchangeable point, that I have resolved to derive the knowledge of God, of yourself, and of all that the world contains' (HR1, 316; AT10, 515). And it agrees with the order of the third of the *Meditations*: '. . . in some way I have in me the notion of the infinite earlier than the finite—to wit, the notion of God before that of myself' (HR1, 166; AT7, 45).

III

REASON AND DESCARTES'S
CONCEPT OF METHOD

In this chapter I will elucidate the nature of Descartes's general
method in terms both of what it is and of what it does. In the first
section I will show that Descartes holds to an identity of reason
and method in the sense that a proper account of the activity of
reason in its pursuit of knowledge is at the same time a definition
of method. It can thus be said that Descartes's concept of reason
determines his concept of method. From this point on one can
speak either of the relation of reason to science or of method to
science. However, since we are now discussing specifically reason's
manner of operation, concepts that come under the heading of
'method' are best suited to further the argument. Hence these
concepts will predominate in the rest of the chapter. The reasoning presented in section 2 leads to the conclusion that method
determines the nature of science. By this I mean that, according
to Descartes, method accounts for the certainty of science, method
determines the nature of the contents of a scientific system, and
method dictates in part the form which a scientific system comes
to possess. Furthermore, by determining certain aspects of what
is to be known, method delimits the nature of the objects which
the science in question is to investigate. In section 3 I present my
first concrete illustration of the fact that Cartesian method fixes
the character of science. I take as my point of departure a discussion of the relationship which, according to Descartes, holds
between the general method and particular techniques or manners
of procedure within a particular science. This illustration of some
of the ways in which method determines the nature of science is
in terms of arguments presented by Descartes in his *Geometry*.
Finally, in section 4 I fill out this discussion of method by examining how the 'method of doubt', the 'hypothetical method', and the
'experimental method' function as part of, or within the confines
of, the general method. This part of the discussion does more
than merely fill out the account of method so far provided; for it

introduces the concepts of 'doubt', 'imagination', and 'sense'—concepts which are needed for the argument in Chapters IV and V.

1. Reason as determining the nature of method

What reason is determines the conditions under which it can obtain knowledge. For Descartes, the nature of reason is expressed in its intuitive and deductive functioning. In order for a thinker to be able to have an intuition, the item to be intuited must have a clear and distinct presentation. 'I term that clear which is present and apparent to an attentive mind. . . . But the distinct is that which is so precise and different from all other objects that it contains within itself nothing but what is clear' (*Principles*, I, 45). If clarity and distinctness are to be obtained, the problems which are to be examined must be divided or analysed into, or resolved or reduced to, their parts until we reach those parts that are the simplest, that cannot be divided further. At this point the doubt disappears; we have attained clarity and distinctness; we can intuit. The procedural order here is from the complex and obscure, through analysis or resolution, to the simple and clear and distinct. For the purpose of constructing systematic knowledge the most crucial of all the clear and distinct items of knowledge is the *Cogito*, 'the first and most certain of all that occurs to one who philosophizes in an orderly way' (HR1, 221; AT8-1, 7). From this point we proceed compositively or deductively 'commencing with objects that were the most simple and easy to understand, in order to rise little by little, or by degrees, to knowledge of the most complex' (HR1, 92; AT6, 18). The procedural principle of order here consists in 'putting forward those things first that should be known without the aid of what comes subsequently, and arranging all other matters so that their proof depends solely on what precedes them' (HR2, 48; AT7, 155; cf. also HR1, 212-13, AT9-2, 16-17). Implicit in all this is the thesis that methodological principles are not external to reason but are the expression of the very nature of reason. Examination of a few passages from Descartes's works will show us this relation between reason and method explicitly.

In the *Rules* Descartes expounds a 'science' whose 'province ought to extend to the eliciting of true results in every subject' (i.e. the method). This science 'should contain the primary rudiments of human reason' (HR1, 11; AT10, 374). Since method has to *contain* (*continere*) these 'rudiments', the relation between method and reason is of an internal, rather than of an external nature. A different interpretation would be possible if, rather than 'contain' Descartes had used a word like 'direct' or 'guide'. When such a word is used, as in the title of this work—*Regulae ad Directionem Ingenii*—it does not introduce an external relationship between method and reason. Rather, in view of the contents of the *Rules*, the title is to be interpreted as an announcement that in this work we are going to be concerned with how reason functions in its pursuit of knowledge. For it is not reason, but the *mind* (including reason or understanding, sense, imagination, and memory) which is to be *directed*. The mind is to be directed in such a way when it attempts to gain the truth of things, that it makes proper use of imagination and sense (what this proper use is will be explicated in section 4 of this chapter) and that it curtails, as much as possible, the role of memory. These directions are to lead the philosopher or scientist to the realization that 'it is the understanding alone which is capable of knowing', of grasping items intuitively, and of grasping the connections between these intuited items; and they are to lead him to an understanding of when, and how, the understanding is to be helped by imagination and sense. (Cf. HR1, 27; AT10, 389.) For reason to be able to function, it must establish a certain *order* in or among the problems towards which it directs itself. This order is attained through the resolution of what is involved and obscure into what is simple, so that we can have an intuition of these simple elements and begin to reconstruct the problems through rigorous use of deduction. Such deduction results in complex items which are clear and distinct, and hence fully intelligible. The three previous sentences are in part a paraphrase of the heading of Rule 5, where we read:

Method consists entirely (*Tota methodus consistit*) in the order and disposition of the objects towards which our mental vision must be directed if we would find out any truth. We shall comply with it exactly if we reduce (*reducamus*) involved and obscure propositions step by step to those that are simpler, and then starting with the intuitive apprehension of all those that are absolutely simple, attempt to ascend to the knowledge of all others by precisely similar steps.

Thus, the heading of Rule 5 *presents this activity of reason as a definition of method.* And whereas the heading of Rule 4 states the necessity of method if we are to get at the truth of things (*Necessaria est methodus ad rerum veritatem investigandam*), this necessity, in Rule 12 is put in terms of the two aspects of reason, intuition and deduction: 'mankind has no road towards certain knowledge open to it, save those of self-evident intuition and necessary deduction' (HR1, 45; AT10, 425).

This doctrine of the identity of method and reason we find stated in other works as well. Suffice it at this point to introduce two passages from the *Principles of Philosophy.* (i) In *Principles,* I, 42, we read that 'it even frequently happens that it is the very desire for knowing the truth which causes those which are not fully aware of the order in which it should be sought for, to give judgment on things of which they have no real knowledge and thereby fall into error'. Since, as is stated in the very next principle, reason 'cannot be fallacious', we cannot conclude that those who 'fall into error' because they judge without being 'fully aware of the order' have *reasoned* incorrectly. Instead, we must conclude that it cannot have been reason that was exercised here. And since Descartes always presents *order* as the essence of method, we must conclude that what may have been called the unmethodical exercise of reason is not really the exercise of reason at all; that the absence of method and the absence of reason go hand in hand. (ii) In *Principles,* I, 13, Descartes writes that when the mind remembers the conclusion of an argument but 'cannot recollect the order of its deduction', there is 'great cause to doubt the truth of such conclusions'. On the basis of this principle some critics have argued, erroneously, that Descartes's attempt to show the trustworthiness of reason was really an attempt to show the trustworthiness of memory.[1] Of course it is correct to say that even if we *could* remember the order of deduction we have some cause to doubt the trustworthiness of our conclusions, for Descartes holds memory to be fallible; that is one reason why, in the *Rules,* he introduces a kind of enumeration which is to eliminate dependence on memory as much as possible (cf. HR1, 19; AT10, 387). The point of *Principles,* I, 13, however, is that since we cannot 'recollect the

---

[1] Cf. e.g. A. K. Stout, 'The Basis of Knowledge in Descartes', in Willis Doney's *Descartes, A Collection of Critical Essays,* pp. 169–91 (first published in *Mind, N.S.,* Vol. XXXVIII, Nos. 151 and 152, 1929, pp. 330–42, 458–72); and Willis Doney, 'The Cartesian Circle', *Journal of the History of Ideas,* Vol. XVI, 1955, pp. 324–38.

order', we do not know whether the conclusions have been reached through reason.

The point I am here making, namely, that there is an identity of method and reason, has been argued before by some commentators on Descartes. Of particular interest are comments made by L. J. Beck, A. Koyré, and Norman Kemp Smith. About *'Mathesis Universalis,* the science of order and measure' Beck writes that it 'exemplifies *sub specie puritatis* the activity of mind itself, that is, the method'.[2] Koyré writes about the method as 'a new logic which gives us the pattern of intelligibility and the true norm of reason'.[3] And Kemp Smith states that '. . . it is not true that the method is merely an instrument for constructing knowledge. Rather . . . it expresses the innermost essence of mind.'[4] These expressions of the last two critics imply that unless we deal with any problem in terms of the method, the problem will remain unintelligible. Descartes himself provides good grounds for presenting the matter the way Koyré and Kemp Smith put it. In the *Rules* he writes that without the method 'study seems to be harmful rather than profitable' and that, to the extent that 'the greater minds of former ages' did make advances in knowledge and did resolve problems intelligibly, they must have had some knowledge of the method (HR1, 10; AT10, 373). And in the *Discourse on Method,* after the introduction of his four methodological principles, he writes that since 'it has been the mathematicians alone who have been able to succeed in making any demonstrations, that is to say producing reasons which are evident and certain', he 'did not doubt that it had been by means of a similar kind that they carried on their investigations' (HR1, 93; AT6, 19). With method as 'the true norm of reason', as the expression of 'the innermost essence of mind', what has been thought of as the unmethodical use of reason is not the use of reason at all, and cannot lead to knowledge. Or, since reason is the 'faculty of knowledge' which 'cannot be fallacious', it follows that to the extent we obtain results which are 'fallacious' we have not gone about our business methodically; we have not been reasoning.

In the preceding chapter it was asserted that, for Descartes,

[2] Beck, *The Method of Descartes,* p. 205.

[3] The *Introduction* to Anscombe and Geach, *Descartes, Philosophical Writings* (London, 1954), p. xxv.

[4] Kemp Smith, *Studies in the Cartesian Philosophy* (New York, 1962; first published in 1902), p. 23.

reason is autonomous. In the next chapter this assertion will be shown to be justified. The outlines of the argument have already been presented: reason, as the understanding in its function of intuiting items known *per se*, will be seen to be immune to all possible doubt, and is therefore absolutely trustworthy. Reasoning, the understanding functioning deductively, is to be justified as truthworthy, but its justification will not introduce elements extraneous to human reason. Thus the justification of reason will turn out to be a self-justification, and reason's autonomy will remain intact. If this can indeed be shown to be Descartes's argument, an important consequence follows with regard to the status of method. Any knowledge of any object can be obtained only through reason. This statement has been shown to be equivalent to the statement that any knowledge of any object can be obtained only methodically. Thus, given that method is the 'innermost essence' of reason and that reason is autonomous, method as well is autonomous. This entails that no justification for the universal applicability of the method to any object that can become an object of knowledge is called for, once it is realized that method is reason's 'innermost essence' and that reason is autonomous. When, therefore, in the first three of the *Meditations*, Descartes provides a validation of reason, this at the same time constitutes a justification for the imposing of his method. To this point I shall return in the next chapter.

2. Method as determining the nature of science

A scientific system, for Descartes, is the result obtained through the methodical, intuitive, and deductive use of the mind. In terms of reason we can say that the exercise of reason is scientific activity, and the product of the exercise of reason is science as a body of knowledge. For the justification and implication of these remarks, let us consider a number of passages from Descartes's writings.

Immediately after the introduction of the methodological principles in the *Discourse* Descartes writes that 'those long chains of reasoning . . . of which geometricians make use in order to arrive at the most difficult demonstrations, had caused me to imagine that all those things which fall under the cognizance of man might very likely be mutually related in the same fashion . . .' (HR1, 92; AT6, 19). This statement says much about the nature of science, as well as about the nature of the object in which the scientist is interested. Whatever is said is, however, introduced as a supposition. For he writes that the geometricians' reasoning 'had caused me to *imagine* . . '. What is necessary to get rid of the suppositional nature of this statement about the sciences? The answer to this question is given by Descartes in the rest of this sentence, where he writes that 'provided only that we . . . always retain the order which is necessary in order to deduce the one conclusion from the other, there can be nothing so remote that we cannot reach it, nor so recondite that we cannot discover it'. It is through following the right order or method that the geometricians have been able 'to arrive at the most difficult demonstrations'. As especially the *Rules* make clear, the success of all of the branches of mathematics is the result of method. *Method gives certainty* to mathematics. Or, to put it in the language of a paragraph from the *Discourse,* 'the Method which teaches us to follow the true order and enumerate exactly every term in the matter under investigation contains everything which gives certainty to the rules of Arithmetic' (HR1, 94; AT6, 21). Hence, if only we apply reason (rather than, for example, uncontrolled imagination) in areas other than mathematics or, if only we go about our business in other areas in the same orderly way as we did in mathematics, then these areas too will become areas in which one can obtain certainty, scientific knowledge.

Science is a concatenation of ideas which themselves are clear and distinct and whose connections are clear and distinct as well. Only when things have been made clear and distinct by reason can it function intuitively and deductively. The only way in which reason can attain clarity and distinctness is by functioning methodically. This is the only way in which it can ever function. Since the result of reason's intuitive and deductive activity is science, reason determines the nature of science; or, putting it in terms of method, method gives certainty to all sciences.

To say that 'reason determines the nature of science' is to say more than 'method gives certainty to all the sciences'. There is more than 'certainty' that characterizes the 'nature of science'. Even a statement like Koyré's, when he writes that '. . . it is this science of order which supplies the foundation of rational knowledge',[5] only gives us part of the story. For method, or reason,

[5] Anscombe and Geach, p. xxvii.

not only supplies the *foundation* of rational knowledge, it also dictates the nature of the detailed content of a science.

Care must be taken here to make the proper distinction. If the science in question is, say, applied physics rather than pure mathematics or metaphysics, method or reason does not provide the specific contents of such a science. But it does determine the nature of whatever will turn out to be its contents. Let us call the object of the physicist's interest 'the world' or 'nature'. *Which* world exists, and *which* things exist, and *which* events occur in it, is a contingent matter. Therefore, no knowledge of these specific details of nature can be obtained except through controlled use of imagination and sense, that is, except through experimentation. But given Descartes's view of reason and method, what can be said *a priori* about 'nature', about whichever 'world' exists, is that its laws will be mechanical laws, that these laws can be expressed in a mathematical fashion, and that these laws are based upon ('follow from') the principles which are incorporated in the science of metaphysics. What can be said as well is that method also dictates the form which such a science will ultimately come to possess. By this I do not mean that each science will have the overall pattern of, say, the metaphysical *Meditations*, where one starts with unordered complexity, which is resolved to intelligible simplicity, from which one then makes one's way to ordered intelligible complexity through composition or deduction. What I do mean to say is that advances within a science of nature will come about through confrontation with a complexity which at least initially contains unintelligible elements; that this complexity will be resolved to its simpler or simplest intelligible parts; that these parts will then be composed into intelligible complexity. The statements made in this paragraph can be placed in a broader framework, which will also make explicit further ways in which method determines the nature of science as well as the nature of the object in which the scientist (whether he be metaphysician, mathematician, or physicist) is interested.

When Descartes holds up the 'long chains of reasoning' of the geometricians as a touchstone for the other sciences, he is speaking not just of the nature of knowledge, but also of the nature of what this knowledge is about. (Consider his words: '. . . all those things which fall under the cognizance of man'.) As he states in the *Author's Letter* to the *Principles*, from the 'principles' of 'immaterial or metaphysical things' he deduces the 'principles' of 'corporeal or physical things' ('to wit, that there are bodies extended in length, breadth and depth, which have diverse figures and move in diverse ways'). From these, in turn, he derives 'a knowledge of all things that are in the world' (HR1, 208–9; AT9–2, 10–11). Thus, to isolate one of the elements involved, in this statement from the *Discourse* we have not merely a supposition about the unity within each science or about the unity among the different sciences, but also one about a certain kind of relatedness or unity of the objects in which the scientist is interested. In the *Principles* Descartes makes it quite clear that metaphysics, physics, medicine, mechanics, and morals are all united in the one science of 'true philosophy' (HR1, 211; AT9–2, 14). Physics, for example, is related to metaphysics in that 'the true principles of material things' are found among 'the clear and simple notions that are in us'. It is the business of metaphysics to bring out these 'clear and simple notions'. Once we recognize which of these are 'the true principles' of *material* things, 'we examine generally how the whole universe is composed, and then in particular what is the nature of this earth', of 'air, water and fire, the loadstone and other minerals', of 'plants, animals, and above all of man'. The sciences, united within and among themselves, give us the composition or nature of reality. Here, too, we find that there is a common nature of the objects of scientific inquiry. This becomes very clear in the later parts of the *Principles*. In Part II, 64, the unity of mathematics and physics is expressed in the statement 'I do not accept or desire any other principle in Physics than in Geometry or abstract Mathematics', and the common nature of the objects as 'all the phenomena of nature may be explained by their means'. (They may be explained, that is, by means of geometry or abstract mathematics.) The latter is clarified in the explanation of this principle where Descartes writes: 'I recognize no kind of "matter" in corporeal objects except that "matter" susceptible of every sort of division, shape, and motion, which geometers call quantity, and which they presuppose as the subject matter of their proofs.' He tells us further than 'the only properties I am considering' in corporeal nature 'are these divisions, shapes and motions'—thus at least for all scientific purposes, what is real is what is measurable—'and about them I assume only what can be derived in a self-evident way from indubitably true axioms' (AT8–1, 78–9).[6] These axioms are, of course, the ones presented in metaphysics and derived from man's own rational nature. (Compare, for example, *Principles*, Part III, 1.)

Although all things in nature as the objects of science are mutually related like the elements in the different parts of the long chains of reasoning of the geometricians, the ideas we have of these related objects—like those of mathematics—allow both of analysis or resolution into intuitable, discrete elements and of deductive reconstitution into complexity. We can thus conclude that reason, as characterized in the second and third methodological rules of the *Discourse*, determines the nature of science as well as the relations that hold in corporeal nature. For no certainty can be attained in science unless we approach our field of investigation methodically. And this can be done only if we view the objects in the field of investigation—comprising, ultimately, the whole universe—as being composed out of entities whose nature is reflected in ideas that can be reduced to what is clear and distinct, and reconstituted into intelligible, clear and distinct, complex wholes. The elements which are the limits of resolution are the self-evident simples and the principles which help serve to connect them, and which we derive from reason itself. The order that holds in the universe and that makes knowledge of it susceptible to resolution and deductive reconstruction is the order of reason. Both as to its elementary principles and its complex order, nature's principles are reason's principles, and nature's order is reason's order.

Critics objected to Descartes's reduction of space to extension and his acceptance of extension and the basic principle of his physics. Descartes considered this sort of objection as deserving only of scorn. And to the extent that critics deduced from this reduction that Descartes's 'Physics is but imaginary and fictitious', Descartes's scorn is understandable, for he reiterates time and again that physics in fact gives us the essence of corporeal nature. However, the only serious response which he presents to these critics is in terms of a consolation he finds in their objection, namely: 'my critics here conjoin my Physics with pure Mathematics, which it is my deepest wish my Physics should resemble' (HR2, 131; AT7, 212–13). The implicit argument is that his critics failed to recognize that what makes mathematics certain is

---

[6] Anscombe and Geach, p. 221.

method; that any science, if it is to be worthy of this name, has to be structured by method or reason in the way that mathematics is. A science structured by method is the only science possible for man. Since science gives us the essence of corporeal nature, then the essence of corporeal nature is no less a reflection of the essence of reason. Descartes places four tenets beyond question: that mathematical extension *ought* to be taken as the basic principle of physics in the way that he has taken it; that physical reality is indeed reducible to the principles governing mathematics; that man's capacity to understand reality is indeed that of intuitive and deductive reason; that the method through which to approach any subject-matter is indeed that of resolution and composition. He cannot allow doubt to arise about these tenets because he has given an autonomous status to reason and thus, by implication, to method. Whatever questions of this kind might be raised about method, such as questions about the validity of this kind of approach, or questions about the legitimacy of the extent of this kind of approach, are questions about reason. Reason itself answers these questions by telling the questioner that there are no good grounds for raising these questions, that there are no good grounds for doubting the trustworthiness of reason and hence no good grounds for questioning the correctness of this imposition of method.

3. 'Method' and 'methods'

When we speak of the universal method, no diversity is introduced when this method is applied to different kinds of subject-matter. But this does not mean that one cannot speak of various other 'methods' or 'techniques' which are used within the confines of the universal method, or the use of which is dictated by the application of the universal method. To complicate matters further, commentators sometimes speak of Descartes's 'method of doubt', about his 'hypothetical method', and about his 'experimental method'. Doubt, hypothesis, and experiment function in the context of the application of the universal method. The first of these is intimately related to both resolution and composition; the second and third function especially in the context of composition, and are related to the proper and necessary use of the imagination in all, and of sense in some, of the sciences.

An examination of how and when doubt, hypothesis, and experiment function in the context of the Cartesian method will complete my discussion of method. I will deal with these aspects in the following section (section 4), by offering a further explication of several of the points made earlier in this chapter. In the remainder of the present section I will discuss an aspect of the relation between the general method and other 'methods' or 'techniques' which are introduced in the context of its application.

About the *Discourse on Method* and the three treatises appended to it, Descartes wrote to Mersenne as follows:

However, I have not been able to understand your objection to the title; because I have not put *Treatise on Method* but *Discourse on Method*, which means *Preface* or *Notice* on method, to show that I do not intend to teach the method but only to describe it. As can be seen from what I say, it is a practice rather than a theory. I call the following treatises *Essays in this Method*, because I claim that what they contain could never have been discovered without it so that they show how much it is worth. I have also inserted a certain amount of Metaphysics, Physics, and Medicine in the first Discourse in order to show that my method extends to topics of all kinds.[7]

The method which 'extends to topics of all kinds', the method described in the first parts of the *Discourse*, is exemplified in the arguments of its later parts, and in the arguments of the *Optics*, *Geometry*, and *Meteorology*, the 'Essays in this Method' appended to the *Discourse*. As Descartes wrote to Dinet: '. . . in the Dioptric and Meteors I have deduced . . . many particular things which show what is my manner of reasoning' (HR2, 375; AT7, 602). The insistence on the inability to provide an abstract theory of method, and the insistence on the point that one can master the method only through practice, through following the steps in those sciences which have come about through the application of the method, is a clear echo of the argument presented in the *Rules*. For also in the *Rules* we read that no abstract theory of method was provided because 'nothing can be added to the pure light of reason which does not in some way obscure it' (Rule 4); also in that work, practice in mathematics is advocated in order that one may learn to reason or to proceed methodically (Rules 10 and 14).

[7] See Descartes's letter of 27 February 1637 (AT1, 347). The translation is from Kenny, *Letters*, p. 30.

The contents of the essays appended to the *Discourse* 'could never have been discovered' without the method, and the details of the arguments of these essays 'show what is my manner of reasoning'. As reason goes about its business in the development of a science, other 'manners', 'ways', 'techniques', or 'methods' of doing things are introduced. Unlike the general method, these manners or techniques can be criticized, rejected, or improved. They can be criticized or rejected if they do not follow from the application of the general method. They can be said to be the proper techniques if it can be shown that their use is dictated by the employment of the general method. There are two points that these essays, therefore, bring out very clearly. The first is that the nature of subject-matter, the concepts which are relevant in a science, and the form which a scientific system takes, are determined by the application of the method. The second is that the specific techniques to be used within a particular science are determined by the method. Although the original text of these essays brings out these points clearly, it has become obscured in the only complete translation of the *Discourse* and its *Essays* in English, Paul J. Olscamp's *Discourse on Method, Optics, Geometry, and Meteorology*.[8]

In these *Essays* three technical terms appear regularly: *méthode*, *moyen*, and *façon*. They are used with a good deal of precision by Descartes in the following way: *méthode* is used with the connotation this word has in the title of the general work on methodology (*Discours de la Méthode*); *moyen* and *façon* are used, interchangeably, to refer to specific manners of procedure within a specific science. The relation between *méthode* on the one hand, and *moyen* and *façon* on the other, is that the general *méthode* dictates the particular *moyens* and *façons* to be used in the particular sciences. Olscamp's translation utterly obscures this important point. He appropriately translates *façon* as 'way'[9] or 'manner',[10] and *moyen* as 'means'.[11] In all these cases one could substitute for both *façon* and *moyen* the word *manière* ('manner') without changing Descartes's meaning or intention, because in each of them he is concerned with

[8] Library of Liberal Arts, 1965. Hereafter referred to as 'O'.
[9] See e.g. O 106, AT6, 138; O 127, AT6, 165; O 215, AT6, 424; O 218, AT6, 431.
[10] See e.g. O 107, AT6, 140.
[11] See e.g. O 114, AT6, 147; O 207, AT6, 412; O 218, AT6, 413; O 250, AT6, 475.

a specific manner of procedure within a specific science. This same translation should also be used in all those instances in which Olscamp has translated *façon* as 'method', and the instances in which Olscamp inappropriately renders *façon* as 'method' outnumber those in which he appropriately translates it as 'manner' or 'way'.[12]

Descartes uses the terms 'method' (*méthode*) and 'manner' (*façon, moyen*) consistently in a crucially different way. The former is used to refer to his general methodology and the latter to specific manners of procedure within specific sciences. All this is clear from the relatively few sets of passages in which *méthode* actually occurs. What is clear as well from these passages is that the method (*méthode*) determines what is and what is not a correct procedure (*façon, moyen*) within a specific context. I will now discuss one of these passages in some detail. As I do so, I will present the relevant material in Olscamp's translation: referring to this translation as 'O'. But wherever Descartes's own formulation helps to clarify a point made in this part of his work, I will present that formulation in addition to Olscamp's translation.

The passage I have selected for comment is to be found at O 179–85; AT6, 372–80. Here, the argument concerns the use of equations in solving problems in geometry. Before Descartes introduces the specific problem in terms of which he illustrates the power of his method, he states what the use of such equations involves in general (O 179–80; AT6, 372–4). What Descartes has in mind with respect to the various details of his general statement will become clearer once we see a specific application of this general statement in terms of the particular example which will be provided below. As I present this general statement I will therefore comment only on those important aspects of it which do not find expression in its application in the specific problem. The salient points of the general statement are as follows.

(i) One 'should first of all consider [the problem] solved'.[13] Next,

---

[12] Such inappropriate translation occurs at, e.g., O 162, AT6, 211; O 196, AT6, 397; O 206, AT6, 411; O 232, AT6, 449; O 250, AT6, 473–4; O 254, AT6, 479; O 258, AT6, 484.

[13] In this respect Descartes follows the procedure already known to the Greeks. See e.g. *The Geometry of René Descartes,* translated by David Eugene Smith and Marcia L. Latham, p. 6, n. 9, of the Dover (1954) re-edition of the Open Court edition of 1925. See also Pappus as quoted in *The Method of Analysis* by J. Hintikka and U. Remes (*Boston Studies in the Philosophy of*

(ii) one must 'give names to all the lines', and (iii) create an 'order which most naturally shows the mutual dependency between these lines, until' (iv) 'we have found a means of expressing a single quantity in two ways', that is, in 'an equation, for [in an equation] the terms of one of the two ways [of expressing the quantity] are equal to those of the other'. In order that we may obtain the necessary 'single quantity' we (v) must use 'division wherever possible'.[14] If we follow this procedure 'we will infallibly reach the simplest terms to which the problem can be reduced'.

The use of 'simplest terms', 'division', 'reduction', and 'order' indicates that Descartes is here applying the general method propounded in the *Rules* and the *Discourse*. The specific geometrical problem to which Descartes applies the general method is one which had been of interest to the Hellenistic geometers, and for which they had presented a solution. However, according to Descartes, these ancient geometers did not observe the general methodological principles with sufficient care, for 'the order of their propositions alone makes us aware that they had no true method (*vraye méthode*) for discovering all of them, but that they had only gathered together those propositions they had stumbled upon'. When Descartes here states that the ancient geometers 'had no true method', it must be kept in mind that he does not mean to say that they did not at all use the method which he

---

Science, Vol. XXV; Synthese Library, Vol. 75; Dordrecht and Boston, 1974), p. 8: 'Now analysis is the way from what is sought—*as if it were admitted*—through its concomitants in order to something admitted in synthesis. For *in analysis we suppose that which is sought to be already done,* and we inquire from what it results, and again what is the antecedent of the latter, until we on our backward way light upon something already known and being first in order. And we call such a method analysis, as being a solution backwards.' The phrases which I have placed in italics especially show Descartes's affinity with Pappus. This affinity results from the role which Descartes assigns to the imagination in the context of his method, and this role of the imagination will be discussed in section 4 of this chapter.

[14] The 'division' here in question is the division or resolution of the general methodology .It therefore differs from the use of 'division' in, for example, the second sentence of the *First Book* of the *Geometry,* where 'division' is the purely mathematical procedure represented by the symbol ' $\div$ '. If the latter meaning is read into the passage now under consideration, this passage does not make sense. If, however, we read 'division' as the complete separation of the distinct elements of the problem by giving names to all the lines and by writing down a complete set of independent equations expressing the relations between the lengths of the various lines, the passage makes excellent sense.

himself had articulated. This is clear from the qualification he introduces: *'le seul ordre de leurs propositions nous fait connoistre qu'ils n'ont point eu la vraye méthode pour les trouver toutes, mail qu'ils ont seulement ramassé celles qu'ils ont rencontrées'*. In this way of putting it, Descartes does not really provide grounds to conclude—as Olscamp's rendering of *rencontrées* by means of 'stumbled upon' might lead one to conclude—that he believed that in the ancient geometers' works there was a total absence of the general method. Since Descartes did allow that some of the relevant propositions had been 'encountered' by the ancients, to that extent he would have ascribed to them correct or methodic procedure. In any case, in view of the fact that Descartes did believe that the ancients had indeed found solutions to geometrical problems, he would also have believed that they had found these solutions through the use of reason. For the use of any other faculty, for example the use of imagination without reason's control, would according to Descartes never lead to a solution of any problem— a point to which I will return in section 4 of this chapter. Hence, if one can speak of a 'solution' at all, the ancients must have used reason to arrive at this solution. And to speak of the 'unmethodical use of reason' is, as we have seen, a contradiction in terms for Descartes.

That the passage under consideration ought to be taken as I have just suggested is also clear from what we read about the ancient geometers elsewhere in the *Discourse* (e.g. HR1, 93; AT6, 19), as well as from what we read in the *Rules*. Take, as an example, the following statement from Rule 4:

Since then the usefulness of this method (*hujus methodi*) is so great that without it study seems to be harmful rather than profitable, I am quite ready to believe that the greater minds of former ages had some knowledge of it, nature even conducting them to it. . . . Arithmetic and Geometry, the simplest sciences, give us an instance of this; for we have sufficient evidence that the ancient Geometricians made use of a certain analysis (*analysi*) which they extended to the resolution of all problems, though they grudged the secret to posterity. . . . [Arithmetic and Geometry] are nothing else than the spontaneous fruit sprung from the inborn principles of the discipline here in question (. . . *nihil aliud sunt, quam spontanae fruges ex ingenitis hujus methodi principiis natae*). (HR1, 10; AT10, 373.)

It is not, therefore, as if the ancients worked without method.

Instead they did not use method systematically because they also placed trust in the imagination and the senses, especially in the sense of sight. To the extent that they misplaced their trust in the senses and the imagination, the ancients were bound to 'resort to those superficial demonstrations, which are discovered more frequently by chance than by skill, and are a matter more of the eyes and the imagination than of the understanding'. To the extent that they relied on sight and imagination, they present the picture of one who 'in a sense' 'ceases to make use of one's reason' (HR1, 11; AT10, 375).

Let us return to the passage from the *Geometry*. One way in which, according to Descartes, the unsystematic use of method in the ancients is clear is that they hesitated to use the simpler terms of arithmetic to express the more complex aspects of geometry; they had scruples about using 'the terms of arithmetic in geometry, which could proceed only from the fact that they did not see clearly enough the relation between the two'; and this 'caused (*causoit*) much obscurity and hindrance in the method with which they explained them (*la façon dont ils s'expliquoient*)'. Thus the absence of a systematic application of reason or method (*méthode*) 'causes' an obscure or inadequate explanation through an inadequate manner (*façon*) of exposition. One could extrapolate and say that the systematic application of reason, or of the general method, 'causes' a clear exposition because it would give an adequate manner of exposition, a clear demonstration. This, says Descartes, 'gave me occasion to try and discover whether, through my method (*par la méthode dont je me sers*), I could go as far as they had gone'. He then shows that he could go as far as the ancients. What is more, through his method he could give an explication of the problem which he could call a 'demonstration'.[15]

The specific problem in terms of which Descartes illustrates the application of his method is that of Pappus—a problem of no small importance, in that Descartes's treatment of it put analytic geometry on the map. Descartes provides the accompanying diagram to illustrate the problem (AT6, 382). Pappus's problem,

---

[15] Descartes can identify a 'manner of exposition' with a 'demonstration'. This is because a clear demonstration—'demonstration' in the sense of 'proof'—will always be a *clear* exposition. Conversely, a *clear* manner of exposition of the various relationships between the relevant quantities, or concepts, will be a proof, a demonstration of the required result.

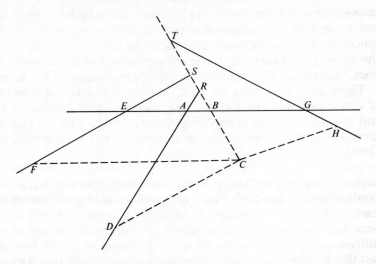

stated in general, is: Given three or more straight lines ('*AB, AD, EF, GH*, etc.'—in Descartes's presentation) to determine the locus of a point *C* such that the lengths of the lines drawn from *C* to cut the given lines at prescribed angles are related as follows: the product of the lengths from *C* to a fixed subset of these intersecting lines is equal to a fixed multiple of the product of the lengths from *C* to the other lines. Descartes's way of solving this problem through use of his method closely follows the general procedure he enunciated earlier. (i) He begins with the assumption that the problem is 'already solved'. (ii) He then gives 'names to all the lines'.[16] (iii) By taking 'one of the given lines' and one of those which it is necessary to find to be the 'principal lines'[17] Descartes creates an 'order which most naturally shows the mutual dependency between these lines'. Once he has made their 'mutual dependency' explicit by determining the lengths of the various intercepts in terms of the lengths '*x*' and '*y*' of the two 'principal

[16] It is clear that Descartes is using symbols such as *x*, *y*, in two different ways: (i) as 'names' ('Let the segment of the line *AB*, which is between points *A* and *B*, be called *x*, and let *BC* be called *y*') and (ii) as algebraic symbols for the lengths ('since *AB* is *x*, *RB* will be $\frac{bx}{z}$'). (O 186–7; AT6, 383.)

[17] These lines were later to become known as the 'Cartesian coordinates'. This move is probably the most important single factor for the development of analytic geometry by the mathematicians who followed Descartes.

lines',[18] he is able (iv) to express 'a single quantity in two ways' and so to obtain 'an equation' connecting 'x' and 'y'. (v) The procedure of 'division wherever possible' is also used to elucidate[19] the signs of the terms in the expressions for the lengths of the lines.[20]

Thus through his method Descartes could give a demonstration of that which the ancients, he believed, had known in part only and had presented somewhat haphazardly. One of the chief ingredients, the presence of which allowed for a demonstration by Descartes and whose absence (according to Descartes) had led to partial knowledge and an unclear exposition on the part of the ancients, is the decision on Descartes's part that the algebraic symbols used to represent the lengths of lines were not necessarily fixed in value.[21] This ingredient became available to Descartes because of a more profound difference, a method-inspired difference, between himself and the ancients. I have in mind the fact that for Descartes there was not only a correspondence between the lengths of lines and numbers, and of numbers to algebraic symbols, but also—and this is in further contrast to the ancients— a correspondence between the products of lengths of lines (i.e.

---

[18] This he does, in effect, through the application of the sine rule of trigonometry.

[19] This 'elucidation' is related to the process of 'enumeration'. There are various cases to be considered, depending upon, for example, whether 'B lies between C and R', or 'R lies between C and B', or 'C lies between B and R'. In these respective cases we have:

$$CR = y + \frac{bx}{z}, \quad CR = y - \frac{bx}{z}, \text{ and } CR = -y + \frac{bx}{z}.$$

Thus what is called for is an exhaustive enumeration of the possibilities together with a correct assignment of the signs in front of y and $\frac{bx}{z}$. Division of the problem in terms of an enumeration of the possibly relevant parts thus leads to an elucidation of the signs.

[20] This elucidation Descartes considered necessary because he was unable to free himself of the restriction that terms represented by a letter could only be positive.

[21] For the Hellenistic mathematicians, e.g. Diophantus, these symbols were necessarily fixed in value, so that, for example, if $AB = x$ and x is two units at some stage, it cannot be five units at a later stage of the demonstration. More importantly, x is not free for them to range over a set of values. None of this holds for Descartes, so that he can say: 'Then, taking successively an infinite number of different values for the line y, we will also find an infinite number of them for the line x; and so we will have an infinite number of different points such as the one marked C, by means of which we will be able to describe the required curved line' (O 188–9; AT6, 386).

areas) and numbers, and again also of these numbers to algebraic symbols. This 'correspondence' is the result of abstraction, of reduction to simplest elements: areas (and volumes) are reduced to lines, lines to numbers, and numbers to symbols. Because of his use of this kind of reduction, Descartes can say: 'Here it is to be noted that by a^2 or b^3 or the like, I ordinarily mean only simple lines, although, in order to make use of the names in algebra, I call them squares, cubes, etc.' (O 178; AT6, 371). In their commentary on this passage, Smith and Latham have noted that 'At the time this was written, a^2 was commonly considered to mean the surface of a square whose side is a, and b^3 to mean the volume of a cube whose side is b; while b^4, b^5, . . . were unintelligible as geometric forms. Descartes says that a^2 does not have this meaning, but means the line obtained by constructing a third proportional to 1 and a, etc.'[22] What is at stake here as a difference between Descartes and the ancients is expressed by another commentator, Hiram Caton, as follows. 'In Greek mathematics, shapes or figures cannot be reduced to magnitudes. . . . the figures themselves are irreducibly primitive.' But Descartes's 'method abstracts no less from figure than from number, because it considers only proportions in general'. For substantiation of this point Caton rightly refers to Rules 14 and 16 (specifically, to HR1, 56, 67; AT10, 441, 454–5). But his point can be made equally well with respect to the passage under consideration. Caton continues:

The algebraic system . . . because it can determine position solely by means of its internal properties, is a representation of space. . . . Cartesian figures, despite the identity of their appearance with Euclid's figures, are not the same. Euclid's figures are given, in the same sense that they are constructed, namely, by the mechanical method of ruler and compass. Descartes' figures . . . are constructed by referring them to an arithmetically constructed coordinate system: the space in which they are constructed is itself constructed.[23]

Caton then aptly quotes Boutroux's statement about Cartesian figures: 'One must never forget that these lines are only there to represent magnitudes in general. For imagination, they are geo-

---

[22] Smith and Latham, op. cit., p. 5, n. 6.
[23] Hiram Caton, *The Origins of Subjectivity* (New Haven and London, 1973), pp. 87–8.

metrical figures, but for the understanding they are pure quantities.'[24]

This leads me beyond the two points about method which I wanted to illustrate in this section. (A) On the one hand, method determines the techniques of a science in the sense that, in terms of geometry, the presence of method allows for a demonstration (allows for a clear exposition and hence a full understanding of the problem). (B) On the other hand, the partial absence of method causes an inadequate exposition (and hence results, at best, in a partial understanding of the problem's solution). The discussion has led me beyond these two points to the extent that it is now becoming clear that also in geometry method determines the nature of the subject-matter itself (rather than merely establishing certain aspects of the theory about the subject-matter). For the subject-matter in geometry consists, for Descartes, of abstract entities which can be related to one another in algebraic equations and which can be related in the space created by the understanding in terms of the coordinate system. There is nothing that is not intelligible with respect to these abstract entities, their relation in algebraic equations, their position in the space of the coordinate system, and the space of the coordinate system itself. All of these items are given to the understanding by the understanding. The objects of interest to the Cartesian geometer therefore have a nature quite different from the objects of interest to the Hellenistic mathematicians; the former only appear to be very similar to the latter. The difference that exists cannot be accounted for except through the introduction of Descartes's method. This is clear from many of the moves Descartes makes throughout the *First Book* of the *Geometry* as he uses Pappus's problem to illustrate the power of his own method. It is, perhaps, clearest from the fact that he feels quite free to consider the generalizations of Pappus's problem which involve the product of more than three lines. For the ancient geometers the product of four lines was something unintelligible. For Descartes, given the methodological

---

[24] This quotation, on p. 88 of Caton's book, is from Pierre Boutroux's *L'Imagination et les mathématiques selon Descartes* (Paris, 1900), p. 31. Caton then refers to Jacob Klein's *Greek Mathematical Thought and the Origin of Algebra* (Cambridge, Mass. and London, 1968), pp. 197–210, especially pp. 203–6. Klein's work presents excellent background material for the topic under discussion.

procedure of resolution to the most simple elements—which in this case involves the separation of name and specific thing named, and of a further abstraction through the symbolic representation of the name itself—this becomes a fully intelligible procedure.

I have used a passage from the *First Book* of the *Geometry* to illustrate the point that the general method determines what is, and what is not, a correct procedure in a specific context within a particular science. There are other passages in the *Geometry* which would lend themselves equally well for the kind of discussion I have just presented. One of these is to be found in the *Second Book* (O 207–14; AT6, 412–23). A detailed discussion of this passage would result in a duplication of points I have just been making in the last few paragraphs. It would thus do little to shed further light on the nature and function of Descartes's method. Something of fresh interest, however, is offered in Descartes's comments at the end of his solution of the problem he presents in that section:

But I should like to inform you, in passing, that the invention of assuming two equations of the same form, in order to compare separately all the terms of the one with those of the other, and to get several equations from one (of which you have seen an example here), can be used in an infinity of other problems, and is not one of the lesser inventions of the method I am using (*n'est pas l'une des moindres de la méthode dont je me sers*).

So, in the *Second Book*, we see the reiteration of a view in the *First*: through the systematic use of the general method one finds the proper technique which is to be used within a specific science. This passage therefore reinforces some of the conclusions reached earlier. Although this is not stated explicitly, the implication is clear. Only the methodic approach to any field of investigation leads to the discovery of techniques which actually further the cause of knowledge in that field. (This remains true whether the technique be forms of exposition or specific ways of proceeding within specific areas of a science.)

More could be said about Descartes's work in mathematics to illustrate that method determines both the nature of the subject-matter and the theory about this subject-matter, as well as the form in which the theory is to be presented in a scientific exposition. It seems to me of greater interest to continue by considering some of these aspects in detail in the context of a discussion of the *Meditations*. For, first, the *Meditations* are far better known among philosophers than is the *Geometry* and, second, in spite of the fact that they are better known, there is still considerable disagreement concerning what, precisely, Descartes intended to do in the *Meditations*. Before I will be able to provide this illustration in terms of the argument of the first three of the *Meditations*, it is necessary to complete the account of Descartes's method by showing how the 'method of doubt', the 'hypothetical method', and the 'experimental method' are related to the general method.

4. Method and doubt, imagination, sense

In the construction of a scientific system, both doubt and imagination play a more fundamental role than sense or experimentation. This holds for Descartes not only in the theoretical sciences like metaphysics or mathematics, but also for an applied physics or mechanics. The reason for this difference in the status of doubt and imagination on the one hand and sense on the other is to be found in the fact that for Descartes only doubt and imagination play a role in the context of the definition of reasoning and hence of method. Sense, or experimentation, does not play a role in the context of Descartes's definition of the general method, and hence it cannot be taken as an integral part of his method. To this assertion I will return later. First, I will discuss the nature and role of doubt, and the role of imagination, in the context of the construction of scientific knowledge.

While treating of these functions assigned to doubt and to the imagination, it is important to keep in mind from the outset Descartes's definition of method, and the relation which this definition of method has to a description of the activity of reason. It is thus important to recall at this point some statements and conclusions already presented in the first section of this chapter. Particularly, we should recall the definition of method as presented by Descartes in the heading of Rule 5:

Method consists entirely in the order and disposition of the objects to which our mental vision must be directed if we would find out any truth. We shall comply with it exactly if we reduce involved and obscure propositions step by step to those that are simpler, and then starting with the intuitive apprehension of all those that are absolutely simple, attempt to ascend to the knowledge of all others by precisely similar steps. (HR1, 14; AT10, 379.)

Next, we should recall that the kind of reasoning which, according to Descartes, gives us science involves, first, the establishing of an order in or among the problems which are considered to be relevant, an order which is obtained through reducing involved issues into simple or simpler ones; and, second, a (re)construction in terms of these simple(r) elements. Putting these statements side by side, we see that a description of the activity of reason coincides in essence with a statement which presents a definition of method. We shall have a good point of departure for a discussion of the nature and role of doubt if we recognize that, implicitly, doubt has a place in the definitional statement of both reason and method. For the 'reduction' involved in both these statements is one pushed to its extreme by the systematic or constant use of doubt.

Because one can speak of the 'systematic or constant use of doubt' the phrase 'universal doubt'—a phrase used by Descartes himself in *The Search After Truth* (HR1, 316; AT10, 515)—is applicable. However, care must be taken about what may be doubted in the use of this phrase. It is used properly in a statement, if the user means to say that doubt can be applied to any belief or to any item of knowledge. It is employed improperly if that statement is meant to imply that none of the items to which doubt is applied are able to withstand the test of doubt. Thus doubt can be applied to any belief, to any item of knowledge, but during the course of this universal application some of these items will show themselves impervious to it. The class of items which is impervious to even the most extreme form of doubt will turn out to be the objects of what I have called intuition$_1$. Thus talk about 'universal doubt' does not conflict with the idea of the autonomy of reason. Throughout the remainder of this discussion it is important to keep in mind the proper use of the phrase 'universal doubt'. Grounds for saying that there is such a proper and improper use in making statements about what may be doubted will be given later on in this section. These grounds will be reinforced in the next chapter.

The definitional statements of method and of reasoning which provide a good point of departure for a discussion of doubt, provide an equally good starting point for a discussion of the role of the imagination. For the imagination plays a necessary role in the 'attempt to ascend to the knowledge of all others by precisely similar steps', in the 'construction' of systematic knowledge 'in terms of these simple(r) items' which one obtains once the process of 'reduction' has run its course. How the imagination functions in the construction of systematic knowledge, and why it is indispensable in the construction of such knowledge, are issues best approached through consideration of the following points.

After the *Meditations* were completed, Mersenne questioned the order of exposition in them. Descartes replied that 'in all my writing I do not follow the order of topics, but the order of arguments'; and 'in orderly reasoning from easier matters to more difficult matters I make what deductions I can, first on one topic, then on another. This is the right way, in my opinion, to find and explain the truth.'[25] Thus the way to find systematic truth involves order and deduction. Deduction consists in a 'train of reasoning', and 'in every train of reasoning it is by comparison merely that we attain to a precise knowledge of the truth'. For 'all knowledge whatsoever, other than that which consists in the simple and naked intuition of single independent objects, is a matter of the comparison of two things or more, with each other' (HR1, 55; AT10, 439). The question is: assuming that one knows one of the two (or more) 'things' to be compared with one another, how does one obtain the relevant 'other thing'? This is a question in the area of composition or, since it concerns 'the right way . . . to find . . . the truth', one might call it a question in the area of the logic of discovery. It is an issue which Descartes took to be of crucial importance. 'In fact practically the whole of the task set the human reason consists in preparing for this operation' of comparing two things or more with each other. When the comparison is 'open and simple' (as it is when one recognizes that there is an immediate logical implication between thought and existence, or between thinking and having ideas) 'we need no aid from art, but are bound to rely upon the light of nature alone, in beholding the truth which comparison gives us' (ibid.). Deductive thought is not that of recognizing immediate logical relations. It therefore involves 'art', involves reliance upon 'aids' to 'the light of nature'. One of these aids is the imagination. Imagination functions in, for example, metaphysics, where it helps reason in proposing judgements as

[25] Kenny, *Letters*, p. 87; AT3, 264.

'things' to be 'compared' with whatever is already known, in order to continue the train of reasoning. It also functions in, for example, 'applied' physics where, with the help of sense, the imagination presents reason with models and experiments. The judgements, models, and experiments have to be presented in a certain order so as not to 'interrupt the flow and even destroy the force of my arguments'.[26] Thus questions about right order, and about the proper use of the imagination, are questions about how to 'find truth', questions about the compositive aspect of the method.

As we saw in the third section of Chapter I there are, according to Descartes, two 'orders' of exposition, those of 'analysis' and 'synthesis'. Of these, only 'analysis' 'shows the true way by which a thing was methodically discovered and derived, as it were effect from cause'. Thus analysis is held to be not just a method of exposition; it is also taken to be the method of discovery. For analysis involves a double achievement. There must be a reduction of the unintelligible or only partially intelligible complexity which initially confronts the thinker, to the fully intelligible starting-point(s) for his composition. And there must be an actual composition of systematic knowledge on the foundation of this starting-point (or on the foundation of these starting-points). If we look at some of the details which Descartes presents with respect to 'analysis' as the method of discovery, this will allow us to say more about both doubt and imagination. Some of these details are presented in the *Discourse* and in the *Rules*. In the *Discourse* (HR1, 92; AT6, 18–19) we read that there are four precepts which, if one does not 'fail, even once, to observe them', are quite sufficient as methodological principles for the discovery of truth. The first two of these precepts are about resolution. While he is discussing resolution as he enunciates the first precept, Descartes explicitly introduces the principle of doubt. The third precept concerns composition. In spelling it out Descartes makes an implicit reference to the role of the imagination. For there he states that one must direct one's 'thinking in an orderly way, by beginning with the objects that were simplest and easiest to understand, in order to climb . . . to the knowledge of the most complex (*des plus composez*) . . . assuming an order among those objects which do not naturally precede each other'. The assumption of order involves the formation of hypotheses; and that is the work of the

[26] Ibid.

imagination. For the assumed order is an 'imaginary' order, and the 'things' that 'follow' once the order is assumed are 'conjectures', *praejudicia* (cf. for example HR1, 31; AT10, 404–5). Through intuition and doubt one determines whether the assumed order is the right order, and whether the conjectures formed with the help of the imagination constitute correct judgements.

The role assigned to doubt within the context of composition may be indicated in the following way. The first methodological principle stated in the second part of the *Discourse* is restated in a somewhat truncated form in its fourth part, where Descartes writes that in his 'search for truth' he decided to 'reject as absolutely false everything about which I could conceive the least doubt' (HR1, 101; AT6, 31). The full statement of this principle in the second part of the *Discourse* gives grounds for the statement made earlier about the phrase 'universal doubt', in that it gives us the extent of 'everything' in to 'reject as absolutely false everything . . .'; 'never to accept anything as true that I did not know evidently to be such; that is to say, carefully to avoid haste and bias, and to include nothing more in my judgments than that which presented itself to my mind so clearly and so distinctly that I had no occasion to place it in doubt'. With respect to most judgements I introduce to further my train of reasoning I can, prima facie, conceive some ground of doubt. If I can conceive some ground of doubt then these judgements must be hypotheses. *Hence the methodological exercise of doubt shows up judgements as, prima facie, hypothetical.* If we ask the question 'Why is there some ground for doubt with respect to these judgements?' the answer is that there remains a ground for doubt because these judgements, rather than being given by the understanding alone, are produced with the help of the imagination. It is for this reason that judgements which state a 'truth known *per se*'—for example, 'there must at least be as much reality in the efficient and total cause as in its effect'— are not hypothetical and hence can withstand the test of doubt. They are not the result of the activity of the imagination; there was no 'comparison', and there were no steps of reasoning which led to their apprehension. Instead, they are singly 'manifest by the natural light' (HR1, 162; AT7, 40).

It is not, in the first place, through doubt that Descartes attempts to make progress in philosophy and the sciences. He holds that it is the imagination which plays the more fundamental role in the development of knowledge. It is through the imagination that we generate our 'enumerations', our lists of items possibly relevant to the argument. Since what is enumerated must be prima facie relevant to the particular problem, the use of imagination does not introduce an element which leads to 'vague and blind enquiries . . . relying more on good fortune than on skill'; it is not as if we proceed 'at random and unmethodically' (HR1, 30, 31; AT10, 403, 405). What is called for is a controlled, disciplined use of the imagination. How Descartes relates reason, method, and imagination is indicated especially in the *Rules*. The opening paragraph of Rule 9 states:

> We have now indicated the two operations of our understanding, intuition and deduction, on which alone we have said we must rely in the acquisition of knowledge. Let us therefore in this and in the following proposition proceed to explain how we can render ourselves more skilful in employing them, and at the same time cultivate the two principal faculties of the mind, to wit perspicacity, by viewing single objects directly, and sagacity, by the skilful deduction of certain facts from others.

Rule 9 then deals with 'perspicacity', which as is stated also in Rule 11 constitutes a further discussion of intuition. Rule 10 deals with sagacity. Its references to 'play', 'invention', and 'imaginary order' indicate that Descartes is here dealing with the use of imagination. Since 'sagacity' is 'one of the two principal faculties of the mind', and since a discussion of 'sagacity' is a discussion of the proper uses of the imagination, imagination must be taken to be subsumed under 'one of the two principal faculties of the mind'. How it is thus subsumed is indicated in Rule 10. For Rule 10 deals with the imagination. But in Rule 11 Descartes writes that Rule 10 deals 'with enumeration alone'. The function of the imagination therefore is to provide 'enumerations'. The examples given in Rule 10 make clear that Descartes is here concerned with the kind of enumeration which can be called 'inductive enumeration', with the 'enumeration or induction' which is an 'inventory (*perquisitio*) of all those matters that have a bearing on the problem raised' (HR1, 20; AT10, 388). Only a disciplined or controlled imagination can provide the relevant inventory. That the imagination must be disciplined is stated many times in Rule 10. It obtains its discipline especially from 'all play with numbers and everything that belongs to Arithmetic, and the like'; for 'It is wonderful how all these studies discipline our mental powers, provided that we do not know the solutions from others, but invent them ourselves'. Thus, in general, the relation between reason, method, and imagination can be put as follows: imagination is necessary to generate deductions; it can fulfil its role only if it is disciplined; and it is disciplined by the mathematical sciences which themselves are structured by method. We can say that inductive enumerations are generated through a methodic use of the imagination. Since in deduction or composition one searches for 'causes' of certain 'effects', what is presented by the imagination to the understanding will be possible 'causes' for experienced 'effects'.

This gives us the general answer to the question raised earlier in this section: given that the mind has before it one of the 'things' to be compared, how does one obtain the other 'thing' which is relevant? The general answer is that for the simple or simpler 'effect' the imagination will present as simple a 'cause' as possible, or a number of alternative 'causes'. These 'causes' are presented as hypotheses, conjectures, *praejudicia*. That 'cause' which can be seen (i.e. intuited) to have a necessary connection with the 'effect' is the 'cause' which can withstand the test of doubt. In that case the 'cause' or hypothesis in question becomes a true proposition; another link has been forged to the deductive chain. If we reformulate the question stated in the first sentence of this paragraph to read: (*i*) *what, precisely, is the next step to be taken in the argument?* and (*ii*) *how does one know that this is the right next step to take?* it will be seen that the general answer provided gives us criteria for answering the second part of the question. However, more needs to be said about both the first and second parts.

The imagination allows the understanding to assume as 'causes' that for which it does not yet have proof. These conjectures are not presented without *some* justification. Just as 'chance circumstances' will 'never bring about' the requisite experiments in the sciences, they will not call to mind the relevant judgements in metaphysics either (cf. HR1, 215; AT9–1, 20). Enumeration of possibly relevant 'causes' is in terms of the contents of the ideas of these 'causes'; and which idea is a possibly relevant one is at least in part determined by the 'effect' to be explained. Thus each inductive enumeration calls for a suitable preparation. Such preparation, besides involving competence in the method, involves thorough familiarity with the details of the argument as far as it has been developed. For, as Descartes writes about 'analysis', about 'the true way by which a thing was methodically discovered': 'it contains nothing to incite belief in an inattentive . . . reader; for if the very least thing brought forward escapes his notice, the necessity of the conclusion is lost' (HR2, 48–9; AT7, 156). Once a complete enumeration of possible 'causes' has been made, the role of the imagination is over. What remains to be done is to find means for elimating those conjectures which are false. In the process of eliminating the false conjectures the deduction is 'discovered'. The means for elimination is provided in the methodological principle of doubt. Suppose that a conjectured 'cause' cannot be seen or intuited to have a necessary relation to the relevant item or items of knowledge already possessed by the mind, or to the relevant parts of the body of knowledge already developed. Suppose that it cannot even be seen to be related to some still only partially intelligible item which is thus only partially incorporated in that body of knowledge. Then such a 'cause' is considered to be dubitable and is rejected as false.

In Rule 4 Descartes states that:

if our method rightly explains how our mental vision (*mentis intuitu*) should be used, so as not to fall into the contrary error, and how deductions should be discovered (*deductiones inveniendae sint*) in order that we may arrive at the knowledge of all things, I do not see what else is needed to make it complete; for I have already said that no science is acquired except by mental intuition or deduction. (HR1, 9–10; AT10, 372.)

The use of 'discovered' in 'how deductions should be discovered' involves another point of importance to be noticed. Descartes uses the same word in his comment on analysis as the method of discovery: 'Analysis shows the true way by which a thing was methodically discovered and derived, as it were effect from cause' (*Analysis veram viam ostendit per quam res methodice et tanquam a priori inventa est*) (HR2, 48; AT7, 155). The Haldane and Ross interpretation of *tanquam a priori* by means of the phrase 'as it were effect from cause' is justifiable in view of what Descartes says elsewhere about the method of discovery, especially in view of *Principles* I, 24 ('in this way we shall obtain a perfect science, that is, a knowledge of the effects through their causes') (HR1, 229; AT9–2, 35). *Invenire* does not mean 'discover' in the sense of 'invent'. Given the philosophical tradition in which this word plays an important role[27] as well as the context in which Descartes uses it, its meaning is 'to find', 'to come upon', that is, to discover something already in existence. Further, the use of 'as if' in *tanquam a priori* seems to indicate that Descartes is using '*a priori*' in a somewhat metaphorical way. Finally, since in its usual sense *invenire* is an achievement-verb, it must be understood as doing duty here for itself and for some activity-verb, such as 'seeking', 'looking for', 'following'. For it is such a verb which would naturally receive the adverbial modifications *methodice* and *tanquam a priori*. Thus *methodice* pertains not to a mode of discovery but to a mode of proceeding in order to make the discovery possible—that is, to a way of seeking-and-discovering; and *a priori* qualifies a description of the method and not of the result or achievement attained by following it. Hence a pedantic but properly clear translation of the whole sentence would be: 'Analysis shows the true way through which a thing has been sought-and-discovered methodically and, as it were, *a priori*.' In the light of the qualifications just introduced, its meaning would be: Analysis shows us the true way which, if followed methodically and, as it were *a priori*, leads the seeker to the discovery of a thing. 'Following methodically' would include the controlled use of imagination to give an inductive enumeration of all the relevant (i.e. *possibly* necessary) 'causes'. To this work of the imagination attaches an 'as it were, *a priori*' element: *which* of the several 'causes' it proposes will be the correct one is to be settled through subsequent doubt and final intuition. Whichever of the 'causes' can withstand the test of doubt will be intuited as the correct one(s). In metaphysics there will be only one such 'cause'. In theoretical physics there may be several 'causes'. If we want to develop an 'applied' physics, we will have to ask which of these several possible 'causes' is the actual 'cause'. This question is to be settled through experimentation, that is, through the use of imagination and sense combined.

A few comments are still in order about the role assigned by

[27] See e.g. Boethius's comments in the First Book of the second *Commentaries* on the *Isagoge* of Porphyry, readily available in Richard McKeon's *Selections from Medieval Philosophers*, Vol. I (Modern Student's Library, Scribner's), p. 74.

Descartes to sense and experimentation. Particularly, grounds have to be given for the assertion, made in the opening paragraph of this section, that sense and experimentation do not enter the picture in the context of the definition of Descartes's general method, and hence cannot be taken as an integral part of it. When we look at the role Descartes assigns to experimentation, this assertion will be seen to be justified.

Professor Gewirth has written that there is 'a non-mathematical, or specifically physical, application of the method, wherein the centre of consideration is not the general formal relation of intelligible essences, but those specific essences, and consequences thereof, which exist in the material universe'.[28] The use of 'mathematical' in 'non-mathematical' is unfortunate. But, quite apart from the word's occurrence, this is a statement which tends to confusion. It appears in the context of Gewirth's (correct) description of experimentation as the activity which is to provide an answer to the question: which 'causes', methodically obtained, actually exist in the material universe? The confusion enters when he makes experimentation a part of Descartes's general method. It is *not* Descartes's view that experimentation plays a fundamental role in the *construction* of any scientific system, or certainly not when 'construction' means 'initiation' or 'creation'. Rather, experimentation tells something about scientific systems *once they have been constructed or,* more practically, *as they are being constructed.* In the latter case, that of the scientist's reflection on a *step* already taken in the construction of a system, experimentation does play a very important role. For it tells the scientist which of the possible 'causes' are actual 'causes', and thus it determines the direction which the scientist takes as he forges new links to his deductive chain. However, the starting point for the chain is given by intuition alone, each successive link is initially provided by intuition or by the imagination followed by the application of doubt and, if the item provided by the imagination can withstand the test of doubt, by subsequent intuition. The actual process of forging link to link is accomplished by intuition-on-the-move, by deduction. Only the question: which link is to be added, *this* or *that*? is answered by experimentation. But the question is asked only under certain circumstances (namely, when

[28] 'Experience and the Non-Mathematical in the Cartesian Method', *Journal of the History of Ideas,* Vol. 2, 1941, pp. 183–210, esp. p. 188.

one wants to develop an applied science) and it is answered after intuition, imagination, doubt, and further intuition or deduction have played their role. The question whether a body of knowledge is or is not about the material universe is a question which is external to that body of knowledge. The procedure which leads to an answer to that question is, therefore, also external to the methodic procedure which resulted in the existence of that body of knowledge. Descartes consistently holds that experimentation is extrinsic to the method. This is the doctrine of the *Rules* (cf. HR1, 47; AT10, 427–8), the *Discourse* (cf. HR1, 120–2; AT6, 63–5), the *Principles* (cf. Part III, 4) and other writings. Of the latter, consider the following.

In a letter to Mersenne[29] Descartes writes about Galileo: '. . . it seems to me that he is continually wandering from the point and does not explain any matter thoroughly; which goes to show that he has not examined the points in order and, without having considered the first causes of nature, he has merely looked for the causes of particular facts, building thus without any foundation'. To the extent that one does not examine 'the points in order' one is working unmethodically, and hence one cannot then develop a thoroughly systematic account. It is for this reason that, according to Descartes, Galileo 'is continually wandering from the point and does not explain'—or demonstrate—'any matter thoroughly'. Thorough demonstration is methodic explanation. Only in the context of methodic explanation does attention to 'particular facts' make scientific sense. Only in the context of demonstration does it become meaningful to look for an answer to the question whether the 'causes' introduced as explanation 'of particular facts' are indeed the explanation. We may thus conclude that, for Descartes, applied physics is as 'deductive' as any of the theoretical sciences. The relation between deduction and experimentation may be put as follows.

A hypothesis introduced with the help of the imagination in an applied science loses its hypothetical status only after it has withstood *two* tests. The first is that of doubt and, if the hypothesis can withstand that test, it will be intuited as a possible next link in the chain. It is still a *possible* next link, because deduction alone

[29] This letter, written in 1638, can be found at AT2, 380. A part of it has been translated by L. J. Beck, and is printed in his *The Method of Descartes*, pp. 241–2. I have quoted Beck's translation.

cannot provide 'causes' for particular 'effects'. The second test is, therefore, observation or experimentation, to see whether these particular 'effects' are indeed explained by a 'cause' already intuited as possibly the right one. Only after this second process is the proposed hypothesis or 'cause' rejected as irrelevant or accepted as the right one. In the latter case, the proposed 'cause' loses its hypothetical status, and another link has been forged to the body of knowledge which is about the world in which we live. This process of the *two* tests Descartes calls (i) 'to explain effects by a cause' (this is the intuitive and deductive part of the 'demonstration'; it involves the imagination and doubt, but does not involve sense), and (ii) 'to prove the cause by the effects' (this is the empirical part which tells something about the 'demonstration', and which is necessary in applied sciences because deduction alone does not tell us whether the knowledge of 'effects' through the deduced 'cause' is knowledge of the particular and contingent 'effects' which are part of the world in which we live).[30]

One comment should be added as a corollary. For the contemporary scientist, experimentation is often employed as a means of verifying the correctness of results obtained. For Descartes, however, experimentation is not a tool which provides evidence for the correctness or incorrectness of science as a whole or of parts thereof. Instead, it only provides evidence for the correctness or incorrectness of a judgement made about the scientific system or about a part of the system, namely, of the judgement: it is an account of the world in which we live. This conclusion is inescapable. For if autonomous reason (which is infallible) or autonomous method determines the nature of science, a consequence is that science becomes unverifiable in the sense that there is no further test beyond doubt and intuition of results within the system, no test of them outside the system, and no test of the system as a whole. Science, the system constituted by reason or method, is absolute to the extent that Descartes considers it neither desirable, necessary, nor possible to test the results obtained, either within the system or outside it. In this respect also science is autonomous. Of course, to say that the results obtained in a science need not, or cannot, be submitted to a *further* test is not to say that one scientist need not, or cannot test the results

[30] These statements are from Descartes's letter to Morin, 13 July 1638. Cf. AT2, 196; and Kenny, *Letters*, pp. 57–8.

obtained by another. For although reason is held to be infallible, scientists are not. Hence results obtained by a scientist need to be tested by others because one does not know, beforehand, whether these results have in fact been obtained through the rigorous application of reason alone. One might suspect that a scientist has allowed himself to be led by 'the eyes and the imagination' rather than by 'the understanding' (Rule 4). The results obtained in that way would not be 'science'. However, the only test available is: to try and rethink the other's argument. Since it is reason which tests results which have purportedly been reached by reason, the autonomy of reason, and thus of science, remains intact.

IV

MEDITATIONS I AND II
The Trustworthiness of Intuition and the Justification of Resolution

In my second chapter I asserted that, according to Descartes, reason in its intuitive function of grasping truths known *per se* does not stand in need of validation. When I made this assertion about what I termed intuition$_1$, I introduced only a few items of evidence to give some grounds for it.[1] And at that time I did not at all attempt to show in detail why Descartes considered himself to be right in his belief about the absolute trustworthiness of intuition$_1$. In both my second and third chapters I made the point that the universal applicability of method is justified for Descartes because of the identity of method and reason.[2] Merely to make this point does not provide any justification for the imposition of the method. For such a justification can be shown to exist only after the trustworthiness of reason has been established. These statements about the two preceding chapters imply most of the tasks to be taken up in this chapter, and the next.

The trustworthiness of intuition$_1$ is established in the context in which Descartes comes to terms with the sceptic's doubt. In section 1 of this chapter I will therefore state the main reasons for the presence of 'universal doubt' in the *Meditations*. In section 2 I will make clear what it was that, in Descartes's view, ought to be doubted. I will seek also to establish, beyond all further question, that Descartes held certain items of knowledge to be impervious to doubt. In section 3 I will argue that for Descartes the recognition that certain items can withstand the test of universal doubt establishes the absolute trustworthiness of intuition$_1$, and that this recognition at the same time provides the grounds which justify the imposition of the principle of resolution. In the course of the position to be presented in sections 2 and 3 it will become clear that Descartes's argument in these *Meditations* is itself structured

---

[1] See Chapter II, section 3.
[2] See Chapter II, section 3; and Chapter III, section 1.

by his method. These are the tasks I have set myself in this chapter. Since all these tasks can be accomplished within the framework of a discussion of *Meditation I* and the first part of *Meditation II*, the subsequent *Meditations* will enter my discussion only to the extent that they help clarify my argument about the first two.

Throughout this chapter and the next I will be employing 'intuition' only in the sense of 'intuition$_1$'. It will therefore be easier and more aesthetic to use the word 'intuition' with no qualifying marks. So I request the reader to understand that in all its occurrences in these two chapters 'intuition' means 'intuition$_1$'. (There is one exception to this, in the next chapter, but it will be clearly set apart.)

Also, in these two chapters, I will work closely to the text of the *Meditations*. I will therefore adopt a method of reference to this text different from that used in my previous chapters. Instead of identifying parts of Descartes's work by means of page references, I will refer to the individual paragraphs of the *Meditations*; for example, to the first paragraph of the first *Meditation* as 1, 1. In their translation, Haldane and Ross have followed exactly the paragraphing of the Latin edition as presented in Adam and Tannery's *Œuvres de Descartes*. My references will therefore continue to be to both the Haldane and Ross translation and to that standard version. Additions which Descartes made to the subsequent French version of the *Meditations* will be incorporated without further comment about their source. These additions are all given in parentheses in the Haldane and Ross translation; in Adam and Tannery they can be found in Volume 9, part 1.

1. Reasons for doubt in the *Meditations*

'I have used in my *Meditations* only analysis, which is the best and truest method of teaching'. The *Meditations*, therefore, 'show the way in which the matter taught was discovered' (HR2, 49; AT7, 156). What is said to be 'discovered' first of all is the first principle of metaphysics which is to be part of the foundation for a 'firm and permanent structure in the sciences' (1, 1). The *Meditations* show how this first principle is reached, what it is, how one proceeds from it to the rest of the foundation for all the other sciences, and what the rest of that foundation is. Since the foundation is to be 'firm and permanent', it must be certain or indubitable. For that reason the powers of the mind which construct the foundation (intuition and deduction), or the procedures used in the construction of the foundation (resolution and composition) must themselves be shown to be absolutely trustworthy.

There is still considerable debate among commentators about what Descartes intended to call into doubt, or actually did call into doubt in the *Meditations*. Basically, the debate is about the word 'all' in the opening sentence of the 'synopsis' of the *Meditations*: 'In the first *Meditation* I set forth the reasons for which we may, generally speaking, doubt about all things . . .'. Some commentators have argued that Descartes means to raise doubts about all supposed or apparent knowledge to the extent that *memory* plays a role in it. They attempt to show that Descartes is seeking a guarantee for the reliability of memory rather than, say, a guarantee for the reliability of all clear and distinct ideas.[3] Others have attempted to show that 'all' in 'doubt about all things' is a severely restricted 'all' because it refers only to all beliefs acquired through the senses.[4] Most commentators do not restrict the realm of the dubitable in this way. For some have defended the thesis that all of reason needs to be validated and these commentators therefore believe that, in the *Meditations*, the trustworthiness of reason is a working hypothesis whose tenability is itself to be tested by the investigation which Descartes undertakes.[5] Still others have suggested that at times Descartes even doubts the *Cogito*.[6] Although all of these interpretations contain some truth they are also all to a greater or lesser extent misinterpretations.

If we look for the reasons for the application of doubt in the *Meditations* we are a step closer to answering the question of what Descartes intended there to call into doubt, and what he succeeded in doing. Descartes makes clear his belief that there are reasons for

[3] This interpretation, presented by A. K. Stout in his 'The Basis of Knowledge in Descartes' and by Willis Doney in his 'The Cartesian Circle', has been shown to be untenable by Harry G. Frankfurt in his 'Memory and the Cartesian Circle', *Philosophical Review*, Vol. LXXI, 1962, pp. 504–11.

[4] See, for example, Merrill Ring's 'Descartes' Intentions', *Canadian Journal of Philosophy*, Vol. III, 1973–4, pp. 27–49.

[5] See, for example, Harry G. Frankfurt, *Demons, Dreamers, and Madmen* (New York, 1970), pp. 27 ff.

[6] See, for example, Alan Gewirth, 'The Cartesian Circle Reconsidered', p. 679.

taking scepticism seriously: '. . . I feel constrained to confess that there is nothing in all that I formerly believed to be true, of which I cannot in some measure doubt, and that not merely through want of thought or through levity, but for reasons which are very powerful and maturely considered' (1, 10). What are these *reasons* of which he is speaking?

Some of them are already presented in the *Rules*, more than a decade before Descartes wrote the *Meditations*. Consider, for example: 'scarce anything has been asserted by any one man the contrary of which has not been alleged by another' (HR1, 6; AT10, 363). In the *Rules* Descartes relates this lack of agreement to a lack of method. The lack of consistent methodic procedure not only leads to disagreement; it also stands in the way of making progress in the sciences. For in the *Discourse* we read that even in the most secure of sciences, mathematics and geometry, there has been little development since the ancients, and 'the order of their propositions alone makes us aware that they had no true method for discovering' (*Discourse, La Géometrie*, AT6, 376). One reason for doubt is, therefore, the pervasive lack of agreement on most issues of importance. Descartes believes that he can at least begin to remove such a reason for doubt if he can show that each and every belief or any body of 'knowledge' which has not been attained through consistent methodic procedure will always remain susceptible to doubt; or if he can show what amounts to the same thing, that disagreement will always remain possible and that progress will always be hindered as long as we do not apply the method systematically. At least as important a reason for doubt arises from the thinking behind the wholesale rejection of scholastic positions by a number of Descartes's immediate predecessors as well as by many of his contemporaries. To the extent that there was such a rejection the intellectual world had lost its moorings. And through François Sanchez's *Quod nihil scitur* and especially Montaigne's *Essais* ('The Apology for Raimond Sebond', 1576), the sceptical positions of Sextus Empiricus and Pyrrho of Elis were current.[7] This scepticism was sufficiently prevalent to make it obligatory for anyone who 'wanted to establish any firm and permanent structure in the sciences' to present a method for

---

[7] For an informative account of sixteenth- and early seventeenth-century scepticism, see Richard H. Popkin, *The History of Scepticism from Erasmus to Descartes* (New York, 1964).

the discovery of truth which would make 'it impossible for us ever to doubt those things which we have once discovered to be true' (Synopsis of the *Meditations*, 1). If philosophers and scientists have gone about their business in haphazard, unmethodical ways, it is not really surprising that 'scarce anything has been asserted by any one man the contrary of which has not been alleged by another'. But the presence of Pyrrhonic scepticism made it advisable to doubt even the method whose application was to lead to indubitable knowledge, or to doubt the validity of the process which leads to the discovery of systematic truth.[8] Thus Descartes believes he will be successful in his attempt to remove the reasons for doubt only if, in his *Meditations*, he will be able to present a justification for trust in the general method, or a validation of the process of reasoning.[9] If we look at what, precisely, is doubted in the *Meditations*, we shall be able to see that doubt is indeed directed to method or the reasoning process. And we shall be able to see how, for Descartes, trust in the efficacy of method and in the validity of reasoning becomes justified.

2. The extent of doubt in the *Meditations*

In *Meditation I* Descartes introduces three kinds of knowledge. He speaks of knowledge of things that are 'hardly perceptible', or 'very far away', of knowledge of being 'seated by the fire, attired in a dressing gown, having this paper in my hands' (1, 4–5). This is what we take to be ordinary knowledge which is gained from the

[8] That, in the *Meditations*, Descartes did indeed intend to defeat scepticism is clear from his comments in the *Discourse* when he offers what one might consider an outline of the position to be presented in the *Meditations*. Consider his statement: 'this truth, "*I think, therefore I am*" was so certain and so assured that all the most extravagant suppositions brought forward by the sceptics were incapable of shaking it' (HR1, 101; AT6, 32). Even more telling is a passage from Descartes' replies to Bourdin's objections to the *Meditations*: 'Neither must we think that the sect of sceptics is long extinct. It flourishes to-day as much as ever, and nearly all who think that they have some ability beyond that of the rest of mankind, finding nothing that satisfies them in the common Philosophy, and seeing no other truths, take refuge in Scepticism. These people are especially such as demand a proof to be given them of the existence of God and the immortality of the soul.' Near the end of this same paragraph Descartes refers to his *Meditations* as 'Arguments by which I, first of all men, upset the doubt of the sceptics' (HR2, 335–6; AT7, 548–50).

[9] James Collins presents a somewhat similar view of the reasons for doubt. See his *Descartes' Philosophy of Nature*, A.P.Q. Monograph No. 5 (Oxford, 1971), p. 42.

senses in everyday experience, rather than from study in the sciences. He also speaks of what we take to be scientific knowledge, specifically, of physics, astronomy, medicine, and mathematics. This (presumed) scientific knowledge is of two kinds which, continuing the use of terminology introduced in previous chapters, I shall call 'applied' and 'theoretical'. I shall use 'applied', for example, in speaking of physics to the extent that it actually describes the world in which we live (1, 8). I shall employ 'theoretical' in referring to any of a number of possible scientific systems about possible worlds or, to stay closer to this *Meditation*, in alluding to mathematics (1, 9). These kinds of knowledge differ in terms of the different elements that enter into their composition. If we distinguish such everyday forms of (presumed) knowledge from instances in applied physics and in theoretical mathematics, what are the reasons for doubt in each of these cases?

The reasons for doubting the three kinds of supposed knowledge in *Meditation I* are as follows. In the case of such everyday forms of what we call *knowledge* we can raise the Cartesian arguments from illusion and from dreaming. We can deal in the same way with presumed knowledge in applied physics to the extent that we speak of it as knowledge in *applied* physics because it introduces sensuous elements. Neither of these two reasons are operative in the case of our directing our doubts to the realm of mathematics. This is not to say that the propositions of this form of science may not be doubted. Rather, it means that such propositions are to be doubted for a reason which has not yet been introduced, for a reason related to the intellectual activity of composition or deduction. It is necessary for us to doubt also such claims to knowledge, although no sensuous elements play a role there, because an evil genius is assumed to be able to tamper with the mental activity of deduction. Of course, since deduction plays a role in the first two kinds of supposed knowledge as well, and since the products of the activity of deduction are now dubitable, we here have an additional reason for doubt of 'knowledge' involving sensation. The important point to be noted, however, is that doubt of the products of reason's deductive activity extends the scope of doubt to all presumed knowledge of a composite nature, including judgements which in no way involve the senses. Since no supposedly systematic knowledge, whether or not it pertains to the world in which we live, is possible without deduction or composition, all of what seems to be our systematic knowledge is untrustworthy, is open to doubt. The text of *Meditation I* supports the picture sketched so far.

In this *Meditation* Descartes, in accordance with the first precept of the method stated in the *Discourse*, decides that he 'must once for all seriously undertake to rid myself of all opinions which I had formerly accepted' (1, 1). In accordance with the *Discourse's* second methodological precept he then proceeds by resolution, that is, by division of all he formerly held true, in terms of the 'principles upon which all my former opinions rested' (1, 2). Initially, Descartes presents only *two* such 'principles': *first*, the 'principle' that what he formerly held to be true involved sensation and, *second*, that it involved complexity and hence composition or deduction. That a *third* 'principle' is relevant as well will become clear in the next section of this chapter.

Arguments from illusion (1, 4) and dreaming (1, 5) are sufficient in Descartes's view to show that any particular sense-based judgement is untrustworthy. Hence the conclusion (stated at the beginning of the argument, at 1, 3) that since 'it is sometimes proved to me that these senses are deceptive', 'it is wiser not to trust entirely to any thing by which we have once been deceived'.

Some critics have assumed that a science like physics cannot withstand the test of doubt because it involves observation and experimentation.[10] Thus it has been assumed that, when Descartes called into question the propositions of all sciences with such obviously empirical domains of application as physics enjoys, he did so by reference to the untrustworthy senses, thus employing his first 'principle' in terms of which doubt is possible. But such critics have failed to distinguish the theoretical from the applied form of a science like physics. In terms of the first 'principle', only the answer to the question 'is this body of alleged knowledge about the physical world in which we think we live?' can no longer be accepted as trustworthy. In *Meditation I*, however, the point is rather that deduction is necessary for gaining scientific knowledge. Not only does reasoning in these sciences necessarily involve deduction or composition, but the very object of this reasoning is complex to begin with, namely, extended corporeal substance—an entity which, by its very nature, is subject to division (cf. HR1,

---

[10] This, for example, is the position taken by Merrill Ring in his article 'Descartes' Intentions'.

264; AT8–1, 51). The latter Descartes makes clear as soon as doubt is brought to bear on these sciences: 'Physics, Astronomy, Medicine, and all other sciences which have as their end the consideration of composite things, are very dubious and uncertain' (1, 8). Since knowledge of what is complex is always composite, the 'principle' in terms of which doubt has a strong foothold is that of composition.

This takes us to mathematics. That discipline is for Descartes a science which differs from the other sciences in that (at least at its foundation) its subject-matter is simple. In terms of subject-matter, therefore, the mathematical sciences initially seem to be able to withstand doubt: 'Arithmetic, Geometry, and other sciences of that kind which only treat of things that are very simple and very general . . . contain some measure of certainty and an element of the indubitable' (1, 8). However, the 'measure of certainty' and the 'element of the indubitable' quickly evaporate when, in that paragraph, the evil genius is introduced. The disappearance of indubitability here is possible, I submit, because mathematics '*treats* of things that are very simple'. Even if we interpret 'very simple' to mean 'absolutely simple', i.e. indivisible, so that the object of mathematics is entirely different from the 'composite things' of the other sciences, doubt is possible because mathematics is the science which *manipulates* these simples by relating them. Deduction, composition, or demonstration is as essential to mathematics as it is to any other science. When, in the *Discourse*, Descartes expresses his delight with mathematics it is 'because of the certainty of its demonstrations and the evidence of its reasoning' (HR1, 85; AT6, 7). For the experienced mathematician it is child's play to understand that 'two and two amount to the same as three and one', let alone that 'two and two make four', and 'three and one make four' ('premisses' from which the first statement was taken to follow before the introduction of the evil genius). For the novice, all three statements need to be worked out. And for both the expert and novice the object grasped in each case is complex. So for *Meditation I* where, with the evil genius on the scene, the question is 'how do I know that I am not deceived every time that I add two and three, or count the sides of a square?' (1, 9). The important words here are 'add' and 'count'. Their presence clearly indicates the necessity of composition or deduction. The emphasis, in paragraphs 8 and 9, on words like 'treat', 'form', 'add', 'count', and 'judge' point to the role of the evil genius: he is assumed to be able to tamper with the activity of composition. The assumption of his existence places in question the trustworthiness of the deductive function of reason.

Before the evil genius is introduced we read that 'For whether I am awake or asleep, two and three together always make five, and the square can never have more than four sides, and it does not seem possible that truths so clear and apparent can be suspected of any falsity' (1, 8). However, what does not seem possible becomes possible in the very next paragraph through the hypothesis about the evil genius.

The claim that 'two and three make five' involves an item of purported knowledge by deduction and hence is dubitable. But even after universal doubt has been introduced in the form of the omnipotent deceiver, we find Descartes saying: '. . . always when I direct my attention to things which I believe myself to perceive very clearly, I am so persuaded of their truth that I let myself break out into words such as these: Let who will deceive me, He can never . . . cause it to be true . . . that two and three make more or less than five . . .' Since I am persuaded of the truth of items like these I am unable, psychologically, to doubt them. The universal doubt is, therefore, 'very slight, and so to speak metaphysical' (3, 4).

Thus one might say that the evil genius makes it possible to doubt at one level (the metaphysical level) what Descartes finds it impossible to doubt at another level (the psychological level). If one wants to adopt the terminology of 'psychological' and 'metaphysical' doubt—the notion of 'metaphysical doubt' introduced by Descartes himself, and that of 'psychological doubt' current in contemporary literature through the use of it, for example, by Professor Gewirth—we must be careful to note what is both metaphysically and psychologically dubitable, and what is psychologically indubitable but metaphysically dubitable. (Later on, we shall have to ask whether there is anything which is both psychologically and metaphysically indubitable.)

'Psychologically and metaphysically dubitable' may now be applied to any particular judgement based on sense experience. Any one of these may be attacked with arguments from illusion or from dreaming. Before metaphysical doubt arrived, before the evil genius was introduced, there was or seemed to be some way, within the relevant set of experiences, to deterimne that some experiences were veridical and some were not. But even before the evil genius is introduced, and also once that hypothesis is again rejected, it is in fact not possible in terms of any particular experience alone further to qualify whether it is veridical or not. This is clear from the final paragraph of the *Meditations* where, with the evil genius again out of the picture, Descartes writes:

And I ought to set aside all the doubts of these past days as hyperbolical and ridiculous, particularly that very common uncertainty respecting sleep, which I could not distinguish from the waking state; for at present I find a very notable difference between the two, inasmuch as our memory can never connect our dreams one with the other, or with the whole course of our lives, as it unites events which happen to us while we are awake.

With the evil genius out of the picture at the end of the *Meditations* there still remains the possibility of one's being deceived in terms of any one of our experiences. There thus remains psychological doubt. But this doubt can be removed through showing that there is a coherence (or lack of coherence) in the judgement made about that particular experience and the set of judgements made about the set of experiences we have during our life or during a substantial part of it. With the evil genius in the picture, the possibility of showing such coherence (or lack of coherence) becomes irrelevant because the total set of experiences, and hence the total set of judgements based upon them, has itself become problematic. For once the evil genius is on the scene, the question arises 'How do I known that He has not brought it to pass that there is no earth, no heaven, no extended body, no magnitude, no place, and that nevertheless I possess the perceptions of all these things and that they seem to me to exist just exactly as I now see them?' (1, 9). It is not the case that I am no longer psychologically certain of the set of experiences, for 'they seem to me to exist just exactly as I now see them'. Through metaphysical doubt, however, the relevance of the coherence test has been lost. For though the judgement based on any one of my experiences may cohere with a large set of other judgements about other experiences, *all* members of this set may be about what 'seems to be' rather than about what 'is' the case.

Comparison of this situation in the realm of what is presumed to be sense-based knowledge with that in the area of what is presumed to be deductive knowledge will give us the basis for showing the validity of reduction as a methodological procedure. It will at the same time provide the grounds for showing the trustworthiness of the intuitive function of reason.

The best place from which to start this part of the argument is in the third *Meditation*, with the paragraph in which Descartes explicitly introduces the concept of metaphysical doubt (3, 4). We there read:

But when I took anything very simple and easy in the sphere of arith-metic or geometry into consideration, e.g. that two and three together make five, and other things of the sort, were not these present to my mind so clearly as to enable me to affirm that they were true? Certainly if I judged that since such matters could be doubted, this would not have been for any other reason than that it came into my mind that perhaps a God might have endowed me with such a nature that I may have been deceived even concerning things which seemed to me most manifest. But every time that this preconceived opinion of the sovereign power of a God presents itself to my thoughts, I am constrained to confess that it is easy to him, if He wishes it, to cause me to err, even in matters in which I believe myself to have the best evidence. And, on the other hand, always when I direct my attention to things which I believe myself to perceive very clearly, I am so persuaded of their truth that I let myself break out into words such as these: Let who will deceive me, He can never . . . cause it to be true . . . that two and three make more or less than five. . . . And, certainly, since I have no reason to believe that there is a God who is a deceiver, and as I have not yet satisfied myself that there is a God at all, the reason for doubt which depends on this opinion alone is very slight, and so to speak meta-physical. But in order to be able altogether to remove it, I must inquire whether there is a God as soon as the occasion presents itself; and if I find that there is a God, I must also inquire whether He may be a deceiver; for without a knowledge of these two truths I do not see that I can ever be certain of anything.

That 'two and three together make five' is psychologically certain. However, under one set of circumstances, namely those which introduce the evil genius, I am able to doubt it. It is therefore metaphysically uncertain or dubitable. That 'I am here, seated by the fire, attired in a dressing gown, having this paper in my hands' (1, 4) is both psychologically and metaphysically dubitable. The difference in the status of these two judgements is that the former is a judgement arrived at purely by deduction, the latter a judgement based on sense perception. Before the introduction of the evil genius, any sense-based judgement could be unveridical, and in terms of the particular judgement or the particular perception alone, no conclusive evidence could be found to show that it was, or was not, veridical. But before the introduction of the evil genius, any judgement arrived at purely by deduction was held to be infallibly true, because reason was held to be infallible. Thus, with respect to any item of purely deductive knowledge, the *only* reason for doubt is that the evil genius' possible existence calls into question the validity of *composition*, the trustworthiness of deduction. This last statement calls for justification. Giving that justification will lead to revelation of the validity of the procedure of *resolution*.

The sense-based judgement 'I am here, seated by the fire . . .' is psychologically dubitable. The judgement 'two and three together make five', a judgement based on reason alone, is psychologically indubitable. This is because of the difference in status of sensation and reason before the introduction of the evil genius. The question now needs to be raised: Is there any further difference in status between these two now that the evil genius has been introduced? Is there anything within a particular deduction-based judgement which is impervious to any kind of doubt? As we have seen, within sense-based judgements there is nothing impervious to doubt.

In order to be able to answer this question we need to recall what was said about Descartes's use of the concept *praejudicium*[11] in the last part of my preceding chapter. For Descartes uses this concept in the context of the *Meditations* exactly as we saw him use it in the context of our discussion of his 'logic of discovery': *praejudicia* are hypotheses, or judgements which have not yet been seen to stand in a necessary relation to whatever knowledge we already possess. That Descartes does indeed use the concept *praejudicium* in this way is clear, for example, from an important passage in the *Replies to Objections* (HR2, 127; AT9-1, 205-6).

---

[11] In my third chapter I used 'prejudice' as a translation of *praejudicium*. In that chapter the context made it quite clear that 'prejudice' had a specific technical meaning, rather different from what we usually convey by 'prejudice'. In the pages which follow, as well as in the next chapter, the context may not always bring this special meaning to the reader's mind. Therefore, unless the particular context clearly indicates the technical meaning of this term, I shall use its various Latin forms in the remainder of this chapter, as well as in the next one.

In this passage (which will become central to my discussion in the next part of this chapter) Descartes writes that whatever is 'known without any affirmation or denial' is not a *praejudicium*. *Praejudicia* come into existence through 'affirmation or denial'. In the previous chapter I showed that when a link is to be added to the deductive chain, when there is *no immediate* logical relation between the two items to be joined, then imagination and doubt play a role. The imagination presents items as possibly necessarily related to the knowledge we already possess, and we affirm or deny whether these items have a necessary connection to this knowledge. These items are, then, hypotheses, *praejudicia*. Nothing presented to the understanding by the imagination is, therefore, prima facie, indubitable. If the item thus presented to the understanding is seen to have a necessary connection to some other item of knowledge we already possess, then the item thus presented ceases to be dubitable. But concepts or principles which are known *per se* are not presented to the understanding by the imagination. They are given to the understanding by the understanding, and are held to be indubitable. As we shall see later on, the supposed presence of the evil genius does not affect the status of concepts or principles which are known *per se*. The evil genius' supposed presence is, however, assumed to affect our ability to recognize whether *praejudicia* actually do stand in a necessary relation to whatever knowledge we already possess. For through the introduction of the hypothesis about the evil genius the methodological principle of doubt has come to have a broader application than it had before. It has this broader application only as long as the hypothesis about the evil genius is not rejected. In the context of composition the normal extent of its application, that is, the extent of its application before the validation of reason was deemed necessary by Descartes, and the extent of its application after reason has been validated, is its role of doubting whether anything proposed by the imagination as a possible next link to the deductive chain is indeed such a next link. This function of the principle of doubt is expressed in the words of the first methodological precept of the *Discourse*: doubt is the methodological instrument by means of which I can 'avoid precipitation . . . in judgments, and to accept in them nothing more than what was presented to my mind so clearly and distinctly that I could have no occasion to doubt it'. In attempts at composition, anything presented by the imagination to the understanding is prima facie dubitable. Such prima facie dubitability entails that the item thus presented is psychologically dubitable. Once that item has withstood the test of doubt, it is seen clearly and distinctly to have a necessary connection with the knowledge we already possess, and becomes certain. However, with the evil genius supposed to be on the scene, such a certainty is only a psychological certainty. Further doubt is called for in order to make metaphysically certain what is already psychologically certain. What can be subject to *further* doubt at this stage? Let us assume that the knowledge we already possess is complex. In that case, since we can doubt the trustworthiness of memory, we can also doubt whether this complex item of knowledge has indeed been derived through deduction (for we only *remember* that it has been). However, at least implicitly, memory has already been judged to be untrustworthy.[12] Thus the introduction of doubt about memory is not the introduction of an item of further doubt.

Let us then instead assume that the knowledge we possess is a single item known *per se*, an item of knowledge obtained through intuition. What may be doubted in that case is whether the

---

[12] Since Descartes has always held memory to be fallible (for this reason he introduced a kind of 'enumeration' in the *Rules* which was to curtail and, if possible, even do away with dependence on memory) any particular 'memory' claim may turn out to be invalid. Furthermore, although such an argument is not presented in the *Meditations*, an argument about memory parallel to that about sensation could easily be developed. Any specific 'memory' claim may be false. To check any one of our 'memory' claims, we must compare it with other memory claims and/or with our sense experience. Any particular sense experience, as well as the set of beliefs based on all of our sense experiences (coherent though that set may be) has been shown to be untrustworthy. There is, therefore, no reason why we could not have as well a set of coherent 'memory' claims which are, however, unveridical. For all we know the evil genius may have given us coherent 'memories' of a past which never existed. In fact, if the evil genius has 'brought it to pass that there is no heaven, no earth, no extended body, no magnitude, no place', the argument just sketched is implicit in this statement. For many, if not most, 'memory' claims which make up the set of one's coherent 'memory' claims are about earth, heaven, body, magnitude, place. To check any particular 'memory' claim for its veridity against a set of such claims is therefore as useless as checking a particular sense-based judgement against those based on other sensations I may now be having, or against the coherent set of judgements about my past experiences. (An argument to the effect that it is logically tenable that we may have coherent 'memories' of a past which never existed is also presented by Bertrand Russell in the context of his discussion of the trustworthiness of memory. See his *The Concept of Mind* (London, 1921), pp. 159 ff.; as well as his *Human Knowledge. Its Scope and Limits* (New York, 1948), pp. 189 ff.)

imagination is indeed capable of presenting to the understanding items which are possible links for the making of a deductive chain. We may also doubt that the methodological use of doubt is an efficacious means which must lead to recognition of the presence or absence of a necessary connection between the knowledge already possessed and the items (or parts of the items) presented by the imagination. Thus what can be subjected to doubt is the process of composition or deduction, the process of the construction of the deductive chain. It is in this context that it makes sense to say that metaphysical doubt is methodological doubt pushed beyond its normal boundaries. On the one hand, what has already been doubted and has withstood the initial test of doubt is therefore psychologically certain. On the other hand, it is complex and does not stand in an *immediate* and necessary relation to what is already known, and so it is subjected to doubt once more. So far, however, I have not yet listed any *additional* item which can be submitted to metaphysical doubt.

What will now have been said to be subject to metaphysical doubt is the activity of the imagination, and the normal application of the methodological principle of doubt. But these two items are only two of three which make up the complex situation which we are now considering. The third is the presence of knowledge already possessed, knowledge to which items are to be added through imagination and doubt. This knowledge has been stipulated to be of items known *per se*, of objects of intuition. Can it be doubted? Such knowledge is not, in the case of Descartes, held to be susceptible to further doubt. In fact, it is not ever held to be susceptible to doubt, whether that be doubt of the normal, methodological sort or of the metaphysical kind. To call something 'not to be susceptible to doubt' is not to imply that one cannot attempt to doubt such items. It means that, once the attempt is made, it cannot be successful. For either the items doubted are absolutely simple, are epistemic atoms, and hence cannot disintegrate under the test of doubt; or they are items standing in immediate and necessary logical relation and, for a reason to be introduced later, they too are imprevious to doubt. Consideration of the text of the *Meditations* and of other writings will show that when Descartes submits these items to metaphysical doubt, they can withstand that test.

We have seen that, in *Meditation I*, the propositions of what we take to be everyday sense-based knowledge, or of applied science, or of theoretical science (including mathematics) all admit of being called into some measure of doubt. About mathematics, once the hypothesis about the evil genius is introduced, Descartes asks 'how do I know that I am not deceived every time I add two and three, or count the sides of a square . . .?' Again, note the words 'add' and 'count', for their presence indicates that, as far as the success of metaphysical doubt goes, Descartes draws the line at the intuition of simples, at grasping items known *per se*. The evil genius is given power only over what is composite. What is genuinely simple or known *per se* is held to be not susceptible to metaphysical doubt. When, in the *Discourse,* Descartes comments on the argument to be presented in *Meditation I*, his use of the terms 'reasoning' and 'demonstration' reinforces my interpretation. He there writes that since 'there are men who deceive themselves in their reasoning and fall into paralogisms, even concerning the simplest matters in geometry', and since he considers himself to be 'as subject to error as was any other', he decided to reject 'as false all the reasons formerly accepted by me as demonstrations' (HR1, 101; AT6, 32). There is no hint in these passages that there is any doubt or uncertainty about what we take to be our understanding of simple ideas such as 'one' or 'equal', both of which must be understood before we can say that $2 + 3 = 5$. Hence as intuition reason is held to be autonomous. It still remains to be shown that Descartes considers himself to have good grounds for holding this position. First however I should state, and remove, a possible objection to this part of my exposition.

Some commentators would argue that the point just made is invalid in view of what is said in a passage in the third *Meditation,* a passage which they would interpret as providing evidence that Descartes holds that even items known *per se* are susceptible to metaphysical doubt. The passage in question comes in the third paragraph of *Meditation III.* I have quoted most of this paragraph earlier in this section, but at that time I omitted some important phrases, which now need to be considered. They are: a 'very slight, and so to speak metaphysical' doubt attaches to statements like 'He [God] can never cause me to be nothing while I think that I am' and 'He [God]' cannot 'someday cause it to be true to say that I have never been, it being true now to say that I am'. Professor Gewirth has argued that Descartes here suggests 'that even the

Cogito might be false'.[13] This, however, is not the case, for neither of these statements is an alternative formulation of the *Cogito* principle; neither is an expression of a first principle, of something known *per se*. For whereas in the *Cogito* we have a statement of the immediate implication of thought and existence, in both these statements we deal with something far more complex. In the first we deal with the relations among thought, existence, God, causality, and a time beyond the present. The second is a statement about a future in which there will be a judgement with respect to the existence of the 'I' of the present. The addition of the reference to the future makes both these statements dubitable. For this addition indicates that composition has entered, and that therefore these statements are *praejudicia*.

Support for the interpretation that Descartes envisages no successful doubt of intuition and its objects is present in other passages of *Meditation III*. In paragraphs 8, 9, and 10, so well before the hypothesis about the evil genius has been shown to be untenable, a contrast is drawn between what 'nature' teaches and what the natural light teaches. Nature 'impels one to believe', but the natural light 'makes one recognize' that certain things are true: 'for I cannot doubt that which the natural light causes me to believe to be true, as, for example, it has shown me that I am from the fact that I doubt, or other facts of the same kind'. Descartes qualifies his talk of 'that which the natural light causes me to believe' in terms of a specific example ('that I am from the fact that I doubt') and then says that 'other facts of the same kind', that is, things like the *Cogito*, can withstand the test of metaphysical doubt. This, first, implies that not all things shown by the natural light are beyond metaphysical doubt, and thus implies that reason stands in need of validation. Second, it indicates that some things shown by the natural light are beyond doubt, and therefore implies that not all of reason stands in need of validation. What is pointed at as being beyond doubt are objects of intuition; and therefore what is implied is that reason in its intuitive function does not stand in need of validation.

3. Autonomous intuition and the efficacy of resolution

Before I provide further evidence for the plausibility of my inter-

13 'The Cartesian Circle Reconsidered', p. 679.

pretation, and before I begin the presentation of Descartes's grounds for holding that intuition is autonomous, let me restate the most important relevant points presented so far. If we say that universal or metaphysical doubt is present in the *Meditations,* we must keep in mind that Descartes states explicitly that only *praejudicia* are affected by this doubt. *Praejudicium* is a technical term for a judgement which still has the status of hypothesis: whatever the imagination holds before the understanding as a judgement that may be necessarily related to whatever knowledge we already possess is a *praejudicium.* Such a judgement loses its hypothetical nature once it can withstand methodological doubt, once it is seen as necessarily connected with the knowledge we already possess. *But this was before the evil genius was introduced, before there was metaphysical doubt.* With the introduction of the evil genius such items also become items subject to doubt. Thus, before the hypothesis about the evil genius was entertained, some of the judgements that were introduced by means of the imagination—namely, those that could withstand the test of normal methodological doubt and could be seen to have a necessary connection with what was already known—lost their hypothetical status, ceased to be *praejudicia.* Once the hypothesis about the evil genius becomes relevant, all judgements—including those that were seen as having a necessary connection with items already known—again become *praejudicia.*

Examination of an important set of passages from the letter to Clerselier in which Descartes replies to some of Gassendi's objections, provides further support for my interpretation. These passages are to be found at HR2, 126–7; AT9–1, 205–6. Consideration of these passages will at the same time further the argument. For they will show not only that the objects of intuition remain unaffected by metaphysical doubt; they will also make clear that the methodological principle of resolution is efficacious.

In these passages there are three items of criticism directed against *Meditation I,* as well as a number of objections against *Meditation II.* Of the latter objections the first two are relevant for my exposition. All three items of criticism directed against *Meditation I* are relevant for my exposition: the first two of them at this point, the third after the first two objections against *Meditation II* have been introduced and discussed.

The *first* of the 'three criticisms directed against the first

Meditation' is: 'That I demand an impossibility in desiring the abandonment of every kind of *praejudicium.*' The *second* is: 'That in thinking one has given up every *praejudicium* one acquires other beliefs of a still more prejudiced kind.'[14] The *third* I will state later on. Part of Descartes's reply is:

The first of these criticisms is due to the author of this book [i.e. Gassendi] not having reflected that the word *praejudicium* does not apply to all the notions in our mind, of which it is impossible for us to divest ourselves, but only to all those opinions our belief in which is a result of previous judgments. And since judging or refraining from judgment is an act of the will ... it is evident that it is under our control.[15]

Part of this statement is about the 'body of knowledge' which we already possess, about what was once seen to be clear and distinct and is part of a deductive system which we now remember to be a deductive system. Since the evil genius was introduced all our memories are untrustworthy; and therefore this kind of apparent knowledge must now be labelled a *praejudicium* or something which involves at least one *praejudicium.* But what is the status of the propositions which constitute this 'body of knowledge' if with respect to them we 'resolve to affirm or deny none of the matters we have previously affirmed or denied, unless after a fresh examination'? That is, what is their status as judgements made in the present? The answer is that, with the exception of our entertaining the hypothesis about the evil genius, no proposition *should* be entertained as possibly true or false at all. For the resolution we have formed is that of 'denying or affirming nothing'. This point is reaffirmed in Descartes's answer to the *second* of these two criticisms:

The second objection is nothing but a manifest falsity; for though I said that we must even compel ourselves to deny the things we had previously affirmed with too great assurance [i.e. without considering

[14] Since Descartes wrote this letter in French, he used *préjugé* rather than *praejudicium*. However, in order not to complicate the issue unnecessarily, I have replaced the French by its Latin equivalent in the translation.

[15] The last sentence may indicate that what, in my first Chapter, I have called a 'concomitant notion' (the motif of freedom versus nature) is really more fundamental than that. This may also be implied in the first paragraph of *Meditation I*, where we read that 'I shall ... seriously and *freely* address myself to the general upheaval of all my former opinions.' For the time being, however, I shall reserve judgement on this issue. It does not affect the general thesis I am presenting in this study.

whether they could possibly be metaphysically false] I expressly limited the period during which we should so behave to the time in which we bend our thought to the discovery of something more certain than what we had been able thus to deny: and during this time it is evident that we could not entertain any belief of a prejudicial character.

Thus, during the period in which the hypothesis about the evil genius is in force, the status of any other hypothesis or *praejudicium* is that it is not to be 'entertained'. They are not to be entertained because during this period nothing can be affirmed or denied with any degree of 'assurance'.

We should now turn to the objections to *Meditation II*. The first two of these objections are relevant at this point because their rebuttal explicitly indicates that *praejudicia* are susceptible to doubt, but that anything known *per se*, or that a proposition in which the concepts stand in an immediate and necessary relation to one another, is not susceptible to doubt. The *first* of these two objections is: '. . . in the statement, *I think, hence I exist,* the author of these criticisms will have it that I imply the assumption of this major premiss, *he who thinks, exists,* and that I have thus already espoused a *praejudicium*.' There are, says Descartes, two errors on Gassendi's part which led him to make this objection. Descartes states 'the greater error' second, but it should be considered first in order to see clearly how he deals with the first error. This second error is:

. . . our critics' assumption that the knowledge of particular truths is always deduced from universal propositions in consonance with the order of the sequence observed in the syllogism of dialectic. This shows that he is but little acquainted with the method by which truth should be investigated. For it is certain that in order to discover the truth we should always start with particular notions, in order to arrive at general conceptions subsequently . . .

This is doctrine straight from the *Rules* and the *Discourse*, a doctrine about which Descartes can say 'it is certain that' because this statement was made after the *Meditations* were written and hence after the method was justified. The successfully accomplished justification of method is to be read into Descartes's rebuttal of the criticism. This rebuttal is:

. . . in the statement, *I think, hence I exist,* . . . I imply the assumption of this major premiss, *he who thinks, exists,* and . . . I have thus already espoused a *praejudicium.* Here he once more mishandles the word *praejudicium:* for though we may apply this term to that proposition when it is brought forward without scrutiny, and we believe it merely because we remember we have made this same judgment previously, we cannot maintain on every occasion that it is a *praejudicium,* i.e. when we subject it to examination, the cause being that it appears to be so evident to the understanding that we should fail to disbelieve it even on the first occasion in our life on which it occurred to us, on which occasion it would not be a *praejudicium.*

In view of Descartes's method, if anything is to be deduced from *'he who thinks, exists'*, that statement must be about a 'particular notion'; it cannot be a 'general conception'. Taken as a claim about a particular notion *'he who thinks, exists'* is simply a misleading formulation of the *Cogito. That* proposition is a statement in which there is an *immediate* and necessary implication of concepts, and hence it is not a proposition obtained through the aid of imagination and doubt, is not a proposition involving affirmation or denial. Thus 'it appears so evident to the understanding that we should fail to disbelieve it even on the first occasion in our life on which it occurred to us, on which occasion it would not be a *praejudicium'* —even if that occasion happened to be during the period in which we entertain the hypothesis about the evil genius. The only occasion on which that statement would be a *praejudicium* is subsequent to the first occasion on which we entertained it. For on a subsequent occasion we could entertain it as an unexamined, at that time un-intuited piece of supposed knowledge from memory. And any mnenic presentation is dubitable *qua* mnemic presentation.

   The second of Gassendi's objections to *Meditation II* Descartes reformulates as: 'that, in order to know that I think, I must know what thought is; which I certainly do not know, they say, because I have denied everything'. The rebuttal is unequivocal: 'But I have denied nothing but *praejudicia,* and by no means notions like these, which are known without affirmation or denial.' 'What thought is', like 'what knowing is' and 'what doubt is', is one of the items one is said to know intuitively. Thus, notions like these, simple items known *per se,* cannot be rejected through doubt. Neither, as we have seen, can a proposition be rejected if it is not at any stage of its career presented to the understanding by the imagination, if it has never had the status of hypothesis or *praeju-*

dicium. Thus all the items known through intuition can withstand the test of metaphysical doubt.

There are, in Descartes's works, two arguments in support of the position that all items known through intuition can withstand the test of metaphysical doubt. The first of these is implicit in Rule 12, the second in the first two of the *Meditations.* For my purposes the second of these is more important, for it is here only that metaphysical doubt is explicitly introduced. However, the argument presented in Rule 12 is also important at this stage, even though the notion of metaphysical doubt is not present in the *Rules*, because the doctrine stated in Rule 12 is at the basis of the argument of the first two *Meditations.* In section 2 of my second chapter I have already alluded to this argument. It is now important to give a complete statement of it.

In Rule 12 we read:

. . . all these simple natures are known *per se* and are wholly free from falsity. It will be easy to show this, provided we distinguish that faculty of our understanding by which it has intuitive awareness of things and knows them, from that by which it judges, making use of affirmation and denial. For we may imagine ourselves to be ignorant of things which we really know, for example on such occasions as when we believe that in such things, over and above what we have present to us or attain to by thinking, there is something else hidden from us, and when this belief of ours is false. Whence it is evident that we are in error if we judge that any of these simple natures is not completely known by us. For if our mind attains to the least acquaintance with it, as must be the case, since we are assumed to pass some judgment on it, this fact alone makes us infer that we know it completely. For otherwise it could not be said to be simple, but must be complex—a compound of that which is present in our perception of it, and that of which we think we are ignorant. (HR1, 42; AT10, 420-1.)

'All these simple natures', as Descartes makes clear on the page preceding the one from which I quoted, involves both items like 'what the act of knowing is' and 'what doubt is', as well as what he calls 'common notions'. One of these 'common notions' is like a mathematician's variant on Aristotle's 'Law of Identity': 'Things that are the same as a third thing are the same as one another.' Another one of them is the causal principle. These 'simple natures' are the class of objects known *per se*. 'We may imagine ourselves to be ignorant of these', for example under the pressure of the hypothesis about the evil genius. However, such imagining is fruitless. The evil genius cannot force a wedge between parts of the act by means of which we obtain our knowledge in these cases simply because there are no parts to this act. Even if the item of knowledge is a proposition, 'the proposition intuited . . . must be grasped in its totality at the same time and not successively'. (HR1, 33; AT10, 401.)

That this doctrine is at the basis of the argument in the first two of the *Meditations* seems clear from what Descartes writes in defence of this argument. In his *Reply* to the second set of *Objections* he writes with respect to statements like 'that I, while I think, exist' and 'that what is once done cannot be undone' (items elsewhere listed among the 'simple natures'), that 'we cannot doubt them unless we think them. . . . Hence we can never doubt them without at the same time believing them to be true, i.e. we can never doubt them.' (HR2, 42; AT7, 145.)

If we keep this doctrine in mind it is not difficult to see how the methodological principle of resolution has functioned in the first *Meditation*, and it is easy to show why, in spite of the supposed presence of the evil genius, Descartes believed that he could trust in the efficacy of that aspect of his method.

In the first *Meditation*, I 'seriously and freely address myself to the general upheaval of all my former opinions' (1, 1). All of one's accumulated 'variety of experiences', the totality of what one takes to be one's knowledge, seems open to doubt. 'All opinions' are divided into or reduced to groups in terms of 'the principles upon which all my former opinions rested'. These 'principles' can now be seen to be not just those of *sensation* and *composition*, but also that of *intuition*. The question of the certainty of each of the classes of knowledge related to these 'principles' is reduced to an attack upon these 'principles'. The attack to which both the first and second class succumb is that which has the aid of the hypothesis about the evil genius. The third class can withstand that attack. That it can withstand this attack is shown through a further reduction: as the representative of items known *per se* Descartes selects the *Cogito*. This item of knowledge, though subjected to metaphysical doubt, withstands the test. Resolution or reduction continues only till we reach the objects of intuition. It is a reduction of 'all my former opinions', of all items I once held to be true, to items known *per se*, to items which continue to be true.

It will now be helpful to introduce the *third* of Gassendi's criticisms directed against *Meditation I*. For in it a statement is made about 'the method . . . of doubting'. Descartes's rebuttal of this criticism provides a good indication of how he considered that the resolution-aspect of his method had been shown to be efficacious. Gassendi's criticism is 'that the method I have proposed of doubting everything does not promote the discovery of any single truth'. Descartes takes no objection to the phrase 'the method of doubting'. Since, in *Meditation I*, no composition is attempted, the only aspect of the method which is operative in it is that of resolution. And since Gassendi's criticism is directed specifically to 'the method of doubting' in the *first* of the *Meditations,* the objection against 'the method of doubting' may be said to be Gassendi's way of formulating his misgivings about Descartes's general method to the extent that it operates in *Meditation I*. Whether or not this was Gassendi's intent Descartes in any case would have taken it this way. This is clear from the first two 'precepts' of the method as stated in the *Discourse,* where doubt also plays its role in the context of division or resolution. If there is a question (like: are any of my beliefs true?) and if the understanding does not immediately see (intuit) the answer to the question, methodological doubt enters (I doubt whether any of my beliefs are true; hence I will attempt to reject them all as false). The attempt at rejection is in terms of 'reasons'. These reasons, in *Meditation I*, are related to 'those principles upon which all my former opinions rested'. Once my beliefs have been divided in terms of the 'principles' on which they rest, the understanding examines its former beliefs in terms of the validity of the 'principle' (or of the 'principles') on which they rest. If it does not immediately see (intuit) the validity of the 'principle', methodological doubt again enters: the 'principle' is rejected as invalid. Thus, division or resolution, doubt, and (the attempt at) intuition become a single process. We can now state clearly what Descartes is doing in the first *Meditation* or, to be exact, in the position he presents from the beginning of *Meditation I* to the end of the third paragraph of *Meditation II*. That is, *Descartes attempts through the application of the principle of resolution to attain knowledge which is not susceptible to any kind of doubt.* Suppose it were to happen that once we come to the end of the process of resolution, we can intuit, and once we then doubt the item intuited, the truth of that item is in fact re-established by the application of doubt itself. In that case the methodic process which led to the grasping of that truth has been established as efficacious. This, I believe, is Descartes's view of what, in part, really does take place in *Meditation I*. For, in reply to Gassendi's 'mere cavilling' about 'the method . . . of doubting' he replies: 'True, mere doubt alone does not suffice to establish any truth; but that does not prevent it from being useful in preparing the mind for the subsequent establishment of truth. This is the sole purpose for which I have employed it.'

The practice of resolution leads to the establishment of truth. The application of doubt leads to indubitable items. The constant attempt to gain the certainty of an intuition leads to the grasping of an intuitable item. No matter how one puts it, the efficacy of resolution and doubt, or the validity of intuition, need not be presupposed in the practice of resolution and doubt, in the attempt at gaining an intuition.

The soundness and success of the application of resolution is established under the most adverse conditions, namely, those where the evil genius is supposed to be on the scene. It shows its usefulness through the application of methodic doubt beyond its normal limits: 'two and three make five', formerly held to be clear and distinct and still psychologically indubitable, is doubted and rejected as possibly false. The utter trustworthiness of intuition becomes apparent at the same time and under the same adverse conditions: 'I am, I exist, is necessarily true each time that I pronounce it, or that I mentally conceive it' (2, 3).

Frankfurt (as I pointed out before)[16] has argued that the trustworthiness of reason is, for Descartes, a working hypothesis whose tenability itself is to be tested by the investigation he undertakes. If we adopt this way of talking as a description of how the efficacy of resolution is established, it can be seen that this may indeed be what takes place in the first two *Meditations*.[17] But to

---

[16] *Demons, Dreamers, and Madmen*, pp. 27 ff.

[17] Taking the efficacy of resolution as a 'working hypothesis' involves the acceptance of a hypothesis in addition to the one about the evil genius. The difficulty is, of course, that Descartes has stipulated that *no* hypotheses beyond that about the evil genius are to be 'entertained' until the latter hypothesis has been rejected. I do not see how this difficulty can be evaded. If we were to say that no real difficulty arises because the hypothesis about the efficacy of resolution is *only* a 'working hypothesis', this would be of little help. For the hypothesis about the evil genius may also be seen as a working hypothesis. In fact, any

adopt this way as descriptive of what happens with respect to intuition would be misleading. When there is a question which can be resolved, a number of further resolutions of resulting questions may be called for until we see the efficacy of resolution in its intuited end-product. Until we have obtained this intuition, the efficacy of the procedure of resolution remains in question, and we can only continue the procedure on the assumption that its efficacy will be established in the end. But when there is an item to be intuited, that item, as soon as the mind is aware of it at all, is at that moment intuited. Thus there can be no time during which we are both intuiting something *and* simultaneously treating the efficacy of intuition as a hypothesis. There is no time during which we can actually 'work' with the 'hypothesis', and hence we cannot speak of the trustworthiness of reason in its intuitive function as a 'working hypothesis'. As we are resolving, we can wonder whether this process is getting us anywhere, and we can doubt that it will ever lead us to intuitable items. Thus the value and reliability of the process of resolution, which includes the function of the principle of doubt within its context, can be taken as a working hypothesis. But as we are intuiting, we know we have attained certain knowledge of the object intuited: doubting whether we do have knowledge of some particular intuitable item simply serves immediately to place this item once again before the understanding, which then cannot fail to grasp it intuitively. There is, thus, no reason to speak of the trustworthiness of intuition as a 'working hypothesis'. In fact, speaking this way is misleading because it presupposes a temporally divisible process where, for Descartes, no such process can exist. Intuition is an achievement which arises 'all at once'.

That it is equally misleading (though for a different reason) to speak of the trustworthiness of reason in its deductive function as a working hypothesis, the next chapter will make clear. It will, in fact, be shown that Descartes takes neither the efficacy of deduction nor that of composition to be 'working hypotheses'.

The process which establishes the efficacy of resolution and

---

judgement proposed by the imagination to the understanding as a possible next link in the deductive chain may be seen as a 'working hypothesis'. Perhaps this difficulty indicates that it is wrong to take the efficacy of resolution as a 'working hypothesis'. But it is hard to see how else it can be put without falling into the trap of circularity.

which leads to the recognition of the absolute trustworthiness of intuition, is completed at the end of the third paragraph of *Meditation II*. In *Meditation I* there is no indication that items known *per se* are submitted to doubt. Doubt, therefore, has not yet been explicitly applied to all objects of knowledge and, by the end of that *Meditation*, has not yet been seen to operate as 'universal' doubt. In *Meditation II*, doubt is extended explicitly also to items known *per se*, in terms of attempted doubt concerning the *Cogito*. This item of presumed knowledge turns out to be a case of absolutely certain knowledge. It can withstand doubt. By implication, any item known *per se* can withstand doubt. This is made explicit as the position is further articulated, for in this articulation and before the hypothesis about the evil genius has been shown to be untenable, other items known *per se* are introduced. They are introduced as 'indubitable', that is to say, as items which if we attempted to call them into doubt, would be able to resist all challenges as decisively well as the *Cogito* resists them.

But why does Descartes single out the *Cogito* for doubt? Why cannot any of the other objects of intuition serve as well as the 'Archimedean point' for which he is searching? It would be a mistake to conclude at this point that, since none of the objects of intuition are susceptible to metaphysical doubt, the *Cogito* is not in some sense unique. It would be a mistake which would be indicative of a lack of understanding about how Descartes's method has structured his position up to this point in the *Meditations*. It is because Descartes's argument is determined by his method that not just any one of the objects of intuition becomes an 'Archimedean point', or is such a point at least potentially. In spite of what some have argued[18] only the *Cogito* is held to be 'the first piece of firm ground . . . on which the whole edifice of science can be erected'. It is for the following reason that no other object of intuition can serve as an 'Archimedean point' for Descartes. By means of the attempt to remove all possible error through universal doubt or, what amounts to the same, by means of the attempt to make universal doubt absolute, it becomes clear that we cannot remain in the state of doubt. To quote from *The Search After Truth:* if we make universal doubt a 'fixed and absolute point' it

[18] See, for example, A. K. Stout, 'The Basis of Knowledge in Descartes', pp. 169 ff.

immediately becomes clear that 'you cannot deny that you doubt' which means that it is 'certain that you doubt' and that 'it is likewise true that you are, you who doubt', 'for if I did not exist I could not doubt'. (HR1, 316; AT10, 515.) Descartes places all objects of intuition beyond the grasp of the evil genius but, because the universal application of doubt necessarily involves making one of them, the *Cogito*, explicit, the *Cogito* alone becomes the natural point of departure for the validation of deduction or composition. It is the natural point of departure for one who philosophizes 'in an orderly way'; strict application of the method alone inexorably leads one to it.[19]

[19] There is another reason why the *Cogito* can serve as an 'Archimedean point' where a conceptual truth like that about equals or identity cannot. Of all objects of intuition it is the *Cogito* alone in which there is no distinction between the idea and what it is an idea of. The concept of equality is not itself an instance of equality; but to entertain the concept of thinking is itself an instance of thinking. Hence the *Cogito* is the first certainty involving existence. Since Descartes needs a 'first piece of firm ground . . . on which the whole edifice of science can be erected', and since some of the sciences (like applied physics or mechanics, and medicine) are about a reality which contrasts with concepts or judgements about it, the Archimedean point must be able to function as a point of departure for saying something about what *exists*, rather than for merely saying something about what is *thought*. In this context, see Descartes's letter to Clerselier, June 1646 (AT6, 442–3; Kenny, *Letters*, pp. 196–7).

V

MEDITATIONS II AND III
The Validation of Deduction
and the Justification of Composition

In the first three of the *Meditations* two important activities are to be noted. *First*, Descartes pursues the goal of reducing whatever in one's experience is complex to its simplest parts. This intended reduction stops once he believes that we have reached items known *per se*. At that point Descartes believes that the process of reduction has shown itself to be efficacious, and that intuition is revealed as absolutely trustworthy. This goal he takes to have been reached in *Meditation II* once we come to the *Cogito*. *Second* Descartes intends that, once we have reached the *Cogito*, the construction of the rest of the foundation of the sciences is to take place. However, since such a task requires the use of deduction, which involves the methodological principle of composition, it will first have to be shown that deduction is trustworthy or that composition is the way to obtain systematic knowledge. This task Descartes faces in the second and third of the *Meditations*.

In this chapter I shall show how, by means of resolution and intuition, Descartes attempts to validate reason in its deductive function. Once such a validation has been presented there are, for him, no further problems with respect to the universal imposition of the methodological principle of composition.

I shall argue that Descartes uses only resolution and intuition in the attempt to provide a validation for deduction; and that he therefore believes this attempt at validation not to be open to the charge of circularity. As we shall see, Descartes's position in the second and third of his *Meditations* is that the *intuitive contemplation* of the *Cogito* leads to the validation of deduction. This relationship between the *Cogito* and the validation of deduction will, according to Descartes, be clear to anyone whose mind does not 'wander'. It will be clear to anyone who steadfastly focuses the intuitive power of his mind on the *Cogito* and who is not distracted by all sorts of *praejudicia*, that is, by all sorts of judgements or hypotheses which, because of the presence of metaphysical doubt, are not yet to be entertained. Most people, however, are constantly distracted by such *praejudicia*, and for this reason the relationship between the *Cogito* and the validation of deduction can be grasped only after much hard work. *Praejudicia* constantly distract the mind because of man's habit of trust in the senses, and because of the habit of what must remain a misplaced trust in the validity of deduction until the sceptic's attack on the deductive aspect of reason has been repelled.

In section 1 of this chapter I shall indicate how Descartes attempts to break our habit of relying on the senses, or on anything related to corporeal substance. This exercise would lead us to the intuitive contemplation of the *Cogito* if there were not a further powerful habit which must first be broken. For after our habit of trusting the senses has been checked, there remains our habit of showing a still misplaced trust in the validity of deduction. In section 2 I shall therefore show how, according to Descartes, the rejection of trust in deduction leads to the intuitive contemplation of the *Cogito*. In section 3 I shall make clear how Descartes takes the intuitive contemplation of the *Cogito* to lead to the validation of deduction and hence to the justification of the imposition of the principle of composition. At relevant points throughout these first three sections it will again become clear that Descartes's method structures the argument of the *Meditations*. Lastly, in section 4, I shall present some further grounds for the plausibility of my interpretation; and I shall, once again, identify the 'prejudice' one needs to adopt in order for one to be able to consider anything like the Cartesian position viable.

1. *Meditation II:* rejection of dependence upon anything corporeal as a step to the intuitive contemplation of the *Cogito*

In the first two paragraphs of *Meditation II* Descartes gives notice of the fact that he is explicitly going to submit to metaphysical doubt the objects of intuition: 'I shall proceed by setting aside all that in which the least doubt could be supposed to exist . . . and I shall ever follow in this road until I have met with something which is certain, or at least, if I can do nothing else, until I have learned for certain that there is nothing in the world which is certain.' In the very next paragraph this process comes to an end when it is recognized that, even if there is an evil genius who deceives me, even if I apply metaphysical doubt, it remains a fact that 'I am, I exist, is necessarily true each time that I pronounce it, or that I mentally conceive it.'

Many articles, and many chapters of books on Descartes have been devoted to a discussion of this statement and of what have been taken as its alternative formulations. It is not important for my purpose to spend much time on a similar discussion at this point. All that should be recognized now is that Descartes here presents two concepts, 'thought' and 'existence', in what he takes to be an immediate and necessary connection (the necessity runs from 'thought' to 'existence' and not vice versa: if there is something which thinks, then it must exist; but it does not hold that if something exists, it must be thinking). It should again be recognized that entertaining the *idea* of thinking is itself an *instance* of thinking. And it should be recognized that this item of knowledge is 'certain and indubitable' only when I actually intuit it. In view of these considerations one can say that an initial plausible interpretation of what Descartes has in mind as his first 'certain and indubitable' item of knowledge may be expressed by means of the phrase 'thinking-going-on'. This phrase, inelegant though it is, should serve to capture what Descartes intended at this stage of his presentation: what exists is a thought-process.

In the next paragraph Descartes makes this process into an object of reflection: 'But I do not yet know clearly enough what I am, I who am certain that I am.' The reflection upon 'what I am' introduces the principle of reduction, as is made clear at the end of this paragraph: 'of my former opinions' about 'what I am', 'I shall withdraw all that might even in a small degree be invalidated by the reasons which I have just brought forward'. One of 'my former opinions' is that 'I' am 'a man' or 'a reasonable animal'. Consideration of concepts like these is, however, dismissed immediately as a wrong move. It is a wrong move because it is an attempt to get to know what is less complex in terms of what is more complex—and that is wrong because it is unmethodical. For if we are to gain any systematic truth, we must work methodically; and to work methodically entails that we must move from the simple to the complex rather than from the complex to the simple. Therefore, to explain 'what I am' in terms of 'I am a reasonable animal' (which in turn calls for an inquiry into 'what an animal is, and what is reasonable', which are questions themselves leading 'into an infinitude of others more difficult') is methodically wrong and is labelled as a 'waste' of time.

In this very first move, after he has reached the *Cogito*, Descartes gives us some clues about the strategy he is adopting in his attempt to validate deduction. Although intuition has been shown to be absolutely trustworthy and reduction has been shown to be efficacious, nothing has as yet been proven about the trustworthiness of deduction or about the efficacy of composition in gaining systematic knowledge. Nevertheless, the making of any move in terms of a methodology which was already rejected before the evil genius was supposed to be on the scene—any move in terms of a spurious methodology which would explain what is simple or simpler in terms of what is (more) complex—is again rejected. Does this rejection imply that the methodology adopted before the evil genius was supposed to be on the scene is preferred? That the methodology which dictates that any explanation must have as starting-point the simplest relevant item or items is adopted instead? If the answer to this pair of questions is affirmative, it would seem that Descartes can adopt the principle of composition as a working hypothesis only. Any other move involving its use would constitute a *petitio principii*. But even this move itself would create a difficulty for Descartes. For as we saw in the third section of my previous chapter, the only hypothesis to be entertained at this stage of the argument is the hypothesis about the evil genius. So the clues we have about the strategy to be followed are the following. *First*, no methodology different from that propounded in the *Discourse* is to be adopted. *Second*, with the exception of the hypothesis about the evil genius, no hypotheses are to be entertained at all, and hence no working hypothesis about the efficacy of composition is to be entertained either. This leads to a *third* clue about Descartes's strategy: if we are to advance at all, the only methodological principle we are allowed to use at this stage of the argument is that of resolution, and the only power of the mind to which we can have recourse is that of intuition. The remainder of the second and third *Meditations* will be seen to bear out my contention that this is indeed Descartes's strategy.

Once Descartes has decided not to waste time on an incorrect procedure, he writes: 'But I shall rather stop here to consider the thoughts which of themselves spring up in my mind, and which were not inspired by anything beyond my own nature alone when I applied myself to the consideration of my own being.' Why is it not a waste of time 'to consider . . . thoughts' at this point? This move is justified because, since 'thinking-is-going-on', there must be thoughts or ideas that are being entertained. There is, thus, an immediate and necessary connection between 'thinking-going-on' and 'entertaining ideas'. And since such connections are grasped intuitively, making the move to 'ideas' or 'thoughts' is justified.

One important doctrine which underlies the move made in this part of the *Meditations* is stated by Descartes as early as in the *Rules for the Direction of the Mind*. In Rule 12 we read that we must 'distinguish accurately the notions of simple things from those which are built up out of them.' Descartes adds that 'we . . . shall call those only simple, the cognition of which is so clear and so distinct that they cannot be analysed (*dividi*) by the mind into others more distinctly known'. As we saw when we discussed a part of this Rule in the previous chapter, Descartes gives some examples of what he means by these 'notions of simple things'. Among the examples listed are 'what the act of knowing is', 'what doubt is'; as well as items like 'figure', 'extension', 'motion', 'existence', 'unity', 'duration'; and also principles like 'things that are the same as a third thing are the same as one another'. Elsewhere Descartes adds the causal principle to this list of examples. He then continues in Rule 12 with the statements 'that all these simple natures are known *per se* and are wholly free from falsity', and that 'all the rest of what we know is formed by composition out of these simple natures'. Then follows the important point for our present considerations:

. . . the union of these things one with another is either necessary or contingent. It is necessary when one is so implied in the concept of another in a confused sort of way that we cannot conceive either distinctly, if our thought assigns to them separateness from each other. Thus figure is conjoined with extension, motion with duration or time, and so on, because it is impossible to conceive [distinctly] of a figure that has no extension, nor of a motion that has no duration. (HR1, 42–3; AT10, 419–20.)

Thus this passage states that a 'simple nature' is indeed known *per se*, but for it to be known *per se* and *clearly and distinctly* it may well be necessary to introduce other concepts (other concepts which are also known *per se*). Only when we have introduced this other concept, or these other concepts, can we say that what is known *per se* is also known *clearly and distinctly*. For 'we cannot conceive either distinctly, if our thought assigns to them separateness from each other'. Although the examples given in this passage are of *two* 'simple natures' thus 'united', this does not mean that there could not be more than two involved. It is necessary to keep this doctrine in mind if we are to be able to make sense of Descartes's position in the second and third of the *Meditations*. For this doctrine is not merely behind the move just made (that from 'thinking-going-on' to 'entertaining ideas'). In the same paragraph from which my last quotation from Rule 12 was taken, we also read:

. . . many things are often necessarily united with one another, though most people, not noticing what their true relation is, reckon them among those that are contingently connected. As example, I give the following propositions:—'I exist, therefore God exists . . .'. Finally we must note that very many necessary propositions become contingent when converted. Thus though from the fact that I exist I may infallibly conclude that God exists, it is not for that reason allowable to affirm that because God exists I also exist.

This doctrine is operative in the *Meditations* as soon as Descartes states that 'I am, I exist, is necessarily true each time . . . that I mentally conceive it'; and it remains operative in a crucially important way until, at the end of *Meditation III*, deduction has been shown to be trustworthy. As we shall see later on, Descartes himself points out the relevance of this doctrine to the moves he makes in the second and third of the *Meditations*.

Although the move to 'thoughts' is justified, consideration of just any thought or idea is not helpful or even legitimate at this stage—as Descartes proceeds to point out. For 'the thoughts which of themselves spring up in my mind . . . when I applied myself to the consideration of my being' are thoughts about myself as a being composed of body and soul. But 'body' is for Descartes a term for a complex idea, and anything said or thought about the term or its meaning must be expressed in judgements rooted in concepts which do not stand in immediate, necessary connections. The same is at least in part true for the term 'soul'. To understand 'body' we must understand as well concepts like 'figure' and 'place' (2, 5); and since we suppose the evil genius to be on the scene I cannot 'affirm' that 'what I am' involves 'body', 'figure', and 'place'. Thus, since there is no immediate and necessary connection between 'thinking-going-on' and 'figure' or 'place', 'I cannot say that it' (body) 'pertains to me' (2, 6). What about 'soul'? Consideration of this concept generates an argument which is partly parallel to that about body. For the soul is to be understood in terms of concepts related to its actions: 'that I was nourished, that I walked, that I felt, and that I thought' (2, 5). The first three terms 'nutrition', 'walking', and 'sensation' all serve to express complex concepts, and all of them in turn require us to know the complex concept of a *body* so as to understand them. Hence, since the evil genius is supposed to be on the scene and is supposed to be able to tamper with my power of deduction or composition, I cannot affirm that 'soul', as explicated in terms of these three 'attributes', 'pertains to me' (2, 6). This, however, is not so with respect to the fourth 'attribute'. I can understand 'thinking' apart from any reference to 'body'. Moreover, 'what thought is' (like 'what existence is') has always been held by Descartes to be a concept known *per se*. Therefore, we can conclude 'that thought is an attribute that belongs to me; it alone cannot be separated from me. I am, I exist, that is certain. But how often? Just when I think' (2, 6).

We have thus returned to the basic fact: 'thinking-is-going-on'. Resolution of former judgements has led to nothing intuitable in them beyond this basic fact. Any affirmation made so far can be doubted, and they are therefore all of them rejected. Beyond clarification of the issue in this way Descartes does, however, make one advance. Whereas in the third paragraph of *Meditation II* all we were aware of was that 'thinking-is-going-on', we ought at this point to be ready to make explicit one additional element which is present in it. To the question 'What am I, I who am certain that I am?' we should be able to see that the answer is: 'a thing which thinks', *sum res cogitans*. Because this new formulation involves the concept 'thing', 'substance', *res*, it is not a mere reformulation of the phrase 'thinking-is-going-on'. The introduction of this additional element, Descartes holds, does not involve composition or deduction. For just as he holds that there cannot be 'thinking-going-on' without there being ideas or thoughts, so he holds that there cannot be 'thinking-going-on' without there being 'a *thing* which thinks'. The latter relation as well is held to be one grasped through concepts which stand in an immediate and necessary relation; it is a relation of which one is aware through intuition.

There is, according to Descartes, an immediate and necessary connection between the terms 'thinking-going-on' and 'substance'. By this he does not mean to say that, just as one can 'perceive' ideas or thoughts, so one can 'perceive' this 'substance'. For as he writes in his *Reply* to Arnauld's objections: 'we do not have an immediate cognition of substances . . .; rather from the mere fact that we perceive certain forms or attributes which must inhere in something in order to have existence, we name the thing in which they exist a *substance*' (HR2, 98; AT7, 222). What he does mean to say is that one cannot have a 'complete' conception of 'thinking-going-on' unless one also conceives of a 'substance' which 'supports' this process. Descartes elaborates on the point at issue in a letter to Gibieuf, a letter written in the year following the publication of the *Meditations*. In this letter he comments on the mind's ability to 'abstract'. One can, he says, 'abstract' an idea 'from some more rich or more complete idea which I have in myself'. He continues as follows:

Intellectual abstraction would consist in turning my thought away from one part of the contents of the richer idea the better to apply it to another part with greater attention. Thus, when I consider a shape without thinking of the substance or extension whose shape it is, I make a mental abstraction. . . . although one can think of the one without paying any attention to the other, it is impossible to deny one of the other when one thinks of both together. . . . Now it seems to me very clear that the idea which I have of a thinking substance is complete in this sense, and . . . that I cannot think of the two together while denying the one of the other.[1]

These passages are sufficient to support my claim that Descartes believes there to be an immediate and necessary connection between 'thinking-going-on' and 'substance'. Two further points should be made in this context. First, 'Abstraction', in the passage quoted from this letter, is not synonymous with 'resolution' or 'division'. 'Abstraction' consists in focusing one's attention on only *one* of two (or more) ideas which stand in an immediate and necessary connection. One might call this kind of abstraction 'selective attention'. 'Resolution', on the other hand, applies only

[1] Kenny, *Letters*, pp. 123–4; AT3, 474–6.

to complex (rather than to 'rich') ideas whose constituent ideas either actually stand to one another in *only necessary* relations, or whose constituent ideas are merely *believed* to stand in only necessary relations to one another. *Second,* although the terminology in this letter differs from that used in Rule 12, we here nevertheless have our first clear indication that the doctrine presented in Rule 12—the doctrine which states that although certain concepts are indeed known *per se*, it may well be necessary to introduce *other* concepts (other concepts which are also known *per se*) for one to be able to know these first concepts *clearly and distinctly*—is indeed operative in the position presented by Descartes in the *Meditations*. One could say that, in the *Meditations*, the application of this doctrine presents an order which is the reverse from that in the letter to Gibieuf. For in the *Meditations* one must come to the recognition that to be aware of 'thinking-going-on' is to be aware of an 'abstraction'; and the task in the *Meditations* is to come to notice the 'richer idea' of which 'thinking-going-on' is an 'abstraction'.

I am 'a thing which thinks'. 'And what more?' This question, raised in the seventh paragraph of *Meditation II*, introduces what seems at first sight an attempt at composition: 'I shall exercise my imagination.' The 'imagination' here introduced, however, is the power of forming images. It is the 'corporeal imagination', instead of the purely mental power through which hypotheses are introduced. 'Imagining' as used in this paragraph 'is nothing else than to contemplate the figure or image of a corporeal thing'. Even before the introduction of the hypothesis about the evil genius this 'mode of thought' was not one which was considered useful to develop a body of systematic knowledge. As we read in Rule 4: if one were to 'busy one's self with . . . imaginary figures . . . in a sense one ceases to make use of one's reason' (HR1, 11; AT10, 375). This paragraph therefore really does not present an attempt at pure deduction or composition. Instead, it also constitutes a statement about how not to proceed. The function of this paragraph is, then, like that of the fifth paragraph. Hence we read as its concluding sentence: 'And, thus, I know for certain that nothing of all that I understand by means of my imagination belongs to this knowledge which I have of myself, and that it is necessary to recall the mind from this mode of thought with the utmost diligence in order that it may be able to know its own nature with perfect distinction.' Even if it were legitimate to introduce anything related to 'body' (and paragraph 6 has shown that this is not legitimate) the introduction of the 'corporeal imagination' would not lead to an advance in knowledge.

The next two paragraphs recapitulate what has been established as being absolutely certain and indubitable. In this recapitulation there is one advance, namely, an indication of the connotation of 'think' in 'I am a thing which thinks.' A 'thing which thinks' is 'a thing which doubts, understands, conceives, affirms, denies, wills, refuses, which also imagines and feels'. All but the last two are, according to Descartes, clearly purely intellectual activities. The terms 'imagining' and 'feeling' call for explanation. For whereas the former could be taken as the 'corporeal imagination' and whereas the latter, 'feeling', is a synonym for 'sensing', it might be objected that Descartes here includes more than is warranted. He therefore explains (in 2, 9) that, even if there is no brain and hence no 'figure or image of a corporeal thing' in the brain to which the mind can turn and thus 'imagine', the mind still has the power to turn to this figure or image if there were one, and thus has the power to imagine. And this power is entirely on the side of 'mind' rather than on the side of 'body'. As he writes in one of his letters to Mersenne: 'The sense in which I include imaginations in the definition of *cogitatio* or thought differs from the sense in which I exclude them. The forms or corporeal impressions which must be in the brain for us to imagine anything are not thoughts; but when the mind imagines or turns towards those impressions, its operation is a thought.'[2] Likewise about 'feeling' or 'sensing': even if there are no eyes, and no objects to be seen, still 'it seems to me that I see light' and thus it is clear that the mind possesses the power to see objects if there exist objects to be seen and if there exists a body which can be affected in the relevant way by these objects. The doctrine behind this position is presented more clearly elsewhere. In a letter to Plempius[3] we read that animals do not 'see just as we do, i.e. feeling or thinking they see'; 'animals do not see as we do when we are aware that we are, but only as we do when our mind is elsewhere'. Thus, whether we say 'I see' or 'I seem to see', in either case we

[2] Kenny, *Letters,* p. 100; AT3, 361.
[3] Kenny, *Letters,* p. 36; AT1, 413–14. A similar statement may be found in the *Principles of Philosophy I,* 9.

are exercising a power of the mind, and in either case we exist as conscious beings. Therefore 'think' in 'I am a thing which thinks' refers to any act of consciousness. Thus another restatement of what he takes to be the basic truth of *Meditation II* is: 'I exist as a conscious being.'

The remainder of the second *Meditation* is primarily meant to reinforce the attitude we ought to take up. Although it has been established that the only certainty I have is that I exist as a conscious being, 'my mind loves to wander' and 'I cannot prevent myself from thinking, that corporeal things are much more distinctly known' than the fact that I exist as a conscious being (2, 10). Well, let it wander. Let it examine an ordinary object, like a piece of wax, and let it find out what it knows about it. This examination, presented in paragraphs 11 to 15, serves to strengthen the conclusion already reached that all I know for certain at this stage is: 'I am a thing which thinks.' The examination is intended to break our strong habit of trust in the senses to give us certain knowledge, and thus is intended to lead us back to trust in intuition alone and to the intuitive contemplation of the *Cogito*. The examination does not, however, quite achieve the latter objective. For even though it has been shown that we cannot trust the senses, we are still left with deduction as something else which we have habitually trusted to give us knowledge. Reference to deduction is implicit in these paragraphs: if external objects exist, and if we know them at all, then we know them through reasoning rather than through sensing. But in the face of the sceptic's attack, our habitual trust in deduction must also be surrendered. The attempt to break that habit is made especially in *Meditation III*. Nevertheless, the examination of the piece of wax has made clear some additional important points: if an object exists, awareness of such an object at the same time involves the revelation of the existence of the subject; and even if it were the case that objects don't exist, so that I don't see, but only think I see an object, the existence of the one who thinks he sees is assured. This exercise therefore has led us back to the *Cogito* (even though, as will be clear from the sequel, it does not lead directly to the sustained intuitive contemplation of the *Cogito*). Moreover, we now ought to realize that we know more about the subject than we know about any object, for with respect to the latter we are not even certain about its existence, and we cannot with confidence make any judgement about it—for the hypothesis about the evil genius is still unrejected (2, 15). In fact, says Descartes, this exercise has made clear 'that there is nothing which is easier for me to know than my mind' (2, 16) 'since all the reasons which contribute to the knowledge of wax, or any other body whatever, are yet better proofs of the nature of the mind' (2, 15). Why this is so is stated in the *Reply to Objections V*. If there is wax, and if it is white and hard, then we must concede that the mind possesses 'the power of being aware of the whiteness' and that it possesses 'the power of recognizing its hardness'. Since different objects possess different properties and since it is the mind which recognizes these different properties, one can ascribe a different property or attribute to the mind whenever it is clear that it has the power to recognize different properties in each successive new object that is presented to it. And since 'our comprehension' of the nature of anything 'is more perfect in proportion to the number of its attributes which we discern', therefore 'nothing yields the knowledge of so many attributes as our mind, because as many can be enumerated in its case as there are attributes in everything else, owing to the fact that it knows these; and hence its nature is best known of all' (HR2, 213; AT7, 360).

2. *Meditation III*: rejection of trust in deduction leads to intuitive contemplation of the *Cogito*

The first paragraph of *Meditation III* again presents a recapitulation of 'All that I really know, or at least all that hitherto I was aware that I knew' (3, 2): I exist as a conscious being. The phrase 'or at least all that hitherto I was aware that I knew' is important. It hints at the fact that, without going beyond the 'I' and its ideas, without introducing a hypothesis, I may be able to discover something important about that which I already know. Hence the next move is to say: 'In order to try and extend my knowledge further, I shall now look around more carefully and see whether I cannot discover in myself some other things which I have not hitherto perceived' (3, 2). The additional item of knowledge which is implicit in what we already know but which needs to be noted explicitly is that since 'I am certain that I am a thing which thinks' it follows that 'I . . . likewise know what is requisite to render me certain of a truth.' In spite of the supposition of the evil genius' presence, I can be absolutely certain that whenever I intuit anything known *per se*, such an item of knowledge is not susceptible to doubt. This still obtains whether we are dealing with a single concept (like one expressed by 'thought' or 'existence'), or with a principle in which concepts are in immediate and necessary connection (as in the principle expressed by 'I exist . . . when I think'). Thus he adds: 'it seems to me that already I can establish as a general rule that all things which I perceive very clearly and very distinctly are true' (3, 2). This last sentence calls for comment.

First, it is to be noted that Descartes does not say that whatever he *merely* perceives in a clear and distinct manner is true. There is a qualification: 'things which I perceive *very* clearly and *very* distinctly are true'. Second, there is the qualification that 'it *seems* to me' that all such things are true. The reason for the latter qualification is that there are other things which seemed very clear and very distinct but which are now nevertheless rejected as false. The next two paragraphs therefore constitute an inquiry as to whether, in the case of any of the things which I *thought* I perceived *very* clearly and *very* distinctly but which I now reject as false, I really *did* perceive them *very* clearly and *very* distinctly. What are the 'things' which I thought I perceived very clearly and very distinctly? That there is an earth, that there are stars, that there is a sky—'objects which I apprehended by means of the senses'. Also, 'that there were objects outside of me from which these ideas proceeded, and to which they were entirely similar'. And that 'two and three together make five, and other things of the sort'. What we have here is an enumeration which parallels that of *Meditation I*, in terms of everyday sense-based knowledge, applied science, and the theoretical sciences which include pure mathematics. What they share in common is that they all involve judgement, and for that reason alone they are all susceptible to doubt. It was therefore wrong to think that 'things' like these were known *very* clearly and *very* distinctly. For none of these are items known *per se*; the knowledge of none of them consists in grasping relations between a set of concepts which stand in an immediate and necessary connection. Therefore the last sentence of this part of Descartes's presentation of his position states that since there may be a God who is a deceiver 'I do not see that I can ever be certain of anything' (3, 4). That is to say, of course, I cannot be certain of anything of *this* sort. That I *can* be certain of anything known *per se* has already been established. Items of *that* sort I indeed know *very* clearly and *very* distinctly. They are not susceptible to doubt.

Is a next move possible 'without interrupting the order of meditation which I have proposed to myself, and which is little by little to pass from the notions which I find first of all in my mind to those which I shall later on discover in it'? (3, 5). In addition we must ask: is a next move possible, using only intuition and resolution, without assuming the validity of the principle of composition, or without assuming the trustworthiness of deduction?

The last sentence of paragraph 4 implies that, if we are to obtain any certainty about deductive knowledge, we shall have to be able to show that the hypothesis about the evil genius is untenable. Can we reject this hypothesis without falling into the trap of circularity? The hypothesis about the evil genius involves the assumption that there actually exists apart from me a being which corresponds to my idea of such a being. Do any of my thoughts warrant the move from the existence of my idea to something existing apart from me which corresponds to my idea? To speak of ideas, as the fifth paragraph reiterates, is quite permissible at this stage. It is quite permissible to speak of ideas, of 'images of things', as long as we take the notion of 'image' in a non-pictorial sense. For if we were to take 'idea' or 'image of a thing' in a pictorial sense we would introduce the corporeal imagination. Therefore, the title "idea"' is 'properly applied' to 'my thought of a man or of a chimera, of heaven, of an angel, or even of God' (3, 5). The introduction of the latter as an example of an idea indicates that we are not meant to introduce anything like a mental 'picture'. This interpretation is reinforced by what we read in later paragraphs: ideas are only 'certain modes of my thoughts' (3, 6), and 'we must remember that since every idea is a work of the mind . . . it is only a mode, i.e. a manner or way of thinking' (3, 14).

Two things can be said about these ideas. First, 'if we consider them only in themselves', i.e. as 'modes of thought', 'and do not relate them to anything else beyond themselves, they cannot properly speaking be false'. The reason is that 'whether I imagine a goat or a chimera, it is not less true that I imagine the one than the other' (3, 6). In either case, they are simply 'works of the mind', they are simply ideas or thoughts. But, second, what if I make any judgements about these ideas? What if, for example, I judge that there exist entities apart from my ideas, and that 'the ideas which are in me are similar or conformable to the things which are outside me'? Then I would make a tactical error. For judgement involves composition or deduction, and any beliefs obtained in this manner are still dubitable. As Descartes says: 'Thus there remains no more than the judgments which we make, in which I must take the greatest care not to deceive myself' (3, 6). The next few paragraphs, those from the seventh to the twelfth, are meant to illustrate the point that if I make use of 'judgment' at this stage I simply do not know whether or not I 'deceive myself'. These paragraphs, therefore, constitute an attempt at composition in this *Meditation*; and Descartes shows that making such an attempt here is premature. At the end of these paragraphs we are therefore again confronted with the position stated in the fourth paragraph: if we want to get beyond the 'I' and its ideas, we shall have to show that the belief 'that there is a God who is a deceiver' is untenable. In addition, we then know through experience (namely, through the experience of attempting to use deduction here) that the use of judgement, the use of deduction or composition, cannot lead us beyond this stage. These paragraphs are therefore meant to break our habit of trusting the validity of deduction, and are meant to force us back to the intuitive contemplation of the *Cogito*. An examination of these paragraphs will support this interpretation.

In paragraph 7 Descartes presents a division of our ideas in terms of three hypotheses about the origins of these ideas: 'some appear to me to be innate, some adventitious, and others to be formed or invented by myself'. The following paragraphs make clear that there are no good grounds for this division. For what reasons do I have for accepting that some of my ideas are adventitious, that they 'proceed from certain objects that are outside me', and that they are 'similar to these objects'? (3, 8). These reasons are twofold. 'It seems to me in the first place that I am taught this lesson by nature; and, secondly, I experience in myself that these ideas do not depend on my will nor therefore on myself' (3, 8). However, 'When I say that I am so instructed by nature, I merely mean a certain spontaneous inclination which impels me to believe', and this 'spontaneous inclination' has 'often enough led me to the part that was worse'. Hence even on this count alone there is no reason for 'following' this inclination now (3, 9). 'And as to the other reason, which is that these ideas must proceed from objects outside me, since they do not depend on my will, I do not find it any the more convincing.' For 'perhaps there is in me some faculty fitted to produce these ideas without the assistance of any external things' (3, 10). For all we know at this stage, all our ideas may be innate or fictitious. We still are where we were when we began this part of the investigation: through the use of judgement 'I have not yet clearly discovered their true origin' (3, 7). Moreover, even if we could show that some of my ideas are adventitious, that does not give me grounds 'to think them similar to these objects'. For the idea I have of the sun, and which I believe to be an adventitious idea, presents the sun as 'extremely small'; while the idea I have of the sun and which is 'elicited from certain notions' which I believe to be 'innate in me' presents the sun as 'several times greater than the earth'. Although 'these two ideas cannot, indeed, both resemble the same sun', I cannot at this time decide which of these two ideas is 'similar' to the object (3, 11).

In paragraph 4 of *Meditation III* it becomes clear that I cannot further my knowledge beyond that of items known *per se* unless I can show that the hypothesis about the evil genius is untenable. I have the idea of God, and I have the idea that God deceives me. The exercise of paragraphs 7 to 11 leads us back to what we already knew in paragraph 4: judgement involves composition or deduction and hence cannot give me any items of knowledge which are *very* clearly and *very* distinctly true. In the case at hand: judgement cannot at this stage tell me even *just* clearly and distinctly whether there is a being, God, apart from my idea of God, let alone whether the nature of this being is 'similar' to my idea of it. The formation of hypotheses about the origin of my ideas, being an attempt at composition or deduction, has led to no advance at all. Whatever judgement has been proposed has been shown to be susceptible to doubt, and has therefore been rejected.

The exercise present in the paragraphs I have just discussed is parallel to that presented in paragraphs 11 to 15 of *Meditation II*. The mind loves to wander because it is often subject to the control of powerful inclinations. In *Meditation II* the inclination that had to be checked was our action on the belief that we can say, before we have countered the sceptic's attack, that we can obtain knowledge through the senses. The argument about the piece of wax showed that if we know external objects at all, we know them through reason rather than through the senses. In *Meditation III* the inclination which had to be checked is the one of hurrying to believe, before we have defeated the sceptic, that we can trust deduction and composition in order to proceed beyond items known *per se*. The argument here shows that if we make judgements before we remove the remaining grounds for scepticism, these judgements result in dubitable items only. (With the exception of my idea of God, it is not until *Meditation VI* that the worry about whether 'there is in me some faculty fitted to produce these ideas without the assistance of any external things', as well as the worry about whether my ideas are 'similar' to these things, can be removed. Cf. HR1, 188–9; AT7, 75–7.)

Because the mind loves to wander and because it is often subject to these strong inclinations, the last part of the second *Meditation* as well as those passages of the third which I have been reviewing, can be seen in various ways as constantly reinforcing the position reached in *Meditation I*. In the first *Meditation* Descartes showed that in the face of scepticism it is wrong to give credence to the deliverances of the senses. But since we have trusted in the deliverances of the senses from our early childhood on, there is a strong inclination not to call them into question. This trust is therefore attacked once more in the discussion of the piece of wax. Also, in the first *Meditation* Descartes showed that we cannot, in the face of scepticism, trust the validity of conclusions derived by means of deduction, irrespective of whether or not such deductions are about what is given by the senses. However, we have accepted as trustworthy our ability to form true judgements from the time we began to use our understanding. There is therefore a strong inclination to continue to use judgement. This trust is attacked once more in the paragraphs of *Meditation III* which we have just now considered. In both cases, the conclusions of the first *Meditation* are re-established by means of an attempt to trust what was shown to be untrustworthy; in both cases, the fact that action based on this trust led to no advance re-establishes the correctness of these conclusions. Finally, in the first *Meditation* nothing was said to indicate that we could not continue to be absolutely certain of whatever is known *per se*. The second *Meditation* explicitly shows that it was correct to consider items like these to be impervious to doubt. At the point we have now reached in our discussion of *Meditation III* we therefore again return to that base of certain knowledge. We return to this base because the application of the principle of resolution—a methodological principle whose continued use was justified once we reached the *Cogito*—inexorably leads us back to it.

There is 'thinking-going-on', and this involves the existence of ideas. Ideas must come from somewhere. It has already been shown that ideas are 'modes of thought'. But is that all we can say about them? Not quite, according to Descartes. 'If ideas are only taken as certain modes of thought, I recognize amongst them no difference or inequality, and all appear to proceed from me in the same manner; but when we consider them as images, one representing one thing and the other another, it is clear that they are very different one from the other' (3, 13). I can account for my ideas *as modes of thought* in terms of the fact that I am a thing which thinks. But can I account in this way as well for these modes of thought if we consider *what they seem to represent or where they seem to point*? Consider the example which Descartes himself presents in the fourth paragraph of the Synopsis: suppose I possess the idea 'of a very perfect machine'—how could I have obtained this idea? To say that this idea is a mode of thought and that therefore it is a product of my mind does not tell the complete story. Any rational being can think thoughts, but not every rational being is able to produce the idea of a very perfect machine. In order to be able to do that one needs a highly developed, well-trained mind. One must be a scientist and, since the idea is 'of a very perfect machine', one must be a very good scientist. Or if one is not a very good scientist and one nevertheless has this idea (which is in part possible because the idea *is* a mode of thought) then one must have 'received the idea' from someone who is a very good scientist, from someone whose mind is more powerful than one's own and sufficiently powerful to be able to produce that kind of idea. This must be so, for else I cannot account for the idea in its *representative* aspect.

Thus it seems clear to Descartes (i) that ideas must come from somewhere, for 'something cannot proceed from nothing' (3, 14); (ii) that to account for ideas merely in terms of 'modes of thought' is insufficient in view of their representative aspect; (iii) that either I must be the 'cause' of my ideas also with respect to their repre-

sentative aspect, or (iv) that if my mind is not sufficiently powerful
to be the 'cause' of any one of these ideas, I must have 'received
the idea' from someone else. I must acknowledge the last two
points because (v) 'it is manifest by the natural light that there
must at least be as much reality in the efficient and total cause as
in its effect' (3, 14). Items (i) to (v) are the salient points of the
fourteenth and fifteenth paragraphs of *Meditation III*. According
to Descartes, it is of crucial importance that none of these points
is an item which is not known *per se;* all of them are known through
intuition. Therefore the introduction of every one of them is
legitimate. The principles that 'something cannot proceed from
nothing'—item (i)—and that 'there must at least be as much reality
in the efficient and total cause as in its effect'—item (v)—have
regularly been stated to be items known *per se*. The introduction of
'ideas'—item (ii)— has already been shown to be legitimate. But
if we were to limit our conception of an *idea* to that aspect of it
which is indicated by the ascription to it of 'mode of thought', we
do not have a clear and distinct concept. For an idea is always a
'mode of thought' about something or of something. This is the
case 'whether I imagine a goat or a chimera' (3, 6). I simply cannot
have an idea that is not an idea of something. Whether that thing
actually exists is not yet at issue at this point. For all we know to
exist at this point is the 'I' and its ideas. Therefore we know *very*
clearly and *very* distinctly that 'I' must be the 'cause' of my ideas
unless any of my ideas is such that the 'I' is not a 'cause' sufficiently
great to account for the relevant representative aspect. This takes
care of items (iii) and (iv). Thus, reflection on the concept 'idea' has
advanced the position. We therefore read in paragraph 16:

And the longer and the more carefully that I investigate (*examino,*
j'examine) these matters, the more clearly and distinctly do I recognize
their truth. But what am I to conclude from it all in the end? It is this,
that if the objective reality of any one of my ideas [i.e. the idea as to
its representative aspect] is of such a nature as clearly to make me
recognize that it is not in me either formally [i.e. I could not *have such*
a mode of thought] or eminently [i.e. I could not *make such* an idea if I
tried in view of the representative aspect of that idea], and that consequently I cannot myself be the cause of it, it follows of necessity that I
am not alone in the world, but that there is another being which exists,
or which is the cause of this idea.

Although this may look like an argument which involves deduction, it is not meant to be one. It is an investigation, an examination, of what we already know *per se*. This examination makes us recognize that there is more to be the intuitive knowledge which I already possess than what I could realize at first. The cluster of concepts in immediate and necessary connection does not consist only of *thought, existence,* and *ideas*; it also includes *cause,* and all that is immediately and necessarily related to that concept.

3. *Cogito,* 'God', the validation of deduction, and the justification of composition

The only judgement which has been seriously entertained up to this point is that which states the hypothesis about the evil genius. It is through taking this hypothesis seriously that Descartes faces the sceptic; and it is because the hypothesis is taken seriously that no other judgement ought to be entertained or that if we entertain seriously any other judgement we do so prematurely. Because the hypothesis about the evil genius is the only judgement we now entertain, it is about the ideas related in this judgement that we must ask whether any of them is such that I cannot be the cause of it.

The hypothesis about the evil genius states that an 'all-powerful God' exists who, rather than being 'supremely good', 'desired that I should be . . . deceived' (1, 9). It supposes the existence of 'not that God who is supremely good . . . but some evil genius not less powerful than deceitful (*summe potentem & callidum*)' who 'has employed his whole energies in deceiving me' (1, 12). I must, therefore, ask 'whether there is a God at all', that is, I must ask whether the idea I have of God could have been caused by a being other than God (by myself, for example). And if the answer to that question is that I could have obtained the idea of God only from God, I must ask whether this idea is 'similar' to the object it represents, whether 'there is a God who is a deceiver' (3, 4).

To say that the hypothesis about the evil genius is the only judgement which has been seriously entertained by Descartes is of course not to say that no other judgements have been introduced at all. These other judgements were, however, introduced prematurely, and they could not contribute to any advance in systematic knowledge as long as the sceptic had not been answered. To drive this point home once more Descartes asks also about the ideas in *these* judgements whether consideration about their 'cause' necessarily leads me beyond the 'I' and its ideas. This question is therefore asked not only about the idea of God, but also about ideas 'representing corporeal and inanimate things, . . . angels, . . . animals, and . . . men similar to myself' (3, 17). Paragraphs 18 to 21 show that I have reasons to doubt whether any of the ideas in the latter category *must* (not *can*) have a 'cause' apart from the 'I'. Therefore no progress may be made through consideration of ideas like these, or of judgements which incorporate ideas like these. Thus paragraph 22 states:

Hence there remains only the idea of God, concerning which we must consider whether it is something which cannot have proceeded from me myself. By the name God I understand a substance that is infinite, eternal, immutable, independent, all-knowing, all-powerful, and by which I myself and everything else, if anything else does exist, have been created. Now all these characteristics are such that the more diligently I attend (*attendo*) to them, the less do they appear capable of proceeding from me alone; hence, from what has been already said, we must conclude that God necessarily exists.

Through paying attention to this idea of God, rather than *through deductive or compositive argumentaion,* 'we must conclude that God necessarily exists'. Why, according to Descartes, must we come to this conclusion? And is it correct to stress *attendo* as I have done? Both of these questions are answered in the next dozen paragraphs of *Meditation III*. These paragraphs make clear as well that what Descartes pays attention to is a cluster of concepts, namely, the cluster including the concepts of *I, thought, ideas, existence, cause,* and *God.* It has already been shown that the first five of these are held to be concepts standing in immediate and necessary relations. Descartes now wants to show that all of these concepts are related in this way.

To make this point Descartes raises two questions. *First:* Could I have the idea of God if God does not exist? This question is answered in paragraphs 23 to 28. *Second:* Could I who have the idea of God exist if God does not exist? This second question is answered in paragraphs 29 to 36. These two questions are implicit in what Descartes writes after he has given us his answers to them. The first is implicit in the words: 'I recognize that it is not possible . . . that I should have in myself the idea of a God, if God did not veritably exist'; and the second is implicit in the words: 'I recognize that it is not possible that my nature should be what it is . . . if God did not veritably exist' (3, 38). Moreover, the second question is stated explicitly at the end of paragraph 28.

First. Could I have the idea of God if God does not exist? The idea of God is the idea of 'an infinite substance'. I can be the 'cause' of the 'substance' aspect of this idea, for I myself am a substance. But I cannot be the 'cause' of the idea of 'infinite substance', and certainly not with respect to its representative aspect; for I myself am a finite substance. Therefore, 'I should not have the idea of an infinite substance—since I am finite—if it had not proceeded from some substance which was veritably infinite' (3, 23). To assert that I could be the 'cause' of the idea of 'infinite substance' would be to espouse a *praejudicium,* as Descartes's next paragraph makes clear. For the only way in which a being who is a finite substance and who knows himself as finite substance could obtain the idea of 'infinite substance' in terms of itself, would be 'by negation of the finite'. But to try and think this way is all wrong. For 'I have in me the notion of the infinite earlier than the finite—to wit, the notion of God before that of myself.' If this were not so, 'how would it be possible that I should know that I doubt and desire, that is to say, that something is lacking to me, and that I am not quite perfect, unless I had within me some idea of a Being more perfect than myself, in comparison with which I should recognize the deficiencies of my nature?' (3, 24). Thus, I cannot have a clear and distinct conception of the existence of a finite, thinking 'I', unless I also conceive of an infinite being who exists. The concepts of an *existing I* and an *existing God* are, therefore, parts of the cluster of concepts in immediate and necessary relation.

The next paragraphs, 25 to 27, serve to remove possible objections. That is, these paragraphs remove further *praejudicia,* or judgements some might still tend to make either through force of habit, or because of the fact that they have not paid sufficient attention. These are, then, judgements some might still want to make in spite of what has just been shown about the relationship between 'I' and 'God' and in spite of the fact that the making of judgements is suspended as long as the hypothesis about the evil genius is not rejected. These *praejudicia* are: 'that this idea of God is perhaps materially false' (i.e. that it represents as existing what does not exist); that we don't really have a true idea of the infinite because a finite mind cannot 'comprehend the infinite' (3, 25); and that I myself am possibly the 'cause' of this idea of God because I am perhaps potentially perfect (3, 26–7). In these paragraphs Descartes shows that if these *praejudicia* are to be entertained at all, their denial in each case makes more sense than their affirmation. Thus, also for this reason they are dubitable, and they are therefore all rejected. The conclusion of this section is therefore that 'I see nothing in all that I have just said which by the light of nature is not manifest to anyone who desires to think attentively (*quod diligenter attendi*) on the subject'. But *diligent* attention is required. For 'when I slightly relax my attention (*sed quia, cum minus attendo*), my mind, finding its vision somewhat obscured and so to speak blinded by the images of sensible objects, I do not easily recollect the reason why the idea that I possess of a being more perfect than I, must necessarily have been placed in me by a being which is really more perfect' (3, 28). *Praejudicia* which we are willing to accept through a long habit of trusting deduction, as well as relaxation of my attention, continue to interfere with my perception of the immediate and necessary connection of 'I', 'thought', 'ideas', 'existence', 'cause', and 'God'. Therefore, once more attention will be focused upon this cluster of concepts, this time in terms of the question 'whether I, who have this idea, can exist if no such being exists?' (3, 28).

Second. Could I who have the idea of God exist if God does not exist? The 'thinking-that-is-going-on' must have a 'cause', for 'something cannot proceed from nothing'. A number of *praejudicia* are examined and, as before, they are shown to be dubitable and hence rejected. These *praejudicia* are: that 'I myself' am 'the author of my being' (3, 30); that 'I have always existed just as I am at present' (3, 31); that 'I am created by my parents or by some other cause less perfect than God' (3, 33, 34, and 36); and 'that several causes may have concurred in my production' (3, 35). The rejection of these *praejudicia* leaves only God as the 'cause' of my existence. Hence 'we must of necessity conclude from the fact alone that I exist, or that the idea of a Being supremely perfect— that is of God—is in me, that the proof of God's existence is grounded on the highest evidence' (3, 36). This 'highest evidence' is that the only way in which I can clearly and distinctly understand the existence of a being like myself is if I see that the existence of this being is necessarily bound up with the existence of 'a Being supremely perfect'.

To prove the existence of 'a Being supremely perfect' is not enough. 'By the name God I understand a substance that is infinite, eternal, immutable independent, all-knowing, all-powerful, and by which I myself and everything else, if anything else does exist, have been created' (3, 22). Conspicuously absent from this list is the attribute 'veracious', or its negative counterpart 'of the utmost power and cunning' (1, 12). But because I am still entertaining the hypothesis about the evil genius, 'utmost cunning' or 'deceit' is still included in my idea of God. Descartes must therefore once more focus upon the idea of God in order to see whether, in this one crucial respect, this idea may be 'materially false'. As he said earlier: 'if I find that there is a God, I must also inquire whether He may be a deceiver; for without a knowledge of these two truths I do not see that I can ever be certain of anything'—that is, of anything not known *per se*.

Therefore the next point Descartes makes is that the God of whose existence he is now certain is:

a God, I say, whose idea is in me, i.e. who possesses all those supreme perfections of which my mind may indeed have some idea . . ., who is liable to no errors or defect and who has none of all those marks which denote imperfection. From this it is manifest that He cannot be a deceiver, since the light of nature teaches us that fraud and deception necessarily proceed from some defect. (3, 38)

Thus, if my idea of God is an idea of an omnipotent or perfect deceiver, it is materially false. Hence there cannot exist an evil genius. An evil genius cannot exist because not only is there no immediate and necessary connection between 'perfection' and 'deception', but because it is contradictory to hold that 'perfection' and 'deception' can go together. The hypothesis about the evil genius, a hypothesis which states that perfection and deception can exist in one and the same being, is therefore self-contradictory.

In the passage I have just quoted it is not stated explicitly that the hypothesis about the evil genius is rejected because it is self-contradictory. That this is nevertheless implicit is clear from comments Descartes makes about this hypothesis elsewhere, especially from statements we find in *Descartes' Conversation with Burman.*[4] When Burman asked Descartes to comment on the phrase 'of the utmost power' which appears in the statement of the hypothesis at the end of *Meditation I* ('I shall then suppose . . . that . . . some evil genius not less powerful than deceitful (*summe potentem & callidum*) has employed his whole energies in deceiving me'), Descartes notes that 'What the author here says is contradictory, since malice is incompatible with supreme power.'[5] Again, when Burman raised a question about the phrase 'and, if I may say so, malicious', a phrase which occurs in the statement of the hypothesis in *Meditation II* ('But what am I, now that I suppose that there is a certain genius which is extremely powerful, and, if I may say so, malicious, who employs all his powers in deceiving me?') (2, 6). Descartes responds as follows: 'The restriction is added here because the author is saying something contradictory in using the phrase "supremely powerful and malicious", since supreme power cannot co-exist with malice. This is why he says "if it is permissible to say so".'[6]

The conclusion, according to Descartes, is clear. As we read in the *Reply to Objections II*: 'after becoming aware of the existence of God, it is incumbent on us to imagine that he is a deceiver if we wish to cast doubt upon our clear and distinct perceptions; and since we cannot imagine that he is a deceiver, we must admit them all as true and certain' (HR2, 41; AT7, 144). The *only* reason for doubting the efficacy of composition, or the only reason for doubting the validity of deduction, is the possible existence of the evil genius. But the hypothesis which states the existence of the evil genius is self-contradictory. There is, therefore, no reason for doubting the efficacy of composition, or for doubting the validity of deduction. The imposition of the general method is completely justified. To hold otherwise would, for Descartes, be inexcusable. It would be inexcusable because, since composition is the way the mind works when it proceeds deductively, and since the validity of deduction has now been established, there are no grounds whatsoever for having qualms about the use of the general method. If we want to 'establish any firm and permanent structure in the sciences' (1, 1) we *must* resolve the complexity which confronts

---

[4] *Descartes' Conversation with Burman,* translated with Introduction and Commentary by John Cottingham (Oxford, 1976)

[5] Ibid., p. 4; AT7, 22; HR1, 148.

[6] Ibid., p. 9; AT7, 26; HR1, 151.

us until we reach those items which are known *per se*, until we can have an intuition. But grasping items known *per se* does not constitute systematic or scientific knowledge. To obtain the latter, we must use the imagination and doubt: the former to introduce items which may qualify as necessarily linked to the knowledge we already possess, the latter to submit these items to the normal methodological test of doubt in order to see whether the items presented by the imagination can indeed be intuited as linked necessarily with what is already known.

If, for a moment, we return to my earlier terminology of intuition$_1$ and intuition$_2$, it is clear that at this stage also intuition$_2$ is held to be absolutely trustworthy. Any particular memory remains potentially unveridical. Thus, whenever we have made a lengthy deduction, we must remember that we did indeed make all the right moves, and that therefore the conclusion follows with necessity. Thus a slight (but not longer metaphysical!) doubt remains. At least in 'medium-length' deductions, this is a doubt which can be removed if one is not 'sluggish'. As we read in Rule 7:

. . . deduction frequently involves such a long series of transitions from ground to consequent that when we come to see the conclusion we have difficulty in recalling the whole of the route by which we have arrived at it. This is why I say that there must be a continuous movement of thought to make good this weakness of the memory. Thus, e.g. if I have first found out by separate mental operations what the relation is between the magnitudes *A* and *B*, then what between *B* and *C*, between *C* and *D*, and finally between *D* and *E*, that does not entail my seeing what the relation is between *A* and *E*, nor can the truths previously learnt give me a precise knowledge of it unless I recall them all. To remedy this I would run them over from time to time, keeping the imagination moving continuously in such a way that while it is intuitively perceiving each fact it simultaneously passes on to the next; and this I would do until I had learned to pass from the first to the last so quickly, that no stage in the process was left to the care of memory, but I seemed to have the whole in intuition before me at the same time. (HR1, 19; AT10, 387–8.)

Since, in intuition$_2$, there is nothing before the mind but what is self-evident and what is seen to be necessarily related to that, there is no room for error in it. For since the power of intuition$_1$ has been shown to be absolutely trustworthy under any circumstances, and the power of deduction has been validated because it has been shown that no evil genius can exist, therefore also intuition₂ is absolutely trustworthy.

4. 'Prejudices' and the intuitive contemplation of the *Cogito*

The position presented in the first three of the *Meditations* is one which, according to Descartes, involves no circular argumentation. My exposition of this position agrees with Descartes's claim about non-circularity. But there is more than this to indicate that my exposition may be said to do justice to Descartes's position in these *Meditations*. Perhaps most important is that my exposition shows how this position is based on and in harmony with doctrines stated in other works (especially with doctrines stated in the *Rules* and the *Discourse*); and that my exposition is supported by what Descartes himself says about his position, especially in the *Replies to Objections*. A final restatement of the most important aspects of my interpretation of the second and third *Meditations*, together with some pertinent comments from the *Replies to Objections* which have not so far been introduced, should confirm the plausibility of the statement that my exposition has done justice to Descartes's position.

I have constantly presented Descartes's position in the second and third *Meditations* as one in which one aspect of reason (deduction) is validated by another aspect of reason (intuition— an aspect of reason which has been shown to be reliable as soon as we reached the *Cogito*). It is not as if, in the second and third *Meditations*, there are no attempts at deduction. But these attempts are recognized by Descartes for what they are: premature. And nothing results from these attempts except that one's recognition that they lead nowhere forces one back to reliance upon intuition. Thus the introduction of the attempts at deduction may be seen as a pedagogical device. The same may be said about the introduction of the senses. In *Meditation II* Descartes introduces the discussion of knowledge of a physical object (a piece of wax) presumably known through the senses, in order to make clear that if we have knowledge of physical objects, such knowledge is obtained through reason rather than through sensation. This passage is present in order to help us to break our habit of trust in the senses, a habit which leads to innumerable *praejudicia*. Similarly, in the second and third of the *Meditations* Descartes introduces deduction in order to attempt to advance beyond the *Cogito*. He shows both that such attempts lead to no advance and, also, that in making the attempts we find they only lead us back to what we already know through intuition. In these two ways Descartes tries to break the reader's well-established habit of reliance upon deduction. He tries to break this habit by showing that, before the full validation of reason any judgement, anything not known *per se*, is a *praejudicium* which cannot lose its status of *praejudicium* until after reason has been fully validated. (Since *prae* often means 'in front of', 'in advance of', the idea of a judgement—*judicium*—coming *too far in front* fits Descartes's use of *praejudicium* very nicely.) The point is that as long as we attempt to use deduction, as long as we retain any of our *praejudicia*, no validation of deduction can take place. We must thus rely on resolution and intuition alone in order to validate deduction and to justify the imposition of the methodological principle of composition. This basic aspect of my exegesis very well fits Descartes's statement which I stressed earlier: 'I have denied nothing but *praejudicia*, and by no means notions . . . which are known without any affirmation or denial.' Once we are free from dependence on sense and once we are free from *praejudicia*, then intuition will reveal to us not only that there is an immediate and necessary connection between 'thinking' and 'existing', but that such a connection exists between 'thinking', 'ideas', 'existence', 'cause', and 'veracious God'. Since *intuition* shows us this, what is grasped in each case is an item known *per se*.

A passage I introduced earlier from the *Rules* made clear that long before he wrote the *Meditations* Descartes took certain clusters of ideas to be knowable *per se* or non-deductively; indeed, that some items known *per se* could not be known clearly and distinctly unless other items known *per se* were introduced as well. This doctrine I then showed to be operative at crucial points in Descartes's position in *Meditation II* and *Meditation III*. When he comments on his position in these *Meditations*, Descartes himself insists on the relevance of this doctrine. This insistence is made especially clear in the material Descartes appended to his *Reply to Objections II*. In this material he presents the position of the *Meditations* by means of 'arguments drawn up in geometrical fashion'. Part of this presentation consists in a statement of relevant definitions and postulates. As *'fifth postulate'* Descartes presents:

I require my readers to dwell long and much in contemplation of the nature of the supremely perfect Being. Among other things they must reflect that while possible existence indeed attaches to the ideas of all other natures, in the case of the idea of God that existence is not possible but wholly necessary. *From this alone and without any train of reasoning they will learn that God exists, and it will* not *be less self-evident* (*per se notum*)[7] *to them* than the fact that number two is even and number three odd. (HR2, 55; AT7, 163–4. My italics.)

And two pages further on we read:

To say that something is contained in the nature of a concept of anything is the same as to say that it is true of that thing. But necessary existence is contained in the concept of God. Hence it is true to affirm of God that necessary existence exists in Him, or that God Himself exists.

And this is the syllogism of which I made use above, in replying to the sixth objection. *Its conclusion is self-evident* (*per se nota*) *to those who are free from prejudices* (*praejudiciis sunt liberi*), *as was said in the fifth postulate.* (HR2, 57; AT7, 166–7. My italics.)

Thus those who are 'free from *praejudica*' will, after 'long and much . . . contemplation', conclude that God necessarily exists. This 'contemplation', in the *Meditations,* is not focused only on the idea of God. 'Among other things they must reflect that . . . possible existence indeed attaches to the ideas of all other natures. . .' In the order of discovery, in the analytic order of exposition, our first item of certainty is that 'thinking-is-going-on'. To entertain the idea of thinking is itself an instance of thinking: so to this ideal actual, rather than merely possible, existence is attached. But this actual existence is not necessary existence, for 'I am, I exist, is necessarily true' *only* 'each time that I pronounce it, or that I mentally conceive it' (2, 3). In the intuition of the fact that the existence of the 'I' is contingent, the idea of necessary existence and thus the idea of God is implied. These statements

---

[7] As Nakhnikian has remarked with reference to a passage in the Synopsis of the *Meditations: scire* is used by Descartes as a technical term for knowledge of *demonstrated* conclusions; and in this use of the word *scientia* is contrasted with *cognoscentia* or *notitia*, which is the immediate apprehension of 'first principles', of anything known 'without affirmation or denial'. Cf. G. Nakhnikian, 'The Cartesian Circle Revisited', p. 252.

have made explicit some of the 'other things' on which we must focus in our contemplation. Once we do that we can come to the conclusion stated at the end of the third *Meditation*. Or at least we can *if we are free from praejudicia, that is, 'without any train of reasoning'*.

If this were a detailed study of Descartes's *Meditations* much more would have to be said even about these first three. My main task in this chapter has been, however, to show how Descartes believed he could justify an absolute trust in the validity of reason, and how this justification at the same time implies a justification for the imposition of his method. This task I have now completed. Questions about many aspects of this part of Descartes's position can certainly be raised. In fact, many of these questions have been raised and discussed by other scholars, even when they did not attempt to develop the kind of interpretation I have presented.[8]

The basic critical questions one could ask at this point have to do with the notion of self-evidence, with the possibility of knowing anything *per se*. To deny that knowledge of anything *per se* is possible is to deny the validity of one of the most important, if not *the* most important, parts of the very foundation of the Cartesian system. At several points in my earlier chapters I have indicated that I believe this important tenet to be indefensible. But Descartes's validation of reason, and his justification for the imposition of his method, is so intricately bound up with the acceptance of this tenet that one cannot conceive of the possibility of such a validation or justification apart from a commitment to the possibility of knowledge *per se*. For one who rejects the possibility of knowledge *per se*, or finds such talk unintelligible, Descartes's attempts to validate reason and justify his method will perforce be unconvincing. This is not surprising. Descartes's concept of reason is one which itself involves the notion of knowledge *per se* through recourse to his special concept of intuition. And one who rejects the notion of knowledge *per se* would therefore also reject Descartes's concept of reason. For such a person the validation of *that* concept of reason would be doomed to failure from the outset[9].

[8] An excellent study of many of the problems I have left unexplored may be found in Anthony Kenny's *Descartes, A Study of his Philosophy* (New York, 1968). A more recent and equally worthwhile study is Bernard Williams's *Descartes: The Project of Pure Enquiry.*

[9] Of course, also the notion of a method of reduction and composition involves the notion of self-evidence. For Cartesian reduction is reduction *of* the com-

How much of the Cartesian method can be adopted by a thinker who is not a Rationalist? If a non-rationalist does adopt the method articulated by Descartes, does this necessarily involve one in the assumption that such a thinker must incorporate into his position some important Rationalist tenets? Is there some way in which the essence of Cartesian methodology can be adopted by one who at the same time rejects the basic tenets of Cartesian metaphysics? Is there some way in which a non-rationalist can adopt the Cartesian methodology while at the same time retaining the integrity of his non-rationalist position?

Providing a full answer to these questions lies outside the scope of this study. To some of these questions an answer will begin to take shape during my discussion of Locke's work. However, my prime interest in the discussion of Locke is not that of providing such answers. Instead, my main goals will be to show *first*, that the Cartesian method is adopted by Locke; *second*, that for Locke as well as for Descartes, the use of this method determines in important ways the theory of the subject-matter to which it is applied; *third*, that Locke follows Descartes still further since, in particular instances, the Cartesian method even determines what is taken by Locke to be the nature of the subject-matter itself. I have made these three goals the main ones of my chapters on Locke because I want to show that two of the most influential seventeenth-century thinkers, although they are so different in many ways, both committed themselves to roughly the same methodology. Thus too many classical contrasts between this 'Continental Rationalist' and this 'British Empiricist' will soon turn out to have been radically misconceived. It is now time to turn to Locke.

---

plexity of what one experiences *to* the irreducible 'foundational' items which are known *per se*. Since Descartes' time many philosophers and scientists have held that if we are to obtain certain knowledge of any subject-matter, we must know its 'parts' before we can know 'the whole'. And the 'parts' thus to be known—whether they took these to be single simple ideas, complex concepts, propositions, or certain kinds of extralinguistic entities—were often held to be known in terms of themselves. Is it a fair generalization to say that whenever a reductionistic method is employed, some form of 'foundationalism' is implicit? One is tempted to answer this question in the affirmative. A categorical statement to this effect is hardly in place without an examination of at least a number of important representative positions in which a method of a reductionistic kind plays a prominent part. And that is a task well beyond the scope of my present study.

VI

METHOD AND 'GENERAL KNOWLEDGE' IN LOCKE'S *ESSAY CONCERNING HUMAN UNDERSTANDING*

In the remainder of this study it is my aim to establish that a methodology which is much like that of Descartes is clearly present in the major works of Locke. In this chapter I shall make it clear that the principles of such a methodology are advocated by Locke in *An Essay concerning Human Understanding*: for there it is Locke's position that we cannot attain 'general knowledge' unless we apply those principles. Chapter VII will attempt to elucidate some major aspects of the argument of Locke's *Second Treatise of Government* in terms of this methodology. I shall then defend the thesis that both the form which Locke's arguments take in the *Second Treatise*, and the conclusions which he reaches in it, are at least in part determined by the principles of this methodology. Chapter VIII deals with an important concern which comes to the fore in Locke's 'theological' works, namely, that of hermeneutics. After dwelling on certain important characteristics which Locke assigns to biblical writings, I shall ask why he chose to stress those particular features. The answer is not trivial. For Locke takes biblical texts to possess at least some of these characteristics because he has already assumed in turning to the Scriptures that they can be understood only by means of the application of certain methodological principles. And the most important of these we will find enunciated in the *Essay* and applied also in the *Second Treatise*.

If I succeed in performing all these tasks, I shall have completed the programme I announced in my first chapter. That is, I shall have shown through a careful review of major writings by Descartes and Locke how likely it is that leading seventeenth-century thinkers believed there to be but one method whose application to the subject-matter of any discipline in which we can expect to gain knowledge, can give us true mastery of the discipline. This programme, as I indicated before, involves a number of tasks. It has to be shown what are the essentials of this method, and how they were taken to be related to a view of reason(ing). In Chapters II and III I have already made good my programmatic responsibilities to Descartes. In the present chapter I shall bring into focus Locke's position on the nature of the method needed to obtain what he calls 'general knowledge'. This will, at the same time, allow me to show that Descartes and Locke propose fundamentally similar methods for approaching any subject-matter of which they believed they could attain knowledge. With respect to Locke, there then remains the task of showing how this methodological stance structures his theory about subject-matter and, indeed, determines to an extent also the nature of this subject-matter, which task will be undertaken in the course of the following two chapters. With respect to Descartes this has already been accomplished: in terms of a discussion of analytic geometry in Chapter III, section 3; and in terms of metaphysics in the two preceding chapters.

This chapter is divided into four sections. In the first, I shall make clear that Locke speaks about the *development* of 'general knowledge', of a science like that of mathematics or 'morals', in a way which implies a methodological principle very much like that of Descartes's principle of composition. However, Locke's methodological affinities with Descartes can be shown more conclusively by reference to numerous passages where he takes the application of the principle of resolution to be indispensable for providing general knowledge with the right *foundations*. To these passages I shall turn in the second section of this chapter. For Locke resolution can only take place when the mind possesses material which can be resolved. My account of Locke's views on the nature and applicability of the principle of resolution will be preceded by an argument to the effect that, according to Locke, the form which our experience at first takes is always characterized by complexity. In other words, Locke's position will be shown to be that simple or abstract ideas—on which all general knowledge is founded— are not immediately present in our experience but are, instead, obtained through a resolution or decomposition of the complex contents of our sentient states. In the third section I shall make clear that the complexity which characterizes our sentient states is held to be of various kinds. Here I shall also draw attention to the fact that the complex abstract ideas which are needed for the development of certain kinds of knowledge are made by the mind in various ways through a combination of the simple abstract ideas obtained through resolution of the complexity obtained through experience. In both the second and third sections it will become clear that, in addition to the methodological principle of resolution, there is another principle of crucial importance to Locke, a principle which may be called the empiricist principle. In the fourth section, it will be argued that several passages of the *Essay* seem to indicate that the definition of general knowledge, as well as the construction of complex abstract ideas, presupposes that one knows the single ideas obtained through resolution. I shall also show that Locke's description of how we know such ideas is very much in keeping with Descartes's description of how we know 'simples' through intuition. If my analysis of these passages is correct, this reveals a further close similarity between Descartes and Locke: adoption of the principle of resolution seems for both of them to be accompanied by the belief that the end results of the process of resolution are simple ideas or concepts each of which may be known in isolation from other concepts. Such belief about the possibility of knowledge of concepts in isolation—a belief unambiguously articulated by Descartes—might well be called a basic Rationalist tenet. So Locke is a thinker who, in spite of strong non-rationalist tendencies, incorporates in his position a basic doctrine of Rationalism. Moreover, this doctrine is accepted in the context of Locke's adopting the Cartesian principle of resolution. It therefore appears as if the adoption of a Rationalist methodology is what leads Locke to incorporate such a crucial Rationalist tenet in the very heart of his intendedly Empiricist theory of knowledge.

1. The development of general knowledge

Locke did not keep it a secret that he was influenced by the works of Descartes. Lady Masham, Locke's close friend and companion during the last years of his life, wrote after his death that 'the first Books, as Mr. Locke himself told me, which gave him a relish of Philosophical studys were those of Descartes. He was rejoyced in reading of these because tho' he very often differ'd in opinion from this writer, he yet found that what he said was very intelligible.'[1] Much of what he found 'very intelligible' in Descartes's works found its way into the *Essay concerning Human Understanding*.

When in recent work on Locke various aspects of his position are explored, one regularly finds a chapter or an article in which Locke's position is explicitly related to Descartes's views on the matter.[2] Many of these studies amply bear out John W. Yolton's contention about Locke: 'It is evident that in philosophy he wrote from an intimate acquaintance with Descartes and the debates among the Cartesians'; they provide at least some of the grounds for Yolton's generalization that '. . . the way of ideas of the *Essay* is Locke's translation of and transmission to Britain of many of the Cartesian concepts and doctrines'.[3]

The affinity between Locke and Descartes with respect to their views on the nature of reasoning and on right method and procedure indicates, in my view, the most important aspect of Locke's 'transmission to Britain of . . . Cartesian concepts and doctrines'. Of course, this affinity has not remained unnoticed in other recent studies on Locke. Richard I. Aaron, for example, writes that 'Apart from the general inspiration which he derived from Descartes Locke was chiefly indebted to him for the details of his account of knowing.' Specifically, Aaron points out that 'Locke's intuitionism on the subjective side is identical with that of Descartes. With him Locke holds that the best instance of knowing is intuiting and that non-intuitive knowledge, for instance, demonstration or indirect knowing, in so far as it is certain, contains also of necessity an intuitive element'. Aaron also writes, with regard to the method to be used in attaining knowledge: 'The guiding concept of the

---

[1] This statement appears in several recent works on Locke. It is quoted, for example, by James L. Axtell, in *The Educational Writings of John Locke* (Cambridge, 1968), pp. 304–5; as well as by Richard I. Aaron, in *John Locke*, 3rd edn. (Oxford, 1971), p. 9. Aaron there also quotes from Locke's first *Letter* to Stillingfleet, in which he speaks about Descartes as one to whom is due 'the great obligation of my first deliverance from the unintelligible way of talking' of the schools.

[2] To mention just one example: in I. C. Tipton's *Locke on Human Understanding* (Oxford, 1977), M. R. Ayers relates Locke's and Descartes's ideas on substance, Henry E. Allison shows to what extent Locke's theory of personal identity is founded on Cartesian notions, and Laurens Laudan argues that Descartes is one of Locke's sources when he formulates his views on the nature of hypotheses.

[3] These phrases are from pp. 3 and 5 of John W. Yolton's *The Locke Reader* (Cambridge, 1977).

age was that of composition. Since Descartes's day, at least, stress
had been put on the need for analysing the complex into its simple
parts. Things were assumed to be either simples or compounds
and the task of the scientist was to reveal the elements out of which
the compounds were made. . . . Locke too was committed to this
theory. . . .'[4] If we begin with Locke's account of how we *develop*
general knowledge, it is easy to see the high degree of similarity
between Descartes and Locke as they write about the nature of
reasoning and method. I shall however, go well beyond commentators like Yolton and Aaron, for I shall show how Locke repeatedly
discusses the necessity of the implementation of a principle like
that of resolution in the contexts where he discusses the possibility
of general knowledge. Once I have presented this aspect of Locke's
position, I shall also raise points of sharp disagreement with Aaron
concerning Locke's doctrine of the extent of our knowledge.

Because Locke writes in greater detail about how one *obtains
the foundations* for general knowledge than about how, through
composition, one develops general knowledge once these foundations have been obtained, I shall not say very much about the
development of general knowledge. I shall, however, introduce
sufficient material to make it quite clear that Locke wrote about
the development of general knowledge in terms which may plausibly
be said to have been adopted from Descartes. Once this material
has been introduced and once some of its implications have been
considered, we shall at the same time possess the framework for
the discussion of the material to be presented in the following
sections of this chapter. In these following sections I shall then
be able to deal in greater detail with the second of the two methodological principles which underlie Locke's account of general
knowledge: that of resolution. And it will become clear how
Cartesian Locke's account of knowledge really is.

As we saw in previous chapters, resolution and composition are
the essential characteristics of the method advocated by Descartes.
For Descartes, reasoning is the construction of intelligible complex
wholes out of the simple elements obtained through resolution.
Composition, the procedural principle of order which governs this
construction, consists in 'commencing with objects that were the
most simple and easy to understand, in order to rise little by little,

⁴ Aaron, op. cit. These passages are from pp. 10, 221, and 111, respectively.

or by degrees, to knowledge of the most complex', or in 'putting forward those things first that should be known without the aid of what comes subsequently, and arranging all other matters so that their proof depends solely on what precedes them'.[5] These statements of procedure define the conditions under which what Descartes calls 'deduction' takes place. They also define the conditions under which what Locke calls 'deduction', 'demonstration', or 'inference' takes place. Some commentators have not been unaware of the fact that Locke's construction of general knowledge, once the 'materials' were available, is like Descartes's in nature. However, there seems to be no general recognition of the extent to which Locke speaks in terms which are descriptive of Cartesian composition when he discusses the method needed for 'demonstration'. It will, therefore, be useful to introduce some of Locke's own statements on this matter.

Demonstration, for Locke, 'is the shewing the Agreement, or Disagreement of two Ideas, by the intervention of one or more Proofs ['intervening' or 'intermediate' ideas (4.2.3)] which have a constant, immutable, and visible connexion one with another' (4.15.1).[6] The focal point of the methodological procedure implied is in the way this 'intervention' of the intermediate ideas is to take place. It consists in 'laying them in a clear and fit Order, to make their Connexion and Force be plainly and easily perceived' (4.17.3; see also 4.8.3). The nature of this order is indicated, somewhat vaguely, in statements like:

. . . Reason . . . so orders the intermediate Ideas, as to discover what connexion there is in each link of the Chain, whereby the Extremes are held together; and thereby, as it were, to draw into view the Truth sought for, which is what we call Illation or Inference, and consists in nothing but the Perception of the connexion there is between the Ideas, in each step of the deduction . . . (4.17.2);

and:

. . . each intermediate Ideas must be such, as in the whole Chain hath a visible connexion with those two it has been placed between . . . (4.17.4.)

---

[5] AT6, 18; HR1, 92; and AT7, 155; HR2, 48.
[6] All quotations from the *Essay concerning Human Understanding* are from Peter H. Nidditch's edition. I have disregarded all of Locke's italicizations (in the few cases in which I have introduced italics they are my own). References are given in terms of Book, Chapter, and paragraph. Thus '4.15.1' refers to Book 4, Chapter 15, paragraph 1.

Thus the order is that of a 'chain' of ideas. A clearer indication of the nature of the order within the 'chain' is given in, for instance, 4.12.7:

By what steps we are to proceed . . . is to be learned in the Schools of the Mathematicians, who from very plain and easy beginnings, by gentle degrees, and a continued Chain of Reasonings, proceed to the discovery and demonstration of Truths, that appear at first sight beyond humane Capacity.[7]

The last of these statements seems no more than a reconstruction in terms of phrases taken from the *Discourse*, where Descartes enunciated his third methodological precept as 'to carry on my reflections in due order, commencing with objects that were the most simple and easy to understand, in order to rise little by little, or by degrees, to knowledge of the most complex . . .', and where he wrote of 'Those long chains of reasoning, simple and easy as they are, of which geometricians make use in order to arrive at the most difficult demonstrations . . .'.[8]

We must, says Locke, begin our 'demonstrations' from 'very plain and easy beginnings'. As will be made clear in the next section of this chapter, the plainest and easiest 'beginnings' are, according to Locke, to be found in the perception of abstract ideas, ultimately, of single simple ideas abstracted from our experience. On the basis of these, we gradually generate greater and greater complexity in terms of the simple modes of mathematics, the mixed modes of morals, and the complex ideas of any area of intellectual endeavour in which man can attain general knowledge. That the order within the 'chains' must be from simplicity to complexity is clear also from the role 'intuition' plays. Intuition, according to Locke, is necessary for the generation of any chain of reasoning, for it alone perceives 'the immediate connexion of each Idea to that which it is applied to on each side, on which the force of the reasoning depends' (4.17.4).[9] And, for Locke as for Descartes, the order of intuition is always from the simple to the complex. If intuition were to attempt to start from a foundation other than that of simple ideas, it would be building on a false foundation, and 'Reason is so far from clearing the Difficulties which the building upon false

---

[7] See also 4.4.9 and 4.17.3.
[8] HR1, 92; AT6, 18–19.
[9] See also 4.2.1. 4.2.7, and 4.17.15.

foundations brings a Man into that if he will pursue it, it entangles him the more, and engages him deeper in Perplexities' (4.17.12).

The way reason goes about its business is thus, for Locke as it is for Descartes, that of 'putting forward those things first that should be known without the aid of what comes subsequently, and arranging all other matters so that their proof depends solely on what precedes them'. This procedure directs Locke's construction of all general knowledge on the foundations of simple ideas.[10]

This last point can also be made in the following way. 'Rational Knowledge', says Locke, 'is the perception of the certain Agreement, or Disagreement of any two Ideas, by the intervention of one or more other Ideas' (4.17.17). The criterion used to decide, in any particular instance in which we attempt to reason, whether we have succeeded or not, i.e. whether 'the Mind has made this Inference right or no' is: 'if it has made it by finding out the intermediate Ideas, and taking a view of the connexion of them, placed in a due order, it has proceeded rationally, and made a right Inference. If it has done it without such a View, it has not... made an Inference that will hold . . .' (4.17.4). Since all general knowledge is the result of inference, and since the only inferences that 'will hold' are those in which the mind has had a view of the connexion of the intermediate ideas 'placed in due order', and since this order is that of proceeding 'from very plain and easy beginnings, by gentle degrees and a continued chain of reasonings', the principle of composition directs the construction of general knowledge.

Before I present Locke's theory of how one obtains the 'plain and easy beginnings' from which all 'deduction' must ultimately start, it is important to make two points. First, it should be realized that since we are trying to determine what are, for Locke, the

---

[10] Sometimes, as in 4.12.7, it looks as if Locke hints at the limitation of this method to the field of mathematics. The point of such passages is, however, that the methods of disciplines distinct from mathematics are merely specific exemplifications of the general method of resolution and composition. The method used to develop 'morals' is that used to develop mathematics, differently manifested because of a difference in subject-matter. Therefore Locke can say: 'Confident I am, that if Men would in the same method, and with the same indifferency, search after moral, as they do after mathematical Truths, they would find them [i.e. "moral ideas"] to have a stronger Connection one with another, and a more necessary Consequence from our clear and distinct Ideas, and to come nearer perfect Demonstration, than is commonly imagined' (4.3.20).

methodological principles for attaining *general* knowledge, this implies a limitation with respect to the application of the principles of resolution and composition. The application of these principles leads to knowledge in the realm of conceptual connections, in realms like those of arithmetic, geometry, and 'morals'. These principles cannot, however, be applied in a realm like that of physics, where we are interested in discovering relations among physical objects or 'substances'. The reason for this limitation is stated clearly by Locke in passages like the following:

In our search after the Knowledge of Substances, our want of Ideas, that are suitable to such a way of proceeding, obliges us to a quite different method. We advance not here, as in the other (where our abstract Ideas are real as well as nominal Essences) by contemplating our Ideas, and considering their Relations and Correspondencies; that helps us very little. . . . By which, I think, it is evident, that Substances afford Matter of very little general Knowledge; and the bare Contemplation of their abstract Ideas, will carry us but a very little way in the search of Truth and Certainty. What then are we to do for the improvement of our Knowledge in substantial Beings? Here we are to take a quite contrary Course, the want of Ideas of their real Essences sends us from our own Thoughts, to the Things themselves, as they exist. Experience here must teach me, what Reason cannot . . . (4.12.9);

and:

Whence we may take notice, that general Certainty is never to be found but in our Ideas. Whenever we go to seek it elsewhere in Experiment, or Observations without us, our Knowledge goes not beyond particulars. 'Tis the contemplation of our own abstract Ideas, that alone is able to afford us general Knowledge. (4.6.16.)

Thus in an area like that of physics, we remain limited to observation of particular instances. If physics is to be developed on the basis of observation of particular instances, physics calls for a method different from that of resolution and composition. This method is the 'historical, plain method'. And this leads me to the second point we should notice before we consider Locke's theory concerning the derivation of the 'plain and easy beginnings' which are to be the starting points for 'deduction'.

Locke's major purpose in the *Essay* is 'to inquire into the Original, Certainty, and Extent of humane Knowledge' (1.1.2). We have already seen that, as far as the development of general knowledge is concerned, Locke introduces a procedure of which he speaks in terms which do not differ from those used by Descartes when the latter discussed the principle of composition. I shall show in the next part of this chapter that the methodological principle which, according to Locke, is to be implemented if we are to obtain the right starting-points for 'deductions', is the Cartesian principle of resolution. If it is correct to say that these two principles are necessary for the possibility of general knowledge, that in fact 'humane knowledge' can have neither 'certainty' nor 'extent' unless one is guided by these principles, then what is the role of the 'historical, plain method' which, as Locke himself states, is the method he uses in the *Essay*? The answer to this question is implicit in the statement in which the phrase 'historical, plain method' first appears. Locke here claims to have attained his purpose if, 'in this Historical, Plain method, I can give any Account of the Ways, whereby our Understandings come to attain those Notions of Things we have, and can set down any Measures of the Certainty of our Knowledge . . .' (1.1.2). All notions or ideas, to the extent that they are simple, are obtained through resolution of our experience, and certainty in knowledge we obtain only if comparison is structured by the application of the principle of composition. This Locke discovers from *observation* of 'the ways' of the understanding's procedure in its pursuit of knowledge. Like Descartes, Locke holds that an abstract theory of method cannot be provided, and that we are therefore obliged to maintain a careful observation of the workings of reason. We are so obliged, that is, if we are to become aware of how reason actually functions as it obtains its 'beginnings' of general knowledge and as it relates these 'beginnings' into an ordered series. This stress upon observing how the understanding actually does proceed is to be found at many crucial points throughout the *Essay*.[11] I suggest that, as it is used in the *Essay*, the word 'plain' in talk of 'historical, plain method' is meant to give us notice of the fact that we are going to be presented with what Locke believes we can *observe*—rather than with what he would take to be speculative and metaphysical reasonings. And by the use of 'historical' we are given notice of the fact that the *order* of the presentation of what we can observe will reflect the order in which the mind itself goes about its business in its pursuit of knowledge: it begins with simple

[11] See 2.11.16, 2.12.18, 4.2.1, 4.17.14.

ideas and, on this basis, proceeds to general knowledge. Thus, it is by his use and mention of this 'historical, plain method' that Locke tries to make us understand the method which is implicit in the argument of the *Essay*, and indicates the results obtained or obtainable through the latter's use. This, in turn, is no more than saying that by means of the 'historical, plain method' Locke describes the way the mind goes about its business in its successful pursuit of general knowledge.

In this context it is to be noted that what is described is an understanding which, if it is to attain knowledge, proceeds according to the method of resolution and composition, and this procedure is described, not evaluated. Evaluation is not Locke's primary aim to the extent that he employs the historical, plain method; instead, the aim is to show how, as a matter of fact, men obtain their ideas and their knowledge: 'I pretend not to teach, but to enquire' (2.11.17). But there is more to it. For what the inquiry brings to light is that only methodical reasoning, only proceeding 'from very plain and easy beginnings, by gentle degrees and a continued chain of reasonings', is worthy to be called *reasoning* at all; for it alone results in inferences 'that will hold'. In other words, for Locke as for Descartes, the unmethodical use of reason is not really the use of reason at all, and cannot lead to inferences 'that will hold'. Again, if we do not obtain inferences that hold, we have not gone about our business methodically, and have not really been reasoning. Proceeding by means of resolution and composition is proceeding rationally; resolution and composition express the essence of reasoning. And since the process of reasoning is held to be infallible, the method of resolution and composition is held to be beyond the bounds of critical evaluation. Like Descartes in the *Rules*, Locke in the *Essay* accounts for error in terms of memory (cf. 4, 1, 9; 4.2.7). And like Descartes in the *Meditations*, Locke supplements this account in terms of judgement: 'Knowledge being to be had only of visible certain Truth, Errour is . . . a Mistake of our Judgment giving Assent to that, which is not true' (4.20.1). By placing the origin of error in 'memory' and 'judgment', and by sharply distinguishing these two functions from reasoning, both Descartes and Locke place beyond question what they take to be the absolute trustworthiness of results obtained through reasoning or through proceeding by means of resolution and composition.

2. Resolution of the complexity of experience

Demonstration, for Locke, is 'the showing of agreement or disagreement of two ideas . . .'. These ideas *must* both be 'founded'
in 'experience' and be 'abstract'. This dual requirement points
to two different aspects of Locke's account of knowledge, and
these different aspects may be easily identified by introducing two
well-known statements from the *Essay*, each one of a group of
statements which express one of these two different aspects. The
first of these statements is from 2.1.2: 'Whence has it [the mind]
all the materials of Reason and Knowledge? To this I answer, in
one word, From Experience: In that all our Knowledge is founded;
and from that it ultimately derives it self. Our Observation . . .
supplies our Understandings with all the materials of thinking.'
The second is from 4.12.7: 'The true Method of advancing
Knowledge, is by considering our abstract Ideas', for 'General
and certain Truths, are only founded in the Habitudes and
Relations of abstract Ideas.' The first of these expresses the
principle that all knowledge begins with experience. I shall refer
to it as the *empiricist principle*. The second involves what I have
already referred to as the *principle of resolution*. The first principle
holds for *all* knowledge, whether sensitive, demonstrative, or
intuitive. Since the assurance of experience does not extend beyond
particulars, and even then (except for intuitive knowledge) we
must draw a distinction between real and nominal essences, sensitive knowledge lacks the generality and certainty of demonstrative
knowledge, and remains 'but judgement and opinion'. Knowledge
properly so called, that is knowledge characterized by generality
and certainty, is found in demonstrative knowledge, in the shape
of universal truths in propositional form (cf. 4.6.16). Since the
abstract ideas which are the concepts linked in these propositions
are the products of the mind's activity, their real and nominal
essences coincide. This helps to account for the certainty of these
propositions. And since these ideas are abstract, they transcend
particularity. This accounts for their generality. Although, through
the process of 'decomposition' or 'abstraction', these ideas are
made by the mind, the 'materials' for them are given in experience.
Since there cannot be abstraction unless the 'materials' for abstraction are given, this is the sense in which also demonstrative knowledge begins with experience.

To gain further insight into Locke's doctrine of general knowledge, it is necessary to say something about both 'experience' and 'abstraction'. Elaboration on the nature of 'abstraction' will provide an opportunity to make clear what is meant by 'the principle of resolution' in the context of Locke's thought.

The ideas related to form demonstrative or general knowledge are 'abstracted' from experience. This implies that we are not immediately presented with such ideas in sensory experience. Moreover, since the simplest of these abstract ideas will turn out to be Locke's 'simple ideas', this implies that we cannot characterize the contents of our sensory states merely (possibly not at all) in terms of simple ideas, that is, in terms of single unanalysable elements. Before I can make clear how the principle of resolution functions in the *Essay*'s account of knowledge, I shall have to show what it is to which this principle is applied. It is applied to our sentient states in which we are aware of ideas that are united together in combinations *given* to consciousness. I shall therefore show first that Locke holds *complexity* to be characteristic of the form which all our experience initially takes; that, because any sentient state is one in which we are conscious of united ideas in such *given* combinations, every sentient state is always characterized by the complexity of coexisting ideas. The application of the principle of resolution to what we experience, namely, to the complexity of coexisting ideas, gives us the abstract ideas needed for the development of general knowledge. We here see the relationship between the principle of resolution and the empiricist principle: we cannot obtain any abstract ideas unless we first have experiences. We must therefore begin by answering the question: If all knowledge arises from experience, what is the form experience takes to begin with? In dealing with this question I shall, in order to avoid repetition, limit myself wherever possible to a part of Locke's picture. I shall not consider the abstract ideas derived from the internal operations of our minds, but will limit the discussion to the abstract ideas originating in the perception of external sensible 'objects', to ideas obtained from sensation rather than to ideas obtained from reflection.

In 2.2.1. Locke writes that 'Though the Qualities that affect our Senses, are, in the things themselves, so united and blended, that there is no separation, no distance between them; yet 'tis plain, the Ideas they produce in the Mind, enter by the Senses simple and unmixed', so that the simple ideas we come to possess are 'perfectly distinct' from one another.[12] The only way in which we can obtain these simple ideas is by the 'impressions Objects themselves make on our Minds' (3.4.11). This means that 'the Mind is wholly Passive in the reception of all its simple Ideas' (2.12.1). And this, in turn, brings us back to the 'objects themselves', for since the mind is passive it cannot make any of its simple ideas and therefore they 'must necessarily be the product of Things operating on the Mind' (4.4.4). There is one further aspect to this part of Locke's position. I now refer to the many different passages throughout the *Essay* wherein Locke states that simple ideas are observed to exist in several combinations united together.

The sentence 'simple Ideas are observed to exist in several Combinations united together' is a direct quotation from the *Essay* (2.12.1). There are many other statements in which Locke draws attention to our experience of several simple ideas in combination. He writes that 'The Mind being . . . furnished with a great number of the simple Ideas . . . takes notice also, that a certain number of these simple Ideas go constantly together' (2.23.1); and '. . . everyone upon Enquiry into his own thoughts, will find that he has no other Idea of any Substance . . . but what he has barely of those sensible Qualities, which he supposes to inhere, with a supposition of such a Substratum, as gives as it were a support to those Qualities, or simple Ideas, which he has observed to exist united together' (2.23.6); he speaks about 'the simple Ideas that are found to co-exist in Substances' (3.9.13), and argues that 'It were . . . to be wished, That Men, . . . would set down those simple Ideas, wherein they observe the Individuals of each sort constantly to agree' (3.11.25); and 'Herein therefore is founded the reality of our Knowledge concerning Substances, that all our complex Ideas of them must be such, and such only, as are made up of such simple ones, as have been discovered to co-exist in Nature', for 'Whatever simple Ideas have been found

---

[12] Although the statement '. . . Ideas . . . enter by the Senses simple and unmixed' may seem to imply a doctrine in which the distinctness of ideas is bound up with the physiological aspect of the involvement of different senses, this is not Locke's intention. For in this passage he also states that the distinctness of ideas is in no way affected by the process involved: whether several ideas enter the mind through different senses, or at the same time through a single sense like that of sight or touch, the simple ideas in each case remain 'perfectly distinct'.

to co-exist in any Substance, these we may with confidence join together again, and so make abstract Ideas of Substances' (4.4.12). These are some of the relevant passages. There are others which contain the same observation but in which, instead of speaking of the unity of ideas of qualities, Locke uses an abbreviated form and simply speaks of the unity of qualities.[13]

Thus, as a summary statement about the form our experience takes to begin with, one can say that we start with a passive mind possessing perfectly distinct simple ideas which are observed to exist in several combinations united together.[14] The important point to be settled now is whether these simple ideas are sometimes, often, or always observed to exist in combinations united together. This point is important because if simple ideas are *always* experienced in combinations united together, then the *single* simple ideas—which are the simplest of the abstract ideas on which all general knowledge is ultimately founded—can be obtained *only* through some process of 'separation' or 'abstraction'.

I believe it can be shown conclusively that Locke holds complexity to be always characteristic of the form our experience takes initially. In 2.8.9 he lists as primary qualities 'Solidity, Extension, Figure, Motion, or Rest, and Number', and states that these qualities produce simple ideas in us, and that 'Sense constantly finds [these qualities] in every particle of Matter, which has bulk enough to be perceived.' That we constantly experience ideas of qualities together is, for Locke, a statement of empirical fact. Of course Locke does not say that experience reveals to us *necessary connections* between certain ideas; he merely reports what he finds to be the case whenever the mind is affected by objects in sensation.[15] Thus, since we cannot obtain any ideas of sensation unless we are affected by objects, and since all objects that affect us possess the primary qualities, it seems to follow that whenever an object affects us we obtain a group of ideas of primary qualities together.

[13] See, for example, 3.6.28, 3.9.17, 4.6.7.
[14] I here use 'passive' in the way Locke uses it, namely, only to indicate that, because of the involuntariness characteristic of sensation, the presence of the ideas of which the mind is conscious must be accounted for in terms of an extra-mental reality (cf. 2.1.25). Being conscious of ideas is, of course, an 'action' of the mind (cf. 2.21.5).
[15] On this point, as well as on the issue of knowledge of the connection between ideas of primary and secondary qualities, see John W. Yolton's 'The Science of Nature', in *John Locke, Problems and Perspectives*, ed. John W. Yolton (Cambridge, 1969), pp. 183–93, esp. pp. 187 ff.

In the very next paragraph Locke connects our ideas of secondary qualities with the primary qualities possessed by objects; the primary qualities are said to 'produce various Sensations in us . . . as Colour, Sounds, Tasts, etc.' Although this is not explicitly stated here, we may perhaps infer that whenever we are affected by objects, we obtain some ideas of secondary qualities as well. If what is stated in this inference does indeed accurately reflect Locke's position, the provision must be entered here as well that experience reveals no necessary connections between primary and secondary qualities; again, the statement embodies a report of what is found to be the case only. Hence Locke's position in passages like these seems to be that we always find groups of ideas of primary qualities together when we are affected by objects and, possibly, that these groups of ideas of primary qualities go together with some ideas of secondary qualities as well.

Although passages like 2.8.9 state that all the primary qualities are present in any object we sense (these qualities are said to be 'utterly inseparable from the Body, in what estate soever it be') we cannot conclude from them that we actually experience *all* of these qualities whenever we sense an object. Take, for example, the idea of solidity. As we read in 2.3.1, solidity is an idea which has 'admittance only through one Sense', that of touch. What solidity is, only our experience can tell us, and it does so when we place a flint or a football between our hands and then try to join the hands together (2.4.6). It is quite plausible that, in this experiment, we have ideas of all of the primary qualities, and quite implausible that we have an idea of solidity only. But when I see a football flying through the air, although I may (and perhaps do) have ideas of extension, figure, motion, and number, I cannot at that time have a sensible idea of the solidity of that object. Thus, although it seems to be Locke's position that we always find groups of ideas of primary qualities together whenever we are affected by objects, these groups do not always include the ideas of all of the primary qualities of which we may become aware when we experience objects under various conditions.

To say that in any particular sentient state we do not necessarily have ideas of all the primary qualities of the object affecting us, does not force upon us the extreme position that in some sentient states we have an idea of only *one* primary (or secondary) quality. For, first, Locke holds that at least ideas of some primary qualities always accompany one another, and ideas of some secondary qualities are always accompanied by ideas of some primary qualities. Second, a passage like 2.16.1 makes clear that even if we can conceive of a sentient state which one might be tempted to characterize as one in which I have an idea of one quality only— as, for example, on a summer evening I may be oblivious to everything but the scent of roses—even this sentient state cannot be characterized by simplicity.

That at least ideas of some primary qualities always accompany one another, and ideas of some secondary qualities are always accompanied by ideas of some primary qualities, is clear from, for example, 2.13.11. Locke there writes that '. . . Solidity cannot exist without Extension, neither can Scarlet-Colour exist without Extension; but this hinders not, but that they are distinct Ideas. Many Ideas require others as necessary to their Existence . . . which yet are very distinct Ideas.' It is clear that, in these sentences, Locke is dealing with ideas of qualities rather than with qualities, with sentient states and ideas rather than with extramental things and their qualities—for he consistently holds that, extramentally, colour exists in bodies only as a dispositional property. Therefore, because both the idea of solidity and the idea of scarlet colour need the idea of extension for their *existence,* this means we cannot be in a sentient state in which we have an idea of solidity or of scarlet colour unless, in this sentient state, we also have an idea of extension. We may generalize the statement about scarlet colour and say that in any sentient state in which we have the idea of any colour we must also have an idea of extension. The generalizations we may make on the basis of the material given in this passage do not allow us to draw the conclusion that, for Locke, *any* sentient state is one in which we are conscious of simple ideas given in combinations united together and that therefore the form our experience at first takes is always characterized by complexity. To be able to draw that conclusion, we need a generalization to the effect that in any sentient state in which we have the idea of any primary or secondary quality, this idea is always accompanied by another idea of a primary or secondary quality or by other ideas of primary or secondary qualities. Grounds for this generalization are given in a passage like 2.16.1.

In 2.16.1. Locke writes that the idea of number, in the form of the idea of 'Unity, or One', accompanies *all* of our ideas: 'every Object our Senses are employed about; every Idea in our Understandings; every Thought of our Minds brings this Idea along with it'—and, of course, whenever an idea is 'brought along', it is 'an actual perception' (1.4.20). Thus, whether we are aware of figure, colour, pain, *whatever* the 'Idea in our Understandings', it brings along with it the idea of number. Also, we cannot be in a sentient state in which we are just aware of 'Unity, or One'. For it is only when our senses are employed about some object, when there is an idea in our understandings, a thought in our minds, that we obtain the idea of 'Unity, or One'. We may therefore conclude that whenever we have the idea of any primary or secondary quality, this idea is always accompanied by the idea of 'Unity, or One', of number; and whenever we have the idea of 'Unity, or One', of number, this idea is always accompanied by the idea of another primary quality or by the idea of a secondary quality.

A passage like 2.7.7 makes the same point, and at the same time makes clear that it is not just the idea of 'unity' which accompanies all other ideas. For we there read:

Existence and Unity, are two other ideas, that are suggested to the Understanding, by every Object without, and every Idea within. When Ideas are in our Minds, we consider them as being actually there, as well as we consider things to be actually without us; which is, that they exist, or have Existence: And whatever we can consider as one thing, whether a real Being, or Idea, suggests to the Understanding, the Idea of Unity.

Therefore, since, for Locke, any sentient state is one in which we are conscious of simple ideas given in combinations united together, we may conclude it to be his position that the form our experience at first takes is always characterized by complexity, namely, by the complexity of simple ideas experienced as co-existing.

It is questionable whether it is correct to say that the form our experience takes at first is that of experiencing *simple* ideas in combination. Some commentators, e.g. Richard I. Aaron and C. B. Martin, take the position that one use of the phrase 'complex idea' is to refer to the simple ideas observed to exist in combination.[16] Professor Martin writes that 'Locke uses the phrase

---

[16] Aaron, op cit., p. 112; C. B. Martin and D. M. Armstrong, *Locke and Berkeley, A Collection of Critical Essays* (New York, 1968), p. 3.

"complex idea" in three ways' and that one of these ways is 'To mean something like "combinations or mixtures of simple ideas or simple aspects of experience" '. That he has here in mind "combinations or mixtures" *presented* to the mind in experience rather than simple ideas combined by the mind itself is clear from the context of his statements. His one example of this use of 'complex idea' is from 2.11.7. Since, as far as I know, this is the only passage in the *Essay* where Locke may be using 'complex idea' in this way, it is important to consider it. The part quoted by Martin reads:

In this also, I suppose, Brutes come far short of Men. For though they take in, and retain together several Combinations of simple Ideas, as possibly the Shape, Smell, and Voice of his Master, make up the complex Idea a Dog has of him; or rather are so many distinct Marks whereby he knows him: yet, I do not think they do of themselves ever compound them, and make complex Ideas.

Since, as the last part of Locke's sentence clearly states, dogs do not make 'complex Ideas', Martin is right in concluding that the first occurrence of 'complex idea' in this sentence must refer to something not compounded out of simple ideas. He therefore concludes that, in this case, 'complex idea' stands for 'combinations or mixtures of simple ideas or simple aspects of experience'. Of course he is correct in holding that since these 'combinations or mixtures' exist in the mind prior to any action of composition on the part of the mind, experience does not initially take the form of 'single unanalyzable elements'. However, the passage quoted is unclear and does not provide good grounds for concluding that Locke uses 'complex idea' to refer to sets of ideas experienced in combination. It may even provide grounds for drawing the conclusion that Locke does *not* use 'complex idea' to refer to simple ideas experienced as coexisting. For immediately after the phrase 'as possibly the Shape, Smell, and Voice of his Master, make up the complex Idea a Dog has of him', Locke as it were corrects himself in mid-sentence by adding 'or rather are so many distinct Marks whereby he knows him'. The sentence following the text of the *Essay* immediately after the last sentence quoted by Martin lends support to the negative conclusion: 'And perhaps even when we think they have complex Ideas, 'tis only one simple one that directs them in the knowledge of several things . . ..' The recurrence to simple ideas stands out clearly.

I believe it is a mistake to apply the phrase 'complex idea' to the simple ideas found to coexist; 2.11.7 offers no clear support for such a use. More important is that when we look at the clear statements in which Locke stipulates the meaning of 'complex idea', it is evident that this phrase cannot be applied to groups of simple ideas found to coexist. For Locke consistently maintains that 'complex Ideas' are 'Combinations of Ideas, which the Mind, by its free choice, puts together . . .' (4.4.5). Thus, whereas the mind is said to be 'wholly Passive in the reception of all its simple Ideas', one of the 'Acts of the Mind wherein it exerts its Power over its simple Ideas', consists in 'Combining several simple Ideas into one compound one, and thus all Complex Ideas are made' (2.12.1; see also 2.11.16). Since the mind is said to be passive in the reception of its simple ideas, and since simple ideas are received in combination with one another, the mind is also passive in its reception of these combinations of simple ideas. It is not the *mind* which, initially, brings these simple ideas together; if this were the case, we would have a kind of activity of the mind of which Locke does give an account, but it is an activity which he allows as a possibility only after the mind has received its simple ideas in combinations united together. Instead of the mind bringing these ideas together in its initial experience of them, it 'observe', 'takes notice of', 'finds', 'discovers' the coexistence of simple ideas. This is Locke's unambiguous position throughout the *Essay*.[17]

We therefore cannot refer to the simple ideas that we perceive in combination with one another as complex ideas. It is still appropriate to ask whether we should then refer to them as *simple* ideas in combination. For if it is the case that, in the form our experience initially takes, there is a complex structure because of the fact that its content is one of ideas *in combination*, we might want to argue that the simple ideas as such, i.e. as single simple ideas, are obtained through a *reduction* of what is experienced in combination into that of the 'elements' originally found in combination. We might want to argue that only the end-products of this reduction, only the 'elements' now uncombined, should be called simple ideas. This would mean that Locke speaks carelessly whenever he speaks of 'simple ideas that are found to co-exist'; for what are then found to coexist are not yet simple ideas. It is a carelessness which consists in using one and the same term to refer to two

[17] Note again, for example, 2.12.1, 2.23.1, 3.9.13, 4.4.12.

quite different things. For the fact that this carelessness is not read into Locke by my exposition but is genuinely present in the *Essay*, I find support from several commentators. Professor Aaron, for example, writes that:

Locke failed to make the nature of the simple idea clear to himself because he meant by the term *simple idea* two quite distinct things: (a) the *given*, (b) the indivisible, the atom. Generally speaking, the simple idea is that which the mind receives; the complex that which it makes, 'the workmanship of the mind'. But the simple idea is also 'the uncompounded', that which 'contains within it nothing but one uniform appearance or conception in the mind and is not distinguishable into different *ideas*'. That is to say, it is the atom. And the atom may be the outcome of a process of abstraction rather than be a *given* of sensation. (a) and (b) are not synonymous, yet Locke means by the term *simple idea* sometimes the one and sometimes the other, and this fact does much to confuse his argument.[18]

We need only take one small further step to say that this way of arguing makes the single simple ideas to be results of a certain kind of activity of the mind, rather than the immediate effect of an object affecting the mind. That this is not at all in conflict with what Locke himself says is one of the items to be made clear in what follows.

As a preliminary move I shall allow here that there are statements which may *seem* to rule out this position. A good example would be his use of the words 'Simple Ideas . . . are only to be got by those impressions Objects themselves make on our Minds . . .' at 3.4.11. But they really do not rule it out at all. For here Locke is only saying that we do obtain simple ideas, and that objects are their 'cause'. If we look carefully at his use of such words, we see that we cannot deduce from this statement any conclusion to the effect that single simple ideas are *directly given* in experience. All we are allowed to conclude is that, without our being affected by objects, we would not have simple ideas: being thus affected is a necessary condition for obtaining a simple idea which need not be sufficient. Moreover, although Locke often says things like 'Simple Ideas . . . are only to be got by those impressions Objects themselves make on our Minds', and 'simple Ideas . . . are imprinted'

---

[18] Aaron, op. cit., pp. 111–12. See also Jonathan Bennett, *Locke, Berkeley, Hume, Central Themes* (Oxford, 1971), pp. 25–30.

(2.1.25), there is no reason to suppose that he then refers to single simple ideas rather than to simple ideas perceived in given combinations. He sometimes also writes that 'simple Ideas, the Materials of all our Knowledge, are suggested . . . to the Mind by . . . Sensation and Reflection' (2.2.2; see also 2.12.2). When Locke so refers to the way in which we obtain single simple ideas, he implies that these ideas are not immediately received from sensation; for they are suggested by sensation.

General knowledge is founded on abstract or single simple ideas. When we ask how the mind proceeds in the pursuit of such knowledge, part of the answer is that 'The true Method of advancing Knowledge, is by considering our abstract Ideas' (4.12.7). The form our experience initially takes is one of perception of simple ideas in combinations united together. These ideas given in combination Locke does not call 'abstract'. Since we are held to possess general knowledge, and since such knowledge is founded on single simple ideas, and since all we initially experience is simple ideas in combination, some process of reduction must have taken place in order for it to be possible that we do in fact possess this knowledge. It is the presence of this process of reduction which allows me to say that the methodological principle of resolution also plays a necessary role in Locke's account of knowledge.

Locke refers to this process of reduction in various ways, by means of the terms 'separation', 'resolution', 'abstraction', 'definition', and 'decomposition'. Examination of passages in which such terms occur will allow the conclusion that these terms do indeed stand for the activity to which I referred as 'resolution' in the context of the discussion of Descartes: division of complexity into as many parts as possible, a process which is to end in the obtaining of the relevant simpler or simplest items which form the starting-points for construction of scientific complexity.

In the passage in which Locke writes that 'simple Ideas are observed to exist in several Combinations united together' he also states that one of the 'Acts of the Mind wherein it exerts its Power over its simple Ideas', is 'separating them from all other Ideas that accompany them in their real existence; this is called Abstraction: And thus all its General Ideas are made' (2.12.1). The phrase 'general idea' Locke uses as interchangeable with the phrase 'abstract idea', as well as with the word 'universal'. In 2.11.9, for example, we read '. . . the Mind makes the particular Ideas, received from particular Objects, to become general; which is done by considering them as they are in the Mind such Appearances, separate from all other Existences, and the circumstances of real Existence, as Time, Place, or any other concomitant Ideas. This is called Abstraction . . . and thus Universals, whether Ideas or Terms, are made.' That such general ideas, such universals, are indeed taken to be the result of a mental operation upon the givens of experience is stated also in a passage like 3.3.11: '. . . General and Universal, belong not to the real existence of Things; but are the Inventions and Creatures of the Understanding, made by it for its own use, and concern only Signs, whether Words, or Ideas'. It is the 'consideration' of these general or abstract ideas, of these universals, which allows for the development of general knowledge. Thus, passages like these state that before we can begin the process of 'reasoning' or 'demonstration', there has to be a process which consists in the reduction of the complexity which characterizes the content of sentient states into simplicity, ultimately, into epistemically atomic items.

A refinement of this position seems to be in order. The ideas which are given to the mind in combinations united together Locke does not call 'abstract'. But ought he to call 'abstract' a single one of these ideas once this idea has been separated from the combination in which it was at first presented? That, one might say, does not really give us a *general* idea or *universal*. A further step seems to be needed to obtain our universals, a step not mentioned in a passage like 2.12.1 but, perhaps, alluded to in a passage like 2.11.9. For in 2.11.9 we read that 'abstraction' is the process 'whereby Ideas taken from particular Beings, become general representatives of all of the same kind; and their Names general Names, applicable to whatever exists conformable to such abstract Ideas'. That he may be alluding to a step beyond mere separation of ideas seems to be indicated by the example he gives in this passage: we may observe the same colour today in chalk or snow which we observed yesterday in milk; the mind then 'considers that Appearance alone' and 'makes it a representative of all of that kind'; to this appearance it attaches 'the Name whiteness' and 'by that sound signifies the same Quality, wheresoever to be imagined or met with: and thus Universals, whether Ideas or Terms, are made'.

The word 'abstraction' thus seems to lead a double life in Locke's position. It seems, first, to be used as interchangeable with 'separation'. But the process of separation gives us single simple ideas obtained from resolution of *this* complex sentient state in which we are *now*. A universal must signify 'the same quality, *wheresoever* to be imagined or met with'. It seems that we have to 'abstract' once more. Using again words from 2.11.9, we must abstract such a single simple idea 'from all other Existences, and the circumstances of real Existence, as Time, Place . . .'. In addition, we must retain this idea in our memory, and must recognize instances of it when we obtain it as the result of separation of ideas given in contents of *other* sentient states. We must then 'abstract' it from all such instances and make it 'a representative of all of that kind'.

If 'abstraction' is indeed used by Locke in this dual manner, this does not call for a basic revision of the picture I have so far presented. For what might be called the second step in the process which gives us our universals presupposes the first step of 'separation'. Thus it remains true that we cannot begin the process of 'demonstration' unless we have general ideas or universals, and we cannot obtain our universals unless we have gone through a complex process whose first step is the reduction of the complexity which characterizes the contents of sentient states into epistemically atomic items.

Amplification of the notion of 'separation' is given through two other words which Locke uses to describe the same process, namely, 'resolution' and 'decomposition'. The notion of 'resolution' occurs in the chapter in which Locke discusses simple modes, more particularly, in a context in which he indicates what is for him the pre-condition for communication ('discourse or argumentation') to be able to occur. He there writes:

I imagine, that Men who abstract their Thoughts, and do well examine the Ideas of their own Minds, cannot much differ in thinking. . . . But if it should happen, that any two thinking Men should really have different Ideas, I do not see how they could discourse or argue one with another. . . . 'Tis not easie for the Mind to put off those confused Notions and Prejudices it has imbibed from Custom, Inadvertency, and common Conversation: it requires pains and assiduity to examine its Ideas, till it resolves them into those clear and distinct ones, out of which they are compounded; and to see which, amongst its simple ones, have or have not a necessary connexion and dependence one upon another. (2.13.27.)

The terminology of 'decomposition' is found in several important passages in the *Essay*. We read, for example, that if a person 'uses his Words as signs of some Ideas' these ideas 'if complex must be determinate, i.e. the precise Collection of simple Ideas settled in the Mind'. For example, 'Justice is a Word in every Man's Mouth, but most commonly with a very undetermined loose signification: Which will always be so, unless a Man has in his Mind a distinct comprehension of the component parts, that complex Idea consists of; and if it be decompounded, must be able to resolve it still on, till he at last comes to the simple Ideas, that make it up' (3.11.9).[19]

It is this process which we have seen Locke describing variously as 'abstraction', 'separation', 'resolution', and 'decomposition', which manifests the application of what I have called the principle of resolution. As we have seen in previous chapters, the term 'resolution', together with the term 'composition', is definitive of the Cartesian method. For Descartes, the mind can obtain certain knowledge only if there is an initial reduction of what is complex, through resolution or division, into what is simple and clear and distinct. Locke presents the same doctrine. We can typify this doctrine, which constitutes one of the two main aspects of the method presented in the *Essay* for the attaining of general knowledge, by saying that it is the reduction of the complexity of the form our experience at first takes, into the simplicity which characterizes the simple ideas. The foundation of all general knowledge

---

[19] It should be noted that Locke does not use the term 'decomposition' univocally. In a passage like 3.11.9 'decomposition' is explicitly used as interchangeable with 'resolution'. In some other passages this synonymity does not hold. In 3.5.13, for example, we read that 'the complex Ideas of mixed Modes, are commonly more compounded, and decompounded, than those of natural Substances. Because they being the Workmanship of the Understanding . . . [it] does with great liberty . . . under one Term, bundle together a great variety of compounded, and decompounded Ideas.' Elsewhere we are told that in the mixed modes of 'moral Names' there are 'many decompositions that go to the making up the complex Ideas of those Modes' (4.4.9). Nidditch, in the *Glossary* to his edition of the *Essay*, correctly identifies the meaning of 'decomposition' as used in 4.4.9 as 'compounding of things already composite', and the meaning of 'decompounded' as used in 3.5.13 as 'made up of parts which are themselves compound' (see p. 834). Nidditch does not, however, list the other meaning of 'decomposition' which is clearly present in the *Essay*; there is no entry in the *Glossary* which identifies 'decomposition' and 'resolution'.

is thus reached by means of division of what is initially given in combinations united together into the simple ideas characterized by indivisibility. That is, the foundation of all general knowledge is reached through the application of the principle of resolution.[20]

3. Various kinds of complexity

One of the two main aspects of the method presented in the *Essay* for the attaining of general knowledge is the reduction of the complexity of the form our experience at first takes. Because the complexity which characterizes the contents of our sentient states is of different kinds, this statement needs further explication. One kind of complexity is that of which we are aware when we perceive a physical object like a stone. Another kind is that of which we become aware through confrontation with actions which might be called 'moral' actions, or with 'mixed modes' of 'morals' of which we become aware through the reading of a discourse on ethics or politics. Yet another kind of complexity is that of which we are aware when we read the Bible. In this part of my chapter, I shall introduce only sufficient material from the *Essay* to make clear that Locke did refer to various kinds of complexity, and to make clear how the principle of resolution functions in this context. I shall do this especially in terms of the second kind, that relate to 'morals', and in the next chapter it will be necessary to say more about this kind of complexity, as it is particularly relevant for coming to an understanding of Locke's *Second Treatise of Government*. I shall not, in this section, expand on the kind of complexity of which we become aware through reading the

[20] Among recent commentators on Locke, J. L. Mackie (*Problems from Locke*, Oxford, 1976) pays a good deal of attention to the material I have just now considered. See especially his fourth chapter 'Abstract Ideas and Universals'. Mackie's account supports my interpretation of these passages. He writes, for example, that on 'Locke's theory' the mind 'is passive in receiving . . . ideas, but is active in . . . separating received complexes of ideas into their simple components (that is, abstracting) . . .' (p. 210). This activity of 'separation' or 'abstraction' Mackie identifies with 'decomposition' and picturesquely describes as a process in which one 'cuts up' received complexes, 'isolates' simple ideas from their complex context, and 'throws away' all those ideas that still remain in the received complex but which one does not need once the simple abstract idea has been obtained through 'cutting out' from the complex context, or which one does not need for the formation of complex abstract ideas (see pp. 112–13).

Bible, for with that we can deal easiest in the context of the position to be presented in Chapter VIII.

One kind of complexity characterizing the contents of our sentient states is that which we obtain when we perceive, for example, the particular combination of ideas to which we refer by means of the term 'pebble': grey, hard, round, smooth. There is no hint of any difficulty in Locke's account here about the mind's ability to distinguish and separate each of the simple ideas making up this particular combination. The reduction which leads to our possession of abstract ideas or universals like 'grey' and 'round' is assumed to be unproblematic. However, not all complex contents which constitute our sentient states to begin with are of this unproblematic nature. For we are born into a world in which men have been and constantly are acting in many ways; a world, also, complete with languages containing many universals. And some of these ways of acting have come to be referred to by universals in these languages. Moreover, often one and the same of these universal terms is used by different men to refer to actions and situations of different kinds. This means that we regularly experience in our day-to-day life complexities which we can only typify as obscure. The universal terms in these cases are names of sets of ideas voluntarily combined by men. But when I have not myself done the combining and am yet confronted with either the universal term or a situation or action to which it is made to refer, the complexity of the ideas obtained is such that it is not at all easy to isolate the constituent simple ideas. Locke deals with cases like these in a way which clearly shows the relevance of the methodological principle of resolution also in their context. The points made in this paragraph may be illustrated by considering 'moral science', which is one of the areas in which Locke believes it possible for man to obtain general knowledge.

'Moral ideas', which are mixed modes, are such that 'their names are of . . . uncertain Signification, the precise Collection of simple Ideas they stand for not being so easily agreed on, and so the Sign, that is used for them in Communication always, and in Thinking often, does not steadily carry with it the same Idea' (4.3.19). As is the case for any area in which man can obtain general knowledge, so also the science of morals must be founded on clear and distinct, general ideas; and as is the case for any other science, so also for the science of morals these clear and distinct general ideas are not the content of our initial experience. We obtain the mixed modes of morals, like all other mixed modes, either (a) through analysis of our experience of particular situations or actions (e.g. 2.22.2,9), in which case it is a matter of the mind voluntarily putting together again those simple ideas which it obtained through abstraction from particular sets of simple ideas it observed to go together in experience; or (b) by 'invention, or voluntary putting together of several simple Ideas in our own Minds', without this particular combination of simple ideas ever having been offered to the mind by experience (ibid.); or (c) by definition or 'enumerating, and thereby, as it were, setting before our Imaginations all those Ideas which go to the making them up' (cf. 2.22.9).

One might say that (c), 'definition', covers both the activities of (a) and (b). It is nevertheless helpful to deal with 'definition' as a separate and distinct way of obtaining mixed modes. In (a) we 'enumerate' all those ideas that we find going together in our experience, and then we put all these ideas, and no others, back together again and thus make a mixed mode. In (b) we legislate which simple ideas, obtained from various and diverse complex sentient states, are to be put together to form a mixed mode; the kind and number of simple ideas combined together in this mixed mode is such that we have not met anything like this combination in our experience. In (c) we 'enumerate' all those ideas (or as many as we possibly can) that we find going together in our experience; some (perhaps many) we reject as irrelevant, some (perhaps many) we retain, and some (perhaps many) new ones obtained from various and diverse sentient states are put together with those we retained to form the new mixed mode. This new mixed mode to at least some degree is like the complexity which we experienced in the first place. That the new mixed mode is at least in some ways like the set of ideas we found going together in our experience is often indicated by the fact that one and the same name (e.g. 'justice', 'ruler', 'state') is given to these different but overlapping sets of ideas.

In all of these ways of obtaining our mixed modes, the principle of resolution clearly plays its role. In the first instance, there is a combination of simple ideas which were already experienced as going together, after these ideas had been abstracted from the unity in which they were originally found. In the second instance also, though not combined in ways previously suggested by experience and hence not initially abstracted from a set of ideas which comes to serve as a pattern for combination, the particular simple ideas have been abstracted from experiences in which they were observed to go together with other simple ideas. It is the third way in which we obtain our complex moral ideas which is of special interest, for here Locke takes account of the fact that we do find ourselves in our daily life confronted with complex situations and actions, and with accounts of or statements about such situations and actions, which are often characterized by lack of clarity. The difficulty here is one of obscurity resulting from the indefiniteness of the number and especially the kind of simple ideas that make up the complexity of our sentient state when we are confronted with such a situation or action, with such an account or statement. This particular difficulty comes about because of the 'Vices, Passions, and domineering Interest' (4.3.18) which influence men in ways such that, for example, where the one may refer to a particular situation or action as 'just', another refers to it as 'unjust'. In addition, 'the desire of Esteem, Riches, or Power, makes Men espouse the well-endowed Opinions in Fashion', for which they then 'seek Arguments, either to make good their Beauty, or varnish over, and cover their Deformity' (4.3.20). Thus confusion and obscurity often reign supreme in the field of morals.

The initial step advocated by Locke to overcome this confusion and to start anew from the foundations is the use of 'definition', the 'setting down that Collection of simple Ideas, which every Term shall stand for' (ibid.). In this way, since definition is, for Locke, never a matter of mere words but always a matter of the ideas for which the words are signs (cf. 3.4.6), we shall be able to obtain a foundation for demonstration in morals once we have reduced the complexity and obscurity initially experienced to the simplicity and clarity of simple ideas. This process of definition, like that of abstraction as discussed in 2.12.1, we may take to be the application of the principle of resolution, for it exhibits this principle's essential characteristic of division or separation. In 3.11.9 Locke himself explicitly refers to this process of definition as one of decomposition.

Only by means of the application of the principle of resolution can we, therefore, obtain the foundations for general knowledge. But as is already implicit in what has just been said, this is not the complete story. In some areas of general knowledge the foundations are *simple* abstract ideas, and for sciences like these (arithmetic, for example) it is correct to say without qualification that resolution provides the foundation for such knowledge. In other areas of general knowledge, for example in 'morals', the foundational concepts are *complex* abstract ideas. And although the basic 'elements' for these complex abstract ideas are obtained through resolution, what is thus obtained cannot function as a foundational concept in such a science. (Why this is so we shall see in the next chapter.) In sciences like these resolution is then followed by a process through which construction of the relevant foundational concepts takes place. This construction of complex abstract ideas takes the various forms of (a), (b) and (c) as described in the previous paragraphs. Thus, in the case of (a), complex abstract ideas are constructed in the presence of an 'archetype' given in one's experience, and in one's construction one follows exactly the pattern presented by that 'archetype'. In the case of (b) these ideas are constructed without there being an 'archetype'. And in the case of (c) they are constructed in the presence of an 'archetype' but in one's construction one does not exactly copy the pattern presented by that 'archetype'. I shall illustrate the manner of construction indicated in (b) and (c) in the next chapter, for this is of importance especially in the context of the development of a political theory. In Chapter VIII I shall discuss the manner of construction indicated in (a), for it functions especially in Locke's account of how one can obtain knowledge of the contents of the Bible. What needs to be remembered is that in all of these cases the construction of complex abstract ideas is, ultimately, to be achieved in terms of single simple ideas obtained through resolution of the materials given in experience. In this sense it remains correct to say that only by means of resolution are we able to obtain the foundations for any area in which, according to Locke, we can attain knowledge.

'The true Method of advancing Knowledge is by considering our abstract Ideas.' Examination of how the mind is said to obtain its abstract ideas makes clear that resolution is the methodological principle operative in this part of Locke's position. Through resolution we obtain the single simple ideas on which all general knowledge is *founded*, whose 'consideration' allows us to advance in knowledge. This 'true method of *advancing* knowledge' is that aspect of the method which I called Cartesian composition. Since, for Locke, resolution allows the mind to obtain the foundations or materials of all its knowledge, and since composition is also for Locke the true method of gaining systematic knowledge once these materials have been obtained, *resolution and composition together express the essence of the method advocated in the 'Essay' for the obtaining of general knowledge*. Only by means of the former can we obtain the foundations for general knowledge, and only by means of the latter can we attain and develop general knowledge.

4. Knowledge of single simple ideas

The *advancement* of general knowledge is through the consideration of our abstract ideas. From this it follows, says Locke, that 'We can have Knowledge no farther than we have Ideas' (4.3.1). Does it also follow for Locke that the possibility of attaining general knowledge presupposes knowledge of single simple ideas? For Descartes, simple ideas like 'unity' and 'equality', or 'thought' and 'existence', were taken to be knowable *per se*, and were viewed as the epistemic atoms to which the process of resolution leads us. Descartes held that they are indispensable, because they are the immediately known foundation of all of our systematic knowledge. The position we have so far seen to be Locke's agrees with that presented by Descartes to a considerable extent. For both Descartes and Locke, resolution of 'experience'[21] leads to the foundation for

---

[21] The explanation of how one obtains 'experience' differs of course from Descartes to Locke. For Locke we obtain experience through sensation (and reflection). Through sensation we obtain the complex contents which characterize our sentient states when, for example, we feel a stone (and thus become aware of 'hard, smooth, round'), or see a procession ('men, flags, drums'), or hear an orator ('Royal prerogative is inviolate') or read (see) a treatise ('Filmer's *Patriarcha* . . . would perswade all Men, that they are Slaves . . .'). No complex sentient states are obtained unless we have experience; sensation and reflection are their only source. For Descartes, the picture differs in part. He resolved to accumulate 'a variety of experiences fitted later on to afford matter for my reasonings', a variety of experiences obtained through education and travel (HR1, 94; AT6, 22): 'not that these extraneous things transmitted the ideas themselves to our minds through the organs of sense, but because they transmitted something which gave the mind occasion to form these ideas, by means of an innate faculty, at this time rather than at another' (HR1, 443; AT8-2, 358-9). But the presence of an innatist doctrine in Descartes, and the absence of it in Locke, does not do away with the fact that for both of them the 'variety of experiences fitted . . . to afford matter for . . . reasoning' presents them with *complexity* which needs to be *resolved* into the relevant simple or simplest items before one can obtain a scientific account about what one experiences.

knowledge; and for both, this foundation includes simple ideas or simple concepts.[22] Does this similarity in methodological stance lead to a futher agreement between Descartes and Locke, an agreement to the effect that both hold we can know ideas in isolation? Generally, commentators have taken the position that Locke rules out knowledge of single simple ideas. Aaron, for example, writes that according to Locke '. . . we never know an idea in isolation', and that 'Locke's account of knowledge implies that the object of knowledge is always a proposition or an inference.'[23] But it is not at all clear that the similarity between Locke and Descartes does not also include the belief that we can know ideas or concepts in isolation.

First of all, it is clear that the similarity in Descartes's and Locke's doctrine about the *nature* of the foundation of knowledge, to the extent that this foundation is taken to consist of ideas and concepts rather than of principles, does indeed exist. For the simple ideas that are the materials of all our knowledge are characterized by Locke as they were by Descartes: they are epistemic atoms, all 'perfectly distinct' from one another, containing in themselves 'nothing but one uniform Appearance', being 'not distinguishable into different Ideas' (2.2.1). That resolution must come to a stop once these ideas have been reached is clear from the last of these phrases, and is reinforced by what we find in other statements: these ideas 'cannot be described, nor their Names defined' (2.20.1; and 3.4.4,14) for 'the several Terms of a Definition, signifying several Ideas, they can altogether by no means represent an Idea, which has no Composition at all' (3.4.7).

Does Locke also agree with Descartes that these epistemic atoms are objects of knowledge? As we have just seen, Locke claims to know a good deal *about* single simple ideas. One might argue that this knowledge is dictated by the particular methodology used: if a process of resolution is to lead us to the foundations for general knowledge, then these foundations cannot themselves be subject to further resolution. Such knowledge need not then be immediate knowledge of each and every one of these single foundational items.

---

[22] That the 'materials' out of which, or the 'foundations' upon which, reasoning constructs its knowledge are indeed the single simple ideas is clear from many passages in the *Essay*. See, for example, 2.1.25, 2.2.2, 2.12.1, 2.12.2, 2.13.1, 2.13.28, 4.1.4, 4.18.3.

[23] Aaron, op. cit., p. 227.

Instead, reflection upon the conditions which are to hold if one is to be able to attain knowledge, which would include reflection upon the conditions which are to hold if a principle like that of resolution is to lead to the foundations for knowledge, might lead one to the conclusion that the foundations must be 'uncompounded' ideas which are 'not distinguishable into different Ideas'. Such knowledge would be *about* the foundations, but need not conflict with Aaron's conclusion that, according to Locke, 'we never know an idea in isolation'. If this were the correct account of how we have knowledge of the *nature* of the foundations, it is to be noted that the methodological principle of resolution explicitly determines the nature of the foundations for general knowledge. But I do not know of any passages in the *Essay* in which Locke accounts for knowledge of the nature of these foundations in terms of methodological considerations. This is, of course, not to say that methodological considerations may not have played a role in the determination of the nature of these foundations. But the account Locke gives of the knowledge which he takes human minds to possess of these foundations differs from that sketched above.

Before I present this account, one might ask why it is that commentators assume it to be Locke's position that 'we never know an idea in isolation'. Since I am not aware of any substantial argument given for this conclusion, I can only surmise that they come to it because of what Locke states in his definitions of knowledge (cf. 4.1.2; 4.17.17). Knowledge is said to be either intuitive, demonstrative, or sensitive. Demonstrative knowledge is general knowledge; it is dependent on intuition. Intuition appears to be a matter of 'seeing' the relations between ideas and *not* one of intuiting these ideas as such. This, then, seems to rule out intuitive knowledge of single simple ideas. Neither do we have sensitive knowledge of single simple ideas, for sensitive knowledge is knowledge of the existence of external objects (or, in terms of a more traditional interpretation, the belief that there is an external world which is the cause of our ideas of sensation) and *not* knowledge of the *ideas* of qualities of external objects. Thus it seems to follow that the materials of knowledge derived from sensation are not themselves known.

However, in spite of what the definitions of knowledge may at first sight seem to imply, there are grounds for saying that Locke holds that we do know the 'materials' of general knowledge. Locke's position seems to be that we know the ideas in combination as we initially experience them, as well as the simple ideas which are the materials of general knowledge. If we did not have knowledge of ideas given in such combinations, there would seem to be no justification at all for the knowledge (or belief) that objects in an external world are the cause of our ideas of sensation. The justification for the knowledge (or belief) that objects exist, or that qualities coexist, is founded on our experience and knowledge of the coexistence of ideas of qualities (cf. e.g. 4.12.9). More important for my argument at this point is whether we know single simple ideas. There are many passages throughout the *Essay* which suggest that we do have this knowledge.

In 4.7.4 Locke writes that:

Every one that has any Knowledge at all, has, as the Foundation of it, various and distinct Ideas: And it is the first act of the Mind, (without which, it can never be capable of any Knowledge,) to know every one of his Ideas by it self, and distinguish it from others. Everyone finds in himself, that he knows the Ideas he has; That he knows also, when any one is in his Understanding, and what it is; And that when more than one are there, he knows them distinctly and unconfusedly one from another.

It is not just the case that we know relations between ideas and know that one idea is distinct from another. The latter we know 'when more than one' idea is in the understanding, and this seems to imply that we know a simple idea even if that idea were to be the *only* one in the understanding. Indeed, 'the first act of the Mind' is 'to know every one of its Ideas by it self'. Although the word 'simple' does not appear in this passage[24] knowledge of single simple ideas seems implied; and there are other passages (e.g. 2.20.1; 2.25.8) where this doctrine is stated explicitly in terms of simple ideas.

If we read the definition of knowledge given in 4.1.2 ('Knowledge then seems to me to be nothing but the perception of the connexion and agreement, or disagreement and repugnancy of any of our Ideas') in the context of some other relevant passages, it becomes plausible to say that this definition does not rule out knowledge of ideas in isolation, but rather presupposes such knowledge. For it

[24] There are other passages which express the same doctrine, but in which the word 'simple' does not appear either' e.g. 2.13.28, 3.11.9, 4.1.4, 4.3.8.

is not the case that the mind imposes relations on ideas that are 'neutral' with respect to one another. Instead, there is something in the nature of the simple ideas themselves that allows the mind to relate them or, alternatively, makes such relating impossible. This seems to presuppose that simple ideas are known in isolation before the mind can perceive agreements or disagreements; and is, I think, the import of a passage like:

It [the mind] requires pains and assiduity to examine its Ideas, till it resolves them into those clear and distinct simple ones, out of which they are compounded; and to see which, amongst its simple ones, have or have not a necessary connexion and dependence one upon another. (2. 13.27.)

That the definitions of knowledge may well presuppose knowledge of single simple ideas can also be shown from considerations like the following. In 4.7.19, after he has shown the uselessness of 'maxims' in the development of general knowledge, Locke sums up his position and states that 'there is little need, or no use at all of these Maxims' if we have our ideas 'determined in our Minds'. Among determined ideas listed as illustrations are 'white' and 'black'. Thus, single simple ideas are among the determined ideas. As we read in the *Essay's* 'Epistle to the Reader', 'By determinate, when applied to a simple Idea, I mean that simple appearance, which the Mind has in its view, or perceives in it self, when that Idea is said to be in it' (p. 13). That determined ideas are known Locke states explicitly in a following paragraph of the '*Epistle*', where he writes that 'determined' or 'determinate' signifies 'Some immediate object of the Mind, which it perceives and has before it distinct from the sound it uses as a sign for it', and 'That this Idea thus determined, i.e. which the Mind has in it self, and *knows,* and sees there . . .'. The last sentence of this paragraph is tantamount to making 'determined' a criterion of intelligibility: 'If Men had such determined Ideas in their enquiries and discourses, they would both discern how far their own enquiries and discourses went, and avoid the greatest part of the Disputes and Wranglings they have with others.'

It is 'upon this ground' of having ideas 'determined in our Minds' that 'intuitive Knowledge neither requires, nor admits any proof, one part of it more than another. He that will suppose it does, takes away the Foundation of all Knowledge and Certainty.' For

'He that needs a probation to convince him, that . . . any . . . two determined distinct Ideas are not one and the same, will also need a Demonstration to convince him, that it is impossible for the same thing to be, and not to be' (4.7.19). This again seems to imply that we must know the 'determined distinct Ideas' in order to know whether they are 'one and the same'. Thus the ground for the validity of intuitive knowledge is knowledge of determined distinct ideas or, ultimately, of determined distinct simple ideas. Knowledge of determined distinct simple ideas 'is so absolutely necessary, that without it there could be no Knowledge, no Reasoning, no Imagination, no distinct Thoughts at all' (4.1.4).

In view of the picture which is now emerging it seems safe to conclude that, according to Locke, the human mind has knowledge beyond the area delimited by the definition given in 4.1.2. This definition is about *general* knowledge, and it presupposes knowledge of *particular* ideas. This conclusion is reinforced if we look at what seems to be involved in the definition of intuitive knowledge. We are said to possess 'intuitive Knowledge' when 'the Mind perceives the Agreement or disagreement of two Ideas immediately by themselves, without the intervention of any other' (4.2.1). As an example of intuitive knowledge he gives: 'White is not Black.' The question is: does Locke believe that for us to be able to know that 'White is not Black', we must also know the single simple idea to which we refer by means of the words 'white' and 'black'? I believe Locke's answer is that unless we know simple ideas singly we cannot know the 'agreement' or 'disagreement' of two such ideas when immediately compared. For he writes ' 'Tis the first Act of the Mind, when it has any . . . Ideas at all, to perceive its Ideas, and . . . to *know* each what it is, and thereby also to perceive their difference, and that one is not another. . . . By this the Mind clearly and infallibly perceives each Idea to agree with it self, and to be what it is . . .'. This 'first exercise' of the mind 'is about *particular* Ideas' (4.1.4). And in the paragraph in which Locke presents his definition of intuitive knowledge, he adds that 'a Man cannot conceive himself capable of greater Certainty, than to know that any Idea in his Mind is such, as he perceives it to be'. As we have seen, these kinds of statements are echoed in more than one place in the *Essay*. It will not do, I think, to say that in a statement like 'A man infallibly Knows, as soon as ever he has them in his Mind, that the Ideas he calls White and

Round, are the very Ideas they are . . .' Locke is concerned merely with knowledge of a propositional or inferential form. If Locke were concerned with propositions here, they would be in the form 'white is white', and the 'agreement' perceived would be of the idea of white (subject) with the idea of white (predicate)—an agreement which would be about nothing in particular unless both subject and predicate terms referred, in this case, to a sense-derived particular idea, and an agreement which could not be perceived or known unless this idea itself were perceived or known. Because Locke is not concerned with propositions here he can, in a different context, say that although 'identical Propositions' 'add no Light to our Understandings, bring no increase to our Knowledge' (4.8.1), they are not without a knowledge content: 'For when we affirm the same Term of it self, whether it be barely verbal, or whether it contains any clear and real Idea, it shews us nothing but what we must certainly know before . . .' (4.8.2). We know that A is A, whatever A is, because we know A. Of 'Universal and Self-evident Principles' Locke says that 'their certainty is founded only upon the Knowledge we have of each Idea by it self, and of its Distinction from others' (4.7.14).

Aaron has written that Locke 'was the happier in his empiricism because for him experience was linked with perception, and because he could be vague and ambiguous about the connotation of the latter term, which certainly carried with it a wider meaning than mere sensation'.[25] That Locke's use of 'perception' is sometimes ambiguous need not be gainsaid; and that it usually has a 'wider meaning than mere sensation' is correct. I believe this 'wider meaning' derives from the fact that, in the end, Locke inclines to the position that whereas sensation 'produces some perception in the understanding', all perception of ideas is knowledge. At least all 'perception' of single simple ideas is 'knowledge' of single simple ideas. To hold this is not to say that Locke also maintained that a stage prior to that of perception of single simple ideas is knowledge. But neither can we say that it is not. The ambiguity of 'perception' remains also in this case. One might argue that this ambiguity arises from considerations like the following. If one says that one knows single simple ideas, and that such ideas are abstract, does not the recognition of their being abstract involve an acknowledgement that other items are known prior to one's know-

[25] Aaron, op. cit., p. 133.

ledge of these abstract ideas? For is there not a difficulty in the conception that, through the mind's activity in the decomposition of some unkown complex content of a sentient state, one obtains simple ideas which are known? It may well have been considerations like these which account for the ambiguity in Locke's use of 'perception', and for his inclining to the position that whereas sensation 'produces some Perception in the Understanding', all perception, also that of the complexity of our sentient states, is knowledge. Of course these statements go well beyond what Locke himself writes. On the other hand, the statement that we at least have knowledge of single simple ideas does not go beyond what Locke states. Therefore, in opposition to Aaron's belief on this point, I conclude that, for Locke, 'perception of ideas in our minds', at least in those instances where ideas have been separated from the complexity which characterizes each sentient state, are instances of knowledge. In further disagreement with Aaron, I think we should say that this perception is not all that different from 'that perception which occurs in knowledge and which is identical with Descartes' intuition'. This, although not always without ambiguity, has now been seen to be Locke's position in Book 2 of the *Essay*. It is the position needed for and stated in the exposition of the argument of Book 4. A final look at some of the latter's passages should convince us of this point.

In 4.2.14 Locke states that 'at least in all general Truths', whatever is not 'Intuition and Demonstration' is 'Faith, or Opinion, but not Knowledge'. He then continues to contrast 'sensitive knowledge', which is based on the 'Perception of the Mind, employ'd about the particular existence of finite Beings without us', with these 'general Truths' which are based on the perception of particular ideas without taking into account the cause of these ideas. About the perception of these particular ideas Locke then writes 'There can be nothing more certain, than that the Idea we receive from an external Object is in our Minds; this is intuitive Knowledge.' Thus the perception of particular ideas is a matter of intuition; and this intuition reveals not just that there is an idea in the mind but, as the context of this statement makes clear, it also reveals the nature of the idea itself. Many other passages in Book 4 state the same doctrine.[26] Consider again 4.1.4, where we read that 'the first act of the Mind' is the perception of 'particular

[26] For example: 4.1.4, 4.2.1, 4.7.10, 4.18.3.

Ideas'. This perception is described entirely in terms definitive of Cartesian intuition: it is a 'clear' and 'infallible' perception, which occurs 'without pains, labour, or deduction; but at first view'; a man 'infallibly knows, as soon as ever he has them in his Mind that the Ideas he calls White and Round, are the very Ideas they are'.

It seems reasonable to conclude, then, that it is Locke's position that we do know single simple ideas and that this knowledge is one of intuitive perception. Of course the statement 'we know simple ideas through intuitive perception' contains a host of problems. It is not necessary for my present purposes to go into any of these. But it should be pointed out that Locke's basic problem is also that of Descartes: both accept the possibility of knowing ideas or concepts in isolation from any other ideas or concepts. It should also be pointed out that when we ask what, precisely, is the nature of the 'act' by means of which we know simple ideas, of this clear, effortless, and infallible intuitive perception, there is no answer beyond a statement of the analogy of intuitive knowledge with vision (4.2.1). This analogy reveals little more than the similarity of Lockean and Cartesian intuition. All we are really presented with is an indication of the starting point from which Locke begins the construction of 'all general Truths'. This starting-point is self-evident intuitive perception of single simple ideas.

What I have not shown in this section is that the adoption of a (Cartesian) reductionistic method *necessarily* leads to the postulation of entities like epistemic atoms as the foundations for knowledge. Neither have I shown that Locke's *Essay* provides clear grounds for saying that it is Locke's adoption of the Cartesian principle of resolution which leads him to his doctrine of simple or abstract ideas as the foundation of general knowledge. What I take to have been made clear is that, in the *Essay*, Locke's adopting the principle of resolution goes closely together with his postulating that single simple ideas are the foundations of general knowledge. To have shown this is to create an important measure of plausibility for the statement that the theses incorporated in the first two sentences of this paragraph may well be correct.

VII

METHOD AND THE ARGUMENT OF LOCKE'S *SECOND TREATISE OF GOVERNMENT*

I shall, in this chapter, defend the thesis that both the form which Locke's arguments take in the *Second Treatise,* and also a significant number of the conclusions he reaches in it, are determined by the principles for obtaining general knowledge which are presented in the *Essay concerning Human Understanding.* If my defence of this thesis is successful, the present chapter will clearly illustrate the correctness of an important element in my general thesis: a particular methodological stance will be shown to structure Locke's theory about subject-matter, and even to affect to a notable extent the nature of this subject-matter. Of course, I do not want to argue that the *Second Treatise* can, or ought to, be explained entirely in terms of methodological considerations. I do believe that we shall better understand the *Second Treatise* if we approach this work in terms of such principles enunciated by Locke in the *Essay.*

Peter Laslett has written that the *Second Treatise* is 'a work of intuition, insight and imagination', rather than a work written by a man who was 'a theorist of knowledge'.[1] If we take this statement as a key to the understanding of the *Second Treatise,* our understanding of it will remain incomplete. For although Laslett is correct in calling it a work of imagination, this does not entail that Locke's methodological principles are not operative in it. To approach this work with some of the *Essay's* principles for the attaining of general knowledge in mind will help us far more than Laslett realizes in coming to an understanding of why Locke said what he did. There is, of course, a good deal of truth in Laslett's statement. Recognizing this will hold one back from an attempt to interpret the *Second Treatise* as if it were a work deliberately and

---

[1] Peter Laslett, Introduction to *John Locke, Two Treatises of Government* (revised edn., Cambridge, 1963), p. 99. All quotations from the *Second Treatise* are from Laslett's edition.

systematically structured by the application of the relevant methodological principles somewhat as were Descartes's *Meditations*. Nevertheless, one can ask whether and, if so, to what extent and in which respects the *Essay's* principles are at work in the *Second Treatise*. This I propose to do in the following pages.

Those of the *Essay's* principles which are especially relevant for coming to an understanding of the *Second Treatise's* arguments will be introduced in the first section of this chapter. In the second section it will be argued that central to the *Second Treatise* is the concept of an individual and that, within the framework of political theory, Locke holds this concept to be irreducible. This concept is, however, a complex abstract idea and *qua* complex it is a construct of the mind. A reconstruction of its 'invention' leads one to see the nature of this concept, and also reveals which methodological principles play a role in this process of 'invention'. Once the concept has been 'invented' the central doctrines of the *Second Treatise* can be seen to be determined by the nature of this complex abstract idea—while the nature of the concept itself is in turn determined by the demands of Locke's methodology. Although the 'invented' concept of an *individual* is central to the arguments of this treatise, the nature of this concept is not made explicit there through a specifically presented 'invention'. Instead, it is made explicit by means of a resolution of the 'Opinions in Fashion' concerning politics. In the third section it will be made clear that, in Locke's day, the opinions on politics of Aristotle, Grotius, and Filmer were pre-eminent. Aspects of these opinions relevant to some of Locke's central arguments are briefly stated. Lastly, in the fourth section it will be argued that resolution of these 'Opinions in Fashion' helps Locke to make clear for the reader what is the nature of the concept of an *individual* and that, in this context of explication, the central doctrines of the *Second Treatise* are articulated. The thesis that the explication of the nature of the concept of an *individual* takes place in the context of a resolution of the 'Opinions in Fashion', and that the nature of this concept determines the central doctrines of this treatise, is illustrated from Locke's text.

1. Relevance of the *Essay's* methodological principles for an interpretation of the *Second Treatise*

'Morality', as a term for a species of general knowledge, is used by Locke in an extended sense, subsuming under it what we today call political theory.[2] As we saw in the previous chapter, the mixed modes of 'morals' are obtained by means of a process which requires the application of what I have called the *empiricist principle*; it also demands the application of the methodological *principle of resolution*. In the context of the present chapter, more must be said about the principle of resolution, and this can best be done as I further clarify the meaning of 'experience' as Locke uses it in the context of applying his empiricist principle in the process of obtaining these mixed modes of 'morals'. Most of what Locke has to say on this is to be found in Book 3, Chapter 5, of the *Essay*.

In this chapter we read that the 'Essences of the Species of mixed Modes, are not only made by the Mind, but made very arbitrarily, made without Patterns, or reference to any real Existence.' For 'in its complex Ideas of mixed Modes, the Mind takes a liberty not to follow the Existence of Things exactly' (3.5.3). However, the principle that all knowledge begins with experience is not, in this process, done away with, for 'this making of these complex Ideas . . . consists . . . not in the making any new Idea, but putting together those which the Mind had before' (3.5.4). Doing this 'without patterns' refers to the doctrine of 'the free choice of the Mind, pursuing its own ends', to the doctrine that 'the Mind, by its free choice, gives a connexion to a certain number of Ideas; which in Nature have no more union with one another, than others that it leaves out'. To sum up, 'in the framing these Ideas, the Mind searches not its Patterns in Nature . . . but puts such together, as may best serve its own Purposes, without tying itself to a precise imitation of anything that really exists' (3.5.6).

---

[2] That 'morality' is used in this extended sense is clear from the *Essay*, Book 4, Chapter 3, where he writes of 'Morality' as being 'amongst the Sciences capable of Demonstration', and then uses propositions from the realm of political theory to demonstrate his point. 'Where there is no Property, there is no Injustice' is 'a Proposition as certain as any Demonstration in Euclid'; 'No government allows absolute Liberty' is such that 'I am as capable of being certain of the truth of this Proposition, as of any in Mathematicks' (4.3.18). It is even clearer from the manuscript piece 'Morality' (Bodleian Library, MS. Locke c. 28, fols. 139–40; published in its entirety for the first time in the *Locke Newsletter*, No. 5, Summer 1974, pp. 26–8). In it, Locke subsumes *contract theory* under 'morality': 'Therefor noe man at his birth can have noe right to any thing in the world more then an other. Men therefor must either enjoy all things in common or by compact determin their rights. If all things be left in common want rapin and force will unavoidably follow in which state as is evident happynesse cannot be had which cannot consist without plenty and security.'

If, in spite of the mind's freedom, it is nevertheless limited to putting together ideas which it obtained from experience, where and how does it obtain these ideas? As we have already noted in the previous chapter, an answer to this question can take several distinct forms. One of these (which, because of the emphasis Locke places on it in the different locations where he discusses 'moral science', seems to be taken by him as descriptive of what occurs most often) is that although the mind does not 'follow the existence of things exactly', it does take its point of departure for the construction of its mixed modes from experiences which provide it with the names of mixed modes, and with relations between these mixed modes, which are commonly believed to be determinate mixed modes, and whose relations are commonly believed to be necessary relations. Another form is that, from any experiences whatsoever, the mind receives sets of ideas in combination with one another; many of these combinations are quite different from anything we would want to classify as a mixed mode of morals; these combinations the mind, through resolution, reduces to simple ideas; and out of these simple ideas the mind constructs a new complex idea—'new' in the sense that this particular combination of ideas, or something like it, had not been met in experience. It is this method of obtaining mixed modes which we have seen Locke call 'invention'. Both of these forms of answer to the question are found in Chapter 5 of Book 3.

About the second form of answer, Locke writes that 'in the beginning of Languages, it was necessary to have the Idea, before one gave it a Name: And so it is still, where making a new complex Idea, one also, by giving it a new Name, makes a new Word' (3.5.15). The need for a new word, for a new name to signify a new complex idea, is indicative of the fact that there is nothing even approximately answering to the idea signified by that new name in the experience one has had so far. The more usual situation is, however, that 'for the most part the Names of mixed Modes are got, before the Ideas they stand for are perfectly known' (ibid.). This leads us to the first form of answer to the question of where and how we obtain our mixed modes.

Although 'the original Patterns' of mixed modes 'are in the Mind', they gain a public dimension through the names they are given. They then come to function in laws, rules, or maxims, and thus come to determine action. In this way, they enter *rerum natura* as 'the well endowed Opinions in Fashion' (4.3.20). Thus, although 'in the beginning of Languages, it was necessary to have the Idea, before one gave it the Name . . . this concerns not Languages made, which have generally pretty well provided for Ideas, which Men have frequent Occasion to have, and communicate' (3.5.15). Hence Locke concludes that 'for the most part the Names of mixed Modes are got, before the Ideas they stand for are perfectly known'. In this form of the answer, Locke is taking account of the fact that in our daily experience we are often confronted with complex situations and actions, and with names for such situations and actions signifying ideas which are often far from determinate. They are indeterminate because I do not yet know the precise number and kind of simple or simpler ideas subsumed under the names in question. They are, further, indeterminate, because different people's vices and desires for esteem (cf. 4.3.18; 4.3.20) make for inconsistency in the signification of one and the same name used by these different people. To make these mixed modes determinate, we have to 'decompose' the complex ideas signified by these names, and to determine which of their simple(r) ideas do and which do not belong to them. Once we know which of the simple(r) ideas do so belong, we may still want to add other ideas to this group before we can say that the mixed modes in question are determinate.[3]

We should now recall that the methodological principle of composition is related to statements like 'the true Method of advancing Knowledge, is by considering our abstract Ideas', for 'General and certain Truths, are only founded in the Habitudes and Relations of abstract Ideas.' We should also recall that the *advancement* of general knowledge consists in 'considering those Ideas, and by comparing them one with another, finding their Agreement, and Disagreement, and their several Relations and Habitudes' (4.12.6), and that because the advancement is that of *general knowledge*, the relations in question must be ones of necessary connections of the concepts related. A necessary pre-condition for being able to trace necessary connections is that the concepts between or among which we attempt to trace such connections be determinate. To use Locke's own words again, 'since the Knowledge of the Certainty of . . . all . . . Truths, depends only upon the perception, we have, of the Agreement, or Disagreement of our Ideas, the way to improve our

---

[3] As in the previous chapter, I again use 'determinate' as this word is defined by Locke in the fifth-from-last paragraph of the *Essay's* 'Espistle to the Reader'.

Knowledge, is . . . to get and fix in our Minds clear, distinct, and complete Ideas . . . and annex to them proper and constant Names' (4.12.6). We have seen that statements like these make it relevant to introduce the methodological principle of resolution. For clear, distinct, and complete ideas we obtain through the resolution or decomposition of the complexity of our experience. If resolution is applied to our experience of the 'well endowed Opinions in Fashion', of what the mind has 'imbibed from Custom, Inadvertance, and common Conversation', it takes the form of showing that what are commonly taken to be concepts in necessary connection with one another are often indeterminate concepts which have no necessary connections with one another at all. *Resolution or decomposition then consists in showing that where necessary conceptual relations are commonly thought to exist, they actually do not exist.* It is this determination of concepts which is the pre-condition for the advancement of general knowledge.

Locke's position in the *Essay* is, thus, that we must comply with two pre-conditions if we are to be successful in developing general knowledge. The two pre-conditions are met by the proper observance of two principles: the *empiricist principle* and the *principle of resolution*.

It will now be possible to present an elucidation of the argument of the *Second Treatise* in terms of these two principles present in the *Essay*. That is, it can now be shown that the form which Locke's arguments take, and also for a significant part the conclusions he reaches, are determined by these principles. By 'the form which Locke's arguments take' I do not so much mean the explicit form in terms of the *overall* order of exposition. It is, for example, not the case that (as a parallel to Descartes's metaphysical *Meditations*) Locke's political *Treatise* actually begins with a resolution of complexity, then finds its fulcrum point in the derivation of an indubitable self-evident item, after which reconstruction follows to the end of the work. Instead, throughout the work the two principles structure the form of reasoning, and help to determine the nature of important conclusions.

In general, I shall argue that one fruitful way in which the *Second Treatise* may be approached is through systematically attending to the assumption that in this work there is a *derivation* of the principles or concepts fundamental to Locke's political theory from what he takes to be *given in experience*. This approach is in keeping with the principle that all knowledge begins with experience, and also with the principle that a pre-condition for the advancement of knowledge is that the givens of experience be resolved into determinate ideas. I shall argue that one important starting point for the argument of the *Second Treatise* is Locke's experience of man, specifically, his experience of those actions of men that can be qualified as 'political'—and not just these actions themselves, but (perhaps more importantly) his experience of the current ('fashionable') and common descriptions of and prescriptions for such actions.[4] And I shall argue that his intended subjection of this experience to the principle of resolution offers a partial but quite significant explanation for some of Locke's most important conclusions about man and society. For example, it helps to explain Locke's radical individualism and his belief that respect for private property must never be violated.

Next let me make my goals somewhat more specific. Let us agree to use the term 'socialism' as indicative of a political theory founded on those characteristics which man is purported to possess as an essentially social being, and let us take the term 'individualism'

---

[4] C. B. Macpherson, in his 'The Social Bearing of Locke's Political Theory' (*Western Political Quarterly*, Vol. VII, 1954; reprinted in C. B. Martin and D. M. Armstrong, *Locke and Berkeley, A Collection of Critical Essays*, pp. 199–230; my references are to the Martin and Armstrong text) is one theorist who is well aware of the importance of 'experience' for Locke's political theory. Throughout his article one meets phrases like '. . . when Locke looked at his own society he saw . . .' (p. 210), and 'What Locke saw in his own society . . .' (p. 212). Macpherson then concludes that 'It would be surprising' if what Locke saw in his own society 'did not somehow affect his premises about society and man as such' (p. 211). This conclusion is correct. Largely incorrect, however, is Macpherson's conclusion that 'what Locke saw' in his society came to function *without substantial transformation* as 'premises' of Locke's argument. For this conclusion assumes that, in the construction of his mixed modes of 'morals' Locke did *not* take the 'liberty not to follow the Existence of Things exactly'; and as we shall see, this is a wrong assumption to make. That it is a wrong assumption is in part evidenced by Macpherson's own argument, for it leads him to the imputation of a fundamental inconsistency in Locke: 'It seems . . . reasonable to conclude that Locke . . . had in mind simultaneously two conceptions of society, which, although logically conflicting . . .' (p. 219); and 'Locke was unconscious of the contradiction between these two conceptions of society . . .' p. 220). We shall see that Locke did indeed have two conceptions of society in mind, but that he considered one of these to be wrong and the other correct. The former Locke takes as one point of departure for the development of the latter. We shall also see that Macpherson is close to the truth when he says of one of these conceptions (the latter) that it 'was the seventeenth-century atomistic conception of society as a mass of equal, undifferentiated beings' (p. 219).

as indicative of a theory founded on a view which considers each person to be essentially autonomous or self-sufficient. We can then say that there is an apparent contradiction between socialist and individualist strains in the argument of the *Second Treatise*. Sometimes, these two strains seem to be present in one and the same paragraph. (One might say, for example, that in paragraph 135 there is an unresolved conflict between the primacy of the principles of 'self-preservation' and 'preservation of mankind'.) If, however, next to Locke's practice in the *Second Treatise* we place the *Essay's* doctrine about how the foundations for general knowledge are to be obtained, a good case can be made for the statement that the conflict between 'socialism' and 'individualism' is indeed only an apparent conflict. Specifically, it can be shown that the 'socialist' strain is present because all knowledge *begins* with experience. And what the political theorist of Locke's day *experiences* when he takes cognizance of the political concepts, maxims, and theories current, even commonplace, is: concepts and maxims embedded in the framework of 'socialist' theories, as well as these 'socialist' theories themselves. One point of departure for Locke's argument therefore becomes these concepts, maxims, and theories. Seen in this light there is, contrary to Laslett's opinion on this point,[5] nothing 'extraordinary' about the fact that the *Second Treatise* 'was at once a response to a particular political situation and a statement of universal principle'. Indeed, Laslett himself provides the clue why this is not extraordinary: 'Only a man of such endowment as an abstract thinker could have transformed the issues of a predominantly historical, highly parochial political controversy . . . into a general political theory.' Also, we need not share Laslett's puzzlement when he writes 'the atmosphere in which its [*Two Treatises*'] doctrines were formulated, [was] an atmosphere of political decision and policy itself. . . . This is not the atmosphere we associate with philosophy, and too often with political thinking, nevertheless this was also the time of Locke's philosophical maturation.'[6] Again, Laslett himself provides the key to the puzzle's solution. In fact, it is already implicit in the last part of the statement just quoted, and it is pointed at even more clearly a few sentences later in Laslett's text, where he states that '*Two Treatises* and the *Essay* were in gestation at the same time. . .'. For the doctrine of the

[5] Laslett, op. cit., p. 91.
[6] Laslett, op. cit., p. 47.

Essay dictates that at least one starting-point for political thinking be the 'atmosphere of political decision and policy itself' or at least the maxims and theories which in turn structure such 'decision' and 'policy'.

To guard against misinterpretation, it should be stated that I do not imply that Locke's political theory can be *deduced* from the *Essay's* methodological principles. Instead, I argue that, given Locke's methodological principles, both the *content* and the *form* of his political theory are to an important extent *determined* by them. For example, given that the application of the principle of resolution is to result in determinate concepts at the foundation of one's theory, we shall find that, at the foundation of Locke's political theory, there is the concept of the autonomous individual. And, given a society to be composed out of autonomous individuals, the only way in which we can give a theoretical account of such composition is through some form of contract theory. For in establishing contracts each party decides *freely* to commit himself to something in order to gain something else. Furthermore, the application of the principle that all knowledge begins with experience does not dictate the precise nature of the content of such experience, and hence the particular content of a political treatise cannot be deduced from it. It does, however, dictate that, for a theorist writing in Locke's day, the starting-point for resolution includes maxims and theories of what I have called a 'socialist' type. In this way, part of the content of the *Second Treatise* is determined by a methodological principle made to apply in a particular historical setting. Given the application of the same principle in a different historical setting, the particular contents of a political treatise written at *that* time might very well differ from that of the *Second Treatise*.[7]

---

[7] I can therefore agree at least in part with Laslett when he writes: 'Filmer . . . set the terms of the argument . . . . It may well be that some of Locke's arguments would never have been developed at all if it had not been for Filmer. We have seen that he [Locke] showed no sign of an interest in the theory of property before he sat down to his polemic, and found himself faced with an argument in favour of primitive communism which was very difficult to refute unless a new justification of ownership was devised' (op. cit., p. 81). Thus if doctrines like those of Filmer had not been part of Locke's world a different political treatise would have resulted simply because there would have been different mixed modes. Locke would have taken them as points of departure to show that these modes did not possess the necessary connections between and among one another which they were commonly taken to possess. He would have used them

2. 'Invention' of the concept of an *individual*

'The true Method of advancing Knowledge, is by considering our abstract Ideas.' How, in the *Second Treatise*, does Locke obtain his abstract ideas? As we saw earlier, abstract ideas are obtained through resolution of complex experience and (if the abstract ideas are complex) recomposition or bringing together a number of the simple or simpler ideas obtained through resolution. Moreover, this recomposition may start after resolution of the kind of experience which has no resemblance to the new complex idea made ('invention'); or it may start after resolution of experience which does have some resemblance to the new complex idea made. In the latter case, however, the mind, in its activity of recomposition, does not 'follow the Existence of Things exactly'. I shall begin by arguing that the process of 'invention' is one way in which Locke could have obtained important complex ideas for his argument in the *Second Treatise*. In this argument, I shall use the fundamental concept of an *individual* to illustrate my point.

How would one 'invent' the concept of an *individual*; and why would one want to 'invent' *that* concept; and what would its determinate nature be? Although answers to these questions will, at this point, be of a somewhat speculative nature and have the form of an imaginative construction, Locke provides sufficient clues to an answer to prevent one from falling into the kind of speculation utterly divorced from anything he may have had in mind.

If we look at the model to which Locke often refers in the *Essay* when he needs an example of general knowledge, namely, mathematics, it is easy to see how *its* most fundamental concepts are obtained. Take, for example, arithmetic. Its fundamental concept is the abstract simple idea of *unity*, which may be abstracted from any one of our experiences. Because the concept unity is a *simple* abstract idea, the question of 'how' one invents is not relevant. However, the question of 'why' this, rather than any other, concept, is relevant. When any of the simple modes of arithmetic is resolved into its constituent parts, resolution must stop at the indivisible,

---

to show that they did not have such necessary connections to the concept which Locke held to be foundational to political theory. However, as long as the methodological principle of resolution is taken to be the right principle to obtain one's foundational concept, Locke's foundational concept would not have varied appreciably with the variations of different historical settings.

simple, abstract idea of *unity*. Or, if we ask how any of the simple modes of arithmetic are made by the mind, the answer is that they are constructed out of the simple idea *unity*. This concept is, thus, fundamental in the realm of arithmetic because all the relevant simple modes are reducible to it, all of them are ultimately composed out of it, and the concept itself is not further reducible and cannot be composed out of others. It is, in arithmetic, the ultimate, atomic building block, the single simple abstract idea whose consideration advances general knowledge in that field (cf. Book 2, Chapter 16).

As a model, arithmetic only partially fits the situation we meet in political theory. But it does fit the situation in at least the following respects. (i) The fundamental concept in political theory (which turns out to be that of the *individual*) must be obtained from resolution of our experience. (ii) Resolution of the different complex modes and of the relations between them must stop when we reach the concept *individual*.

In the field of political theory the concept *individual* is the fundamental abstract idea whose consideration advances general knowledge. If, for example, we ask how the nature and extent of the power of the state is delimited, the answer is that it is delimited by the nature of the concept *individual*. Thus this concept plays as fundamental a role in political theory as does the concept *unity* in arithmetic. Political theory differs from the model of arithmetic at least in the following respect: whereas the fundamental abstract idea in arithmetic is a simple abstract idea, the fundamental abstract idea in political theory is a complex mode. This makes the notion of 'invention' in the latter field a very intricate matter, one which results in potential problems at the foundation of political theory, problems which cannot arise at the foundation of arithmetic. For whereas the ideas both of *unity* and of an *individual* must be clear, distinct, and determinate, only a *simple* idea (like the former) is determinate whenever it is in the mind (since, being *simple*, the mind can only perceive all of it when it perceives it at all). However, 'by determined, when applied to a complex Idea [like that of *individual*], I mean such a one as consists of a determinate number of certain simple or less complex Ideas . . .';[8] and, in political theory, this precise collection of simple(r) ideas is not

[8] *Essay*, 'Epistle to the Reader', p. 13.

'so easily agreed on' (4.3.19). This makes 'invention' in 'morals' an intricate matter.

How, then, would one invent the concept *individual?* We must keep in mind that Locke's method for the advancement of general knowledge dictates that we need a concept in terms of which the different aspects of political thought are to be explained, a concept which, in turn, is not itself further reducible within the area of political thought. Perhaps a rough reconstruction like the following is applicable.

When beings live and act together, their action either is or is not determined by rules or laws. If it is not determined or regulated by laws, there is no structure to their living together, that is, there is no political society or state. If action is determined by laws, beings either live in accordance with these laws, or transgress them. If there is consistent wholesale transgression the situation is one of lawlessness; there is then no structure to living together, and thus no political society. If there is to be no transgression (or punishment following transgression) the laws must be enunciated, recognized, and acted upon, that is, the beings in question will have to be knowing beings, and will have to be able to know whether action is in keeping with, or a transgression of, the laws in question. Moreover, since the concept we are looking for is to be the *fundamental* concept, it must be one in terms of which 'law' and 'lawful behaviour' is to be explained; therefore the beings in question must give laws to themselves, must be autonomous. Let us call an 'autonomous knowing being' a 'rational being'. Although we now have the concept of a 'rational being' this still does not give us the foundational concept for a political theory. Thus we may still ask: with respect to *what* are laws to be kept? If we take a rational being to be a 'mind' or a 'soul', one cannot break laws by transgressing against it through imprisoning it (taking away its freedom) or killing it. Neither can it be robbed, for the products of its action, ideas, are inaccessible to others. What is therefore called for is something public. The freedom of movement of *bodies* can be taken away. *Living bodies* can be killed. And the products of a certain kind of *corporeal* action or disposition, namely, property, can be stolen. Hence the concept we need is that of a *rational corporeal being*. Let us call this kind of being an *individual*. This concept fits Locke's methodological requirements. In terms of it the different aspects of political thought can be explained. (For example, the notion of *autonomy* implicit in that of a *rational being* sets limits to the extent of a government's powers.) Moreover, the concept of an *individual* is not further reducible within the framework of political thought. (For neither the concept of a mere *rational being*, nor the concept of a mere *corporeal being* is sufficient or even relevant as the foundation for a political system—for Locke, the former may be God, the latter a stone or a frog.) Finally, the concept is an abstract concept whose 'invention' presupposes the process of resolution of experience (even the concept of 'law' could have been obtained from experience of this concept in, for example, the realm of physical science, or of religion).

Although the details of this particular 'invention' are speculative, Locke does give some clues that some if not all of its details would be considered relevant by him. In the *Essay*, for example, we read:

For as to Substances, when concerned in moral Discourses, their divers Natures are not so much enquir'd into, as supposed; v.g. when we say that Man is subject to Law: We mean nothing by Man, but a corporeal rational Creature: What the real Essence or other Qualities of that Creature are in this Case, is no way considered. And therefore, whether a Child or Changeling be a Man in a physical Sense, may amongst the Naturalists be as disputable as it will, it concerns not at all the moral Man, as I may call him, which is this immoveable unchangeable Idea, a corporeal rational Being. (3.11.16.)[9]

And in the *Second Treatise* we read that:

To understand Political Power right, and derive it from its Original,

---

[9] There are several other places in the *Essay* where Locke defines 'man' in terms like those of 3.11.6. In 3.6.3, for example, we read that: 'For though, perhaps, voluntary Motion, with Sense and Reason, join'd to a Body of a certain shape, be the complex Idea, to which I, and others, annex the name Man . . .'. And in 4.8.6 he writes: 'That Body, Sense and Motion . . . are three of those Ideas, that I always comprehend and signify by the word Man; and where they are not to be found together, the name Man belongs not to that Thing.' In both of *these* passages, however, Locke takes these statements as *nominal* definitions. Therefore, ' 'tis possible Angels have, and 'tis certain his Maker has . . . a quite other Idea of his Essence' (3.6.3). In these passages Locke deals with 'man' as the name of 'a substance' of interest to, say, the medical practitioner, who knows only man's nominal essence (as distinct from God, who knows man's real essence also when 'man' refers to 'a substance'). 'Invention', therefore, has no place in medicine, for there we are bound to diligent observation of what is 'found together' in experience. In 3.11.16, on the other hand, 'when concerned with moral Discourses', the practitioners 'invent' their concepts, and in them therefore real and nominal essences coincide: 'We mean nothing by Man, but a corporeal rational Creature.'

we must consider what State all Men are naturally in, and that is, a
State of perfect Freedom to order their actions, and dispose of their
Possessions, and Persons as they think fit, within the bounds of the
Law of Nature . . . (§ 4). The State of Nature has a Law of Nature to
govern it, which obliges every one: And Reason, which is that Law . . .
(§ 6)

Given that these two passages, put together, state: (i) that
political power must be explained in terms of pre-political individual beings (in terms of beings who are naturally in a state of
nature); (ii) beings who are corporeal and rational; (iii) who are
subject to law which is not something imposed on them through the
political state (it is the law of the state of nature); (iv) but which is
something imposed upon them by themselves, that is, law here
means 'acting in accordance with one's own nature' (for *reason* is
that law)—given all this, my reconstruction of the 'invention' of
the fundamental concept of Locke's political theory may not be
excessively speculative.

3. Experience of 'Opinions in Fashion'

If it is correct to assume that the argument of the *Second Treatise*
is structured by the *Essay's* principles for the obtaining of general
knowledge, we shall find that this argument starts from the givens
of one's experience (in particular, the 'Opinions in Fashion') and
that there is a constant attempt at resolution of this experience. We
shall find that this resolution of experience takes the form of an
attempt to show that concepts which were generally held to stand
in necessary relations to one another, do not really stand in such
relations at all. Thus, also in the *Second Treatise*, resolution consists
in the separation of ideas which often (if not constantly) are experienced in particular combinations united together. We shall see
that this process either leads to a further explication of the nature
of the foundational concept of an *individual*, or that it allows us to
see what Locke holds to be necessary relations between that foundational concept and ideas which we have thus obtained from experience. We shall find that although experience, especially that of the
relevant 'Opinions in Fashion', is constantly subjected to the process
of resolution, the concept of an *individual* is not. Instead, we shall
find that careful reflection upon it in the context of ideas obtained
from the resolution of 'Opinions in Fashion' is held to advance

general knowledge in political theory. If these statements do indeed describe Locke's practice, it is clear that the concept of an *individual* must already be available to Locke. That is to say, although, in the *Second Treatise*, no attention is paid to the 'invention' of this concept, clearly Locke must have had this concept available to him for it to be possible for him to develop this treatise's theories. Although there is no such 'invention' presented in this treatise, what does happen is that the *nature* of this concept is made explicit in it. This, as I shall show in section 4, takes place through reflection on 'rational' and 'corporeal', and on other ideas held to be necessarily related to these.

Since we now start from the specific context of the ideas present in the *Second Treatise*, we shall be confronted with the picture of a mind which does not 'follow the Existence of Things exactly', of a mind which does not construct its own 'archetypes' to conform exactly with what it experiences to be in 'existence' as 'Opinions in Fashion'. However, in Locke's day there were well-known political theories, and controversial political actions and institutions; and there was much debate about these theories, actions, and institutions. In Locke's 'common Conversation', he was regularly exposed to the experience of these 'mixed modes of morals'. We are therefore confronted with the picture of a mind which, although it does not 'follow the Existence of Things exactly', nevertheless takes its point of departure for the construction of its mixed modes and its tracing of relations between them, from the experience of mixed modes and from the experience of relations between them. It takes its point of departure from the experience of relations between these mixed modes, which were commonly taken to be determinate mixed modes and whose relations were commonly taken to be necessary relations. As we saw, Locke holds that 'for the most part the Names of mixed Modes are got, before the Ideas they stand for are perfectly known'. Therefore, after the introduction of the 'Opinions in Fashion', we shall find the application of the principle of resolution to what is commonly 'known'. Because resolution is to lead to the explication of the nature of the concept of an *individual,* or is to provide us with ideas which are held to stand in a necessary relationship to this concept, the relevant fashionable opinions we are looking for are those which Locke's contemporaries took to make important points about the individual in the context of a state, about man in the context of political theory.

What, then, were the starting-points in the fashionable opinions of Locke's days? That Aristotle's *Politics* was much read needs little substantiation; Locke himself still recommends this work some twenty-five years after completion of his *Second Treatise* (alongside 'Hooker's first book of Ecclesiastical Polity, . . . Two Treatises of Government [and] Pufendorf's Little Treatise, de Officio Hominis et Civis').[10] According to Laslett, Locke while at Oxford read 'such highly respectable, academic authors as Grotius and Pufendorf'.[11] Pufendorf's major work *De Jure Naturae et Gentium* was not published until 1672. Grotius's *De Jure Belli ac Pacis* was published in 1625; and during Locke's lifetime it went through twenty-six editions in Latin and three editions in the English translation (of which Locke possessed those of 1650 and 1680). As fashionable opinion before and during the time when he wrote the *Second Treatise* it was, therefore, more common than Pufendorf's work. In England itself Filmer, rather than Hooker, 'was the man of the moment, a formidable and growing force with those whose political opinions mattered, and representing in himself the *ipsissima verba* of the established order';[12] he was 'the author whose works had become the official exposition of the Royal and Tory view of the basis of governmental power'.[13] In view of the contents of Locke's *First Treatise of Government*, the importance of Filmer's works can hardly be overemphasized in this context.

It therefore seems safe to say that if we look at the doctrines of Aristotle, Grotius, and Filmer, we have a good representative sample of the fashionable opinions of Locke's day. The sample will, of course, have to be narrowed down to opinions relevant to 'inquiring into the ground and nature of civil society' and the 'notions of laws in general; and property, the subject-matter about which laws are made'.[14]

Neither Aristotle, nor Grotius, nor Filmer would deny that man

[10] Letter to the Revd. Mr Richard King, 25 August 1703, *Works* (1823), Vol. X, pp. 305–9; cf. pp. 307–8. See also Locke's *First Treatise*, § 154, where he writes that the heathen Aristotle is 'not rejected by our Zealous Christian Politician', i.e. Filmer, 'whenever' Aristotle 'offer[s] any thing that seems to serve his turn'. Also Hooker, as quoted in the *Second Treatise*, § 74, refers to doctrines from Aristotle's *Politics*.

[11] Laslett, op. cit., p. 34.

[12] Laslett, op. cit., p. 80.

[13] Laslett, op. cit., p. 45.

[14] This is a statement from the same passage of the letter to Richard King quoted in n. 10. See also *Second Treatise*, § 3.

202 METHOD OF LOCKE'S *SECOND TREATISE*

is a corporeal rational being. None of them would deny that man's
rationality enables him to know about justice and injustice and
thus enables him to live according to law. All of them assert that
man has a right to support himself by making use of the fruits of
the earth. All of them declare that whosoever's actions are in
accordance with law has a right to life. But what does it mean for
them, in the context of political theory, to say that man is an intelligent or rational animal? For both Aristotle and Grotius, to say
that man is essentially intelligent or rational is to say that *he is
essentially a social or political being. Reason, for them, is a common
bond which unites men into fellowship and society.* Aristotle, for
example, writes that man is a political animal because man is the
only animal who possesses the gift of speech; and 'the power of
speech is intended to set forth the expedient and inexpedient, and
therefore likewise the just and the unjust'. Because he is a rational
animal, it is 'characteristic of man that he alone has any sense of
good and evil, of just and unjust, and the like, and the association
of living beings who have this sense makes a family and a state'.[15]
And Grotius writes that 'among the traits characteristic of man is
an impelling desire for society, that is, for the social life—not of any
and every sort, but peaceful, and organized according to the
measure of his intelligence, with those who are of his own kind;
this social trend the Stoics called "sociableness".' It is, for
Grotius, the maintenance of this peaceful, intelligently organized
social life, of this 'social order', which is 'the source of law properly
so called'.[16] Secondly, what does it mean for them to say that man
has a right to support himself by making use of the fruits of the
earth? For Filmer, this involved the assertion of a 'primitive
communism', of an 'original communism' which 'could not give
way to private property without the universal consent of mankind'.[17]

[15] Aristotle, *Politics*, 1253a 7–18.
[16] Grotius, *De Jure Belli ac Pacis*, Prolegomena, paras. 6 and 8, respectively.
In spite of statements like these Grotius's arguments are, in important respects,
closer to those of Locke than to those of Aristotle or Filmer. For example, that
a ruler of a nation has rights over the nation's citizens is explained in terms of
arguments which deduce these rights from the rights possessed by the individual
persons who constitute the nation. See *De Jure*, Book I, ch. 3, section 8, sub. 1,
2; Book I, ch. 3, section 10, sub. 5; Book I, ch. 4, section 2, sub. 1; Book II,
ch. 6, section 4.
[17] Cf. Laslett, op. cit., p. 80; also pp. 327–8, notes to para 25, lines 18–21.

It meant that *the earth, and all living beings inferior to man, originally belonged to all men collectively.* Finally, what is implied by saying that a law-abiding person has a right to the preservation of his life? For Aristotle, this implied that *the preservation of the individual is secondary to that of society or the state.* For if society or the state were to be destroyed there would not be any human individuals: '. . . the individual, when isolated, is not self-sufficing; and therefore he is like a part in the relation to the whole. But he who is unable to live in society, or who has no need because he is sufficient for himself, must be either a beast or a god: he is no part of a state'.[18] These statements also revert to the first of the fashionable opinions identified: man is essentially a social being.

These were some of the most important of 'the well endowed Opinions in Fashion' which confronted the political theorist of Locke's day. Certain questions should now be asked. Did Locke in fact take opinions like these as his points of departure? Was he indeed able through their resolution to make explicit the nature of his determined concept of an *individual*? Did this resolution in fact provide him with ideas which he took to have a necessary relation to the concept of an *individual* and which he thus took to lead to an advance in 'general knowledge'? In the course of answering these questions, the contours of what Locke took to be general knowledge in the field of political theory will become apparent. It is, of course, not a part of my task to give an account of all the important details of Locke's political theory. I shall, therefore, leave this theory in contour form.

4. Resolution of 'Opinions in Fashion'

From the text of the *Second Treatise* I shall now illustrate that the fashionable opinions identified are indeed starting points for Locke's arguments. The passages I shall select are some of those which help make explicit the nature of the concept of an *individual* in so far as it is specifically related in thought to certain other concepts. I have in mind the concepts of (i) *reason*, (ii) *communality, labour,* and *property,* and (iii) *self-preservation.*

(i) *Reason.* In the opening paragraph of the *Second Treatise,* 'reason' occupies a prominent position. It is among the 'faculties'

---

[18] *Politics*, 1253a 25–29; see also 1253a 2–5.

which make men share 'in one Community' (§ 6); it is the 'rule' by which men live and thus becomes 'the tye, which is to secure them from injury and violence' (§ 8); it is 'the common Rule and Measure, God hath given to Mankind' which sets them apart from 'Savage Beasts, with whom Men can have no Society' (§ 11). To use the words of a later paragraph, 'Reason' is 'the common bond whereby humane kind is united into one fellowship and societie' (§ 172). This common bond exists whether or not men live in civil society with one another. Civil society is only possible, in fact, because of the prior existence of this common bond, because of a 'symmetry in reason between all of us'.[19] Although this way of speaking may seem to indicate the priority of 'reason' to 'individual' and hence may seem to point to a definition of the individual in terms of the common bond, the opposite is the case.

First, it is to be noted that this symmetry in reason in no way abrogates the individual's epistemic autonomy. Just as in the *Essay* anything taken for true on the word of someone else is not knowledge but is opinion or belief, and knowledge is gained only by each individual when he himself traces the agreement or disagreement of ideas, so also in the realms of ethics and politics: 'each single person has to infer the law of nature from the first principles of nature, not from another person's belief'.[20] It is, therefore, each man's reason which determines the rightness or wrongness of action. Each man's reason is 'a self-dependent source of obligation'.[21] But more than epistemic autonomy is involved. For it is the exercise of reason which makes and keeps men *free*. Reason identified by Locke with the law of nature (§ 8), can without imposition dictate to a man because it is a human quality, because, in fact, it is *the* human quality, for it alone distinguishes between man and beast. 'Thus we are *born Free,* as we are born Rational' (§ 61). It is each man's reason which makes each man free.

Second, and related to this, it is important in the context of the *Second Treatise* to make a distinction between 'reason' or 'rational' and 'knowing' or 'reasoning'. For in the context of this treatise it is not true that the phrase 'corporeal rational creature' is synonymous

---

[19] This is Laslett's phrase, op. cit., p. 124.

[20] *John Locke, Essays on the Law of Nature,* translated and edited by W. von Leyden, p. 177.

[21] W. von Leyden, in the Introduction to the *Essays on the Law of Nature,* p. 52.

with the phrase 'corporeal knowing or reasoning creature'. Whereas the first of these is definitive of a human being, the second is not. Transgressing the law of nature reduces one to a subhuman level (cf. e.g. §§ 10, 11, 16, 181). But only if one transgresses the law of nature knowingly does one become responsible for the transgression and is punishment in order. Already in the *Essays* on the *Law of Nature* Locke had written that the law of nature is 'binding on all those to whom it is given' but that 'it does not . . . bind those to whom it is not given'; this means it does not bind 'children and idiots', for the law 'is not given to those who are unable to understand it'.[22] Criminal action is knowing transgression of the law of nature. 'In transgressing the Law of Nature, the Offender declares himself to live by another Rule, than that of *reason*. . .' (§ 8). Once this kind of distinction is made, it is not difficult to see that the *'common bond whereby humane kind is united into one fellowship' comes about only when individuals act rationally, that is, when each knows the law of nature and each lives by its 'Rule'.*

There are four elements in the preceding paragraph which need to be made more explicit. First, 'reason', in the *Second Treatise,* stands for more than the process of reasoning, the intuiting and demonstrating activity of the mind which is central to the epistemological concerns of the *Essay.* Through the intuitive and demonstrative activity of the mind one can come to know the principles of natural law. 'Reason', on the other hand, covers (a) knowledge of the principles of natural law, (b) knowledge that these principles are normative, binding for action if action is to qualify as human action, as well as (c) individual acceptance of the normative and binding nature of these principles. 'Reason', in the *Second Treatise,* has strong normative overtones. Thus there is nothing wrong with the criminal's capacity to know; what is wrong is that he rejects as normative and authoritative the principles of 'Right Reason'. It is not the absence of an intellectual capacity, but the rejection in thought and ensuing behaviour of these principles as proper norms which makes him subhuman. And he is held responsible for such behaviour precisely because he does know but rejects as binding the principles which rational, human beings knowingly accept as normative for their action.

Second, since 'reason' covers individual knowledge of the

---

[22] *Essays on the Law of Nature,* p. 203.

principles of natural law, individual knowledge that these principles are binding for action if action is to qualify as human action, and individual acceptance of the normative nature of these principles, reason itself becomes a definition of individuality.

Third, the fact that all human beings possess reason does not do away with the fact that the locus of reason is in each individual. Each man is prevented from subordinating the other to himself because each man recognizes that the other possesses the same quality (reason) which he himself possesses. The recognition of reason in the other guarantees that the other is left inviolate by all individuals acting reasonably, that is, by all human beings. In other words, the common bond 'binds' only once individuals act rationally and recognize reason in one another. *The existence of this common bond is dependent on and to be explained in terms of reciprocal individual human action.*

Fourth, although all rational action is, by definition, action within the bounds of the law of nature, not all action is rational action. But this does not imply two extremes of human action, namely, fully rational human action and totally non-rational human action. Rather, in terms of extremes, the dichotomy is between human (rational) action and subhuman (non-rational) action.

(ii) *Communality, labour, and property.* In the very first paragraph of Locke's chapter 'Of Property', the argument begins with the assertion of the fashionable opinion (supported by the authority of the Bible) that 'God . . . has given the Earth to the Children of Men, given it to Mankind in common'. But before the end of this paragraph, Locke's intention to undermine Filmer's position is clear: 'But I shall endeavour to shew, how Men might come to have a *property* in several parts of that which God gave to Mankind in common, and that without any express Compact of all the Commoners' (§ 25). For 'Though the Earth, and all inferior Creatures be common to all Men, yet every Man has a *Property* in his own *Person*. This no Body has any Right to but himself. The Labour of his Body, and the Work of his Hands, we may say, are properly his' (§ 27). '. . . Man (by being Master of himself, and *Proprietor of his own Person*, and the actions or *Labour* of it) had still in himself *the great Foundation of Property*' (§ 44). It is clear from these statements that, from the outset, Locke places severe restrictions on the concept of communality. First, communality extends to the earth and all *inferior* creatures only. Human beings are not 'common' to one another. It is not the case that, for example, the products of one another's labour—even though also these products are part of the earth—are freely accessible for the others' use. The concept of the communality of the earth and all inferior creatures is restricted as soon as it is considered in relationship to the concept of the individual's activity. Strictly speaking, Locke can accept a thoroughgoing communality only as long as one presupposes inactivity on the part of men. Action directed towards taking care even of basic needs—gathering food and fuel—immediately does away with the communality of the earth, for such action is defined as labour and the product of labour is by definition private property. And since human life is impossible without such action, the communality concept cannot function except as *an abstract principle which allows for a theory of independent, individual, self-expression through labour*. In other words, although a statement like '. . . the Earth, and all inferior Creatures be common to all Men' appears at first sight to give grounds for supposing that human beings are tied together and that to theorize about them merely in terms of the concept of *individuality* would be inadequate, all it really does is to allow for theorizing entirely on the basis of a concept like that of an *individual*.

The communality concept functions as an abstract principle which allows for a theory of independent, individual self-expression through labour. For Locke, this implies a distinction between 'having things in common', and 'possessing things' or 'having belongings'. For since the earth is 'in common', it therefore does not yet belong to anyone in particular. But since it does not yet belong to anyone in particular, to any individual, it therefore does not 'belong'. For 'belonging' is taken to come about only through a certain activity of individuals, namely, through the activity called 'labour'. The necessary conceptual connection is held to exist between the concepts of *individual action (labour)* and *property*, rather than between the concepts *mankind* and *property*. Therefore the area in which one has 'things in common' becomes the arena for labour, that is, the arena in which, through labour, one claims parts of what is 'common' as exclusively one's own.[23]

[23] It is clear that in the seventeenth-century debate about 'negative community' versus 'positive community', Locke comes down on the side of the former. Patrick Kelley has pointed out that 'Pufendorf's definition of negative community as "all things lay open to all men and belonged no more to one than another" is

If we focus on *property* and *labour* rather than on *individuality* and *labour*, the conclusion just drawn is reinforced. To use Professor Polin's words 'Property . . . is the external manifestation of freedom, its expression and its very concrete existence for others. . . . Every man, being equal to every other, manifests his liberty by the domination, the ownership of his property.'[24] Or, in Professor Yolton's words, 'It is bodily movement', 'the work I do' which is 'the manifestation of my person as property'.[25] For Locke, the nature of property is such that *'without a Man's own consent it cannot be taken from him'* (§ 193). 'Their *Persons* are *free* by a Native Right, and their *properties*, be they more or less, are *their own, and at their own dispose . . .'* (§ 194). As we shall see, it is not just in the 'state of nature', but it is also in civil society that a man remains 'absolute Lord of his own Person and Possessions' (§ 123). Human individuals are not distinguished from one another in terms of their possession of reason, for *qua* rational being each individual is the same as any other. Individuality, uniqueness, is established through action. And because human (that is, rational) action is by definition within the bounds of the law of nature, each man's action is to be left free. Through the specific action called 'labour' each establishes his property. Thus property is the overt manifestation of each man's freedom, and a man's property constitutes the assertion of his selfhood in the presence of others. Action marks an individual as human or, if he acts constantly in violation of the law of nature, as subhuman. It is reason which determines whether the action is within the law of nature or a transgression of it. Hence it is reason which determines that the product of the kind of action called labour qualifies as property, and the product of the kind of action called aggression as something like 'illegitimate conquest'. *Each* man's reason establishes this a such. Thus what is and what is not 'property' is determined

---

remarkably like Locke's phrase ". . . noe man at his birth can have noe right to any thing . . . more then an other." ' (See n. 2 above.) Kelley presents a brief though interesting sketch of this debate in 'Locke and Filmer; was Laslett so wrong after all?' *Locke Newsletter*, No. 8, 1977, pp. 77–91. The passage I have quoted is on p. 81.

[24] Raymond Polin, 'John Locke's conception of freedom', in John W. Yolton, ed., *John Locke, Problems and Perspectives*, p. 6.

[25] John W. Yolton, *Locke and the Compass of Human Understanding* (Cambridge, 1970), p. 190.

by the nature of the concept of an *individual*: property is the result of a certain kind of corporeal and rational action. Furthermore, because all men possess reason there is the guarantee that, among human beings, there will be agreement in judgement as to what is property and what is illegitimate conquest. In *this* way reason is indeed 'the Rule given between Man and Man' (§ 181). And because the law of nature continues in civil society, property remains inviolate also in society. This means that whenever a man finds himself in a position where he has to ask leave for any of his actions that lead to the acquisition of property or that concern property that he already possesses, he is forced to act against the law of nature (cf. § 57). To comply with the other's will in circumstances like these is to deny one's autonomous nature, to abnegate one's individuality, to perform a non-rational action. Man is, and ought to remain, 'Master of himself, and *Proprietor of his own Person,* and the action or *Labour* of it'. This, in turn, is just one way of saying that the individual remains inviolate as individual in society. Moreover, since the absolute lordship over one's property implies the absolute separation of one man's property from that of all others' and because property constitutes the assertion of selfhood in the presence of others, there is a fundamental separation of each individual from all others.

(iii) *Self-preservation.* Again, in the very opening paragraph of the argument 'Of the Extent of the Legislative Power' we meet a fashionable opinion: '*the fundamental Law of Nature* being *the preservation of Mankind.* . .'. This is a law of nature of which it is said that it 'stands as an Eternal Rule to all Men'. It is a law which embodies both a right and a duty which each human being has to himself, and a duty which each has to 'the rest of Mankind'. When individuals enter civil society and thus, depending on the nature of their activity from that point on, place themselves in the position of gaining society's protection or being subject to society's punishment, the rules which come to govern society's action must be 'conformable to' this fundamental law of nature. These statements seem to indicate that the individual in civil society is to be discussed in terms of societal laws and it seems as if these societal laws, rather than being laws derived from the nature of the individual, are laws derived from the nature of the species: the fundamental law which governs the behaviour of both rulers and citizens in civil society is that of the preservation of *mankind.* However, this fundamental law is taken by Locke not to stand in a necessary connection with the concept of man as a social being; it is not derived from a consideration of the nature of 'mankind'. It is, instead, a law derived from each man's peculiar nature, form the 'power' which each man 'has in himself', from the 'power' which, individually, 'every Member of the Society [has] given up to that Person, or Assembly, which is Legislator' (§ 135).[26] The primacy of the concept of the individual stands out clearly if one considers, first, when an individual actually becomes subject to the power of the state and, second, when the duty which he has to 'the rest of Mankind' becomes effective.

First, only when a man ceases to act rationally does he actually become subject to the state's executive power. The important instance of an individual's ceasing to act rationally is when he becomes an aggressor, when he endangers the other's property. In that case, he has 'quitted Reason', and 'so revolting from his own kind to that of Beasts by making Force which is theirs, to be his rule of right, he renders himself liable to be destroied by the injur'd person . . .' (§ 172). 'Quitting Reason', 'varying from the right Rule of Reason', 'transgressing the Law of Nature' all seem to be synonymous phrases each of which points to the same effect: it makes a man 'degenerate' (§ 128), subhuman. Whoever tries to eradicate all feeling of the law of nature within himself at the same time works at the eradication of his own humanity.[27] It is to be noted that such an eradication of one's own humanity is possible only if we assume that man is, and in civil society remains, *essentially* unrelated to and independent from others. If social or political relationships were *essential* to a human being, he would be able to eradicate his human nature only by breaking these social or political relationships. However, since such relationships are *for Locke* contractual and hence *reciprocal* rather than unilateral relationships, other men, civil society, would have to be called upon for action in order for it to be possible for the first individual's human nature to be eradicated. The magistrate's action would then be an element in making the transgressor subhuman. But this is not the case, for the magistrate's action only becomes legitimate once there is trans-

---

[26] The doctrine incorporated in this paragraph is stated by Locke as early as in the *Essays on the Law of Nature*. See, in particular, Essays VI and VII.

[27] Cf. *Essays on the Law of Nature*, p. 123, from which I have taken this terminology.

gression, once the corporeal being has ceased to act like (and therefore has ceased to be) a corporeal rational being. Thus, Locke does not say that the action of others helps to eradicate an aggressor's *human* nature. Rather, the others act in a punishing role, even up to that of killing the aggressor, because the aggressor has already become subhuman by his own unilateral act of aggression, which constitutes at the same time an act towards the eradication of his human nature. The magistrate does not give orders to kill a human being, but to destroy a beast. Eradication of one's humanity is a possibility only because each human being is, and remains, essentially unrelated, self-sufficient. It is reason, a quality of each human being, which is also the law of nature, the 'measure . . . set to the actions of Men, for their mutual security' (§ 8). The aggressor, living unreasonably, is subject to punishment. Punishment, even destruction, in this case is not the violation of a human self. The aggressor cannot claim protection under the fundamental law of nature for he has unilaterally excluded himself from mankind.

It is only the individual who has 'quitted Reason' who becomes subject to the power of the state. Human beings, to the extent that they live within the bounds of the law of nature, are never subject to this power. For if the state subjects them to its power, the state commits a 'breach of trust' and itself becomes the aggressor; and its power becomes illegitimate (cf. § 230).

Second, self-preservation is both a fundamental right and a fundamental duty. Preservation of others, although a duty, is not a fundamental duty. A man ought 'as much as he can, to preserve the rest of Mankind' but only 'when his own Preservation comes not in competition' (§ 6). Since the law of nature does not cease in civil society we may say, with a variant on words from § 134, that we always ought to work for the preservation of others as far as will accord with the fundamental private good of self-preservation. This is perhaps the clearest instance of the precedence given to the individual over society. Preservation of mankind is a duty which is to be acted out egocentrically.[28]

By considering the concept of an *individual* in the context of

[28] In the context of this, as well as of the preceding section, it is instructive to note how, in the *First Treatise*, Locke argues for the right of children to own the possessions of their deceased parents. 'The first and strongest desire God Planted in Men, and wrought into the very Principles of their Nature being that of Selfpreservation, that is the Foundation of a right to the Creatures, for the particular support and use of each individual Person himself. But next to this

concepts like *reason, communality, labour, property,* and *self-preservation,* we have now established that this is the foundational concept of Locke's political theory. It has a determinate nature, because 'individual' is the name of the mixed mode which includes as simpler ideas those named by 'corporeality' and 'rationality'. That nature has now been further explicated through confrontations with 'Opinions in Fashion' in terms of some other ideas to which it stands in necessary connections. Of these other ideas, many were obtained through a resolution of 'Opinions in Fashion'. Thus the concept of a *corporeal rational being* is further characterized by the necessary connections it is taken to have to the concepts involved in the phrase *inalienable rights to life, liberty, and estate.* It is now clear that this concept determines the nature of the major doctrines of the *Second Treatise.*

Reason is 'the common bond whereby humane kind is united into one fellowship and society'; 'the Earth, and all inferior Creatures' is 'common to all Men'; 'the fundamental Law of Nature' is 'the preservation of Mankind'—these are three principles which are of central importance for the construction of Locke's theory. But if these principles are taken as statements of necessary relationships among the abstract ideas on which Locke's political theory is *founded,* Locke's political thought is full of tension between 'socialist' and 'individualist' elements. For in these principles reason defines man as a social or political being. Also, the earth, being necessary for the sustenance of corporeal beings, binds men in a community because it is common or belongs to all, which implies some form of communism. And since the fundamental law of nature is the preservation of mankind, the preservation of each individual becomes secondary to that of the state. Political theory would then be founded on concepts like *sociableness, communality,* and *mankind.* However, it is clear enough that Locke's theory is not founded on concepts like these. Instead, it is founded on the concept of the autonomous individual characterized by inalienable rights.

God Planted in Men a strong desire also of propagating their Kind, and continuing themselves in their Posterity, and this gives Children a Title, to share in the Property of their Parents, and a Right to Inherit their Possessions' (§ 88). It is thus not civic laws or family relationships which give inheritance rights to the children. Basically, this right is founded on an individual's desire to 'continue' himself in his posterity.

If we take seriously what Locke says in the *Essay* about the method by which to 'advance general knowledge', there is no conflict in his theory between 'socialism' and 'individualism'. For these concepts of *reason, communality,* and *mankind* are foundational to political theories prior to (and in important instances, contemporary with) Locke's. In Locke's theory, they function as points of departure from which, through the application of the principle of resolution, one comes to recognize what is really involved in the foundational concept of an *individual*; they are points of departure for the introduction of many other concepts which are held by Locke to stand in necessary relations with this foundational concept.

We are born into a world in which men have been and constantly are acting in many ways. Some of these actions can be described as 'social' and 'political'. Philosophers prior to Locke have theorized about these actions, and the principles just mentioned have come to occupy a foundational place in their theories. Within the framework of political theory these principles, for Locke, are complex and derived rather than foundational. To single out one aspect common to all three of them, they are about 'humane kind', 'all Men', 'mankind'. General knowledge, however, must start with items that are irreducible. 'Mankind' is made up of 'nations', 'clans', 'families', 'individuals'. The 'individual' is taken to be a 'member of a family', of a 'clan', of a 'nation', of 'mankind'. What happens in the *Second Treatise* is that Locke constantly attempts to show that whatever conceptual connection the concept of an *individual* is commonly believed to have with any of the other concepts is shown to be either non-existent or much looser than political theorists have claimed. Showing that no necessary connections exist between or among concepts where they are traditionally assumed to exist breaks up these complexes of concepts; and this is an exercise in resolution. Thus, the traditional principles, as 'the well endowed Opinions in Fashion', function as a point of departure for a reduction to pure individuality. Once this reduction is complete we have obtained the irreducible abstract concept of an *individual* characterized by inalienable rights. 'General knowledge' starts with the consideration of this concept.

As criticism of Locke's political theory, Aaron has written that Locke:

. . . deals too frequently in artificialities. His individual is artificial. He has no family ties. He tends to be considered as a somewhat isolated being even when he enters into social relations with others. So also Locke's state is artificial. It is a community of free and independent individuals bound together by a compact into which they have entered for the better security of their lives, liberties, and estates—and it is nothing more. But surely a political or civil society is much more.[29]

Aaron is right: 'a political or civil society is much more', indeed, it is (or ought to be) founded on a blueprint very different from that provided by Locke. It is interesting to note that Aaron lists a number of the most fundamental aspects of Locke's political theory and that he criticizes each of them by calling them 'artificial'. It should be clear that Locke would not be perturbed by such criticism, for both his 'individual' and his 'state' are *meant* to be 'artificial': they are names of mixed modes, and all mixed modes are 'artifacts' of the human mind.

   The 'artificiality' of the *Second Treatise's* doctrines has, of course, not been a barrier to their gaining tremendous historical importance. It did not take long for them to enter *rerum natura* as a set of *new* 'Opinions in Fashion'. And once these new 'Opinions in Fashion' were acted upon they helped change the course of history. In fact, Laslett has presented a convincing case for the correctness of the belief that they helped change the course of history even before the *Second Treatise* was published. It was published after 1688, but its central concepts were formulated and discussed well before that date. And, as Laslett writes, '*Two Treatises* . . . turns out to be a demand for a revolution to be brought about, not the rationalization of a revolution in need of defence.'[30] Through his long and intimate relationship with the First Earl of Shaftesbury, Locke's doctrine became fashionable among Shaftesbury's circle of intimates—the Whigs whose political action precipitated the revolution of 1688. Politics in Great Britain before the event of the 'Glorious Revolution' differed markedly from what it has been since that event. And that these 'Opinions' remained 'in Fashion' well beyond the time of Locke's death is borne out by some of the most important documents which history has produced. Locke would have been quite pleased with these words from the opening sentence of the second paragraph of the American *Declaration of Independence*: '. . . all Men are created equal, . . . endowed by their Creator with certain unalienable Rights, . . . among these are

---

[29] Aaron, op. cit., p. 284.
[30] Laslett, op. cit., p. 60.

Life, Liberty, and the Pursuit of Happiness—That to secure
these Rights, Governments are instituted among Men, deriving
their just Powers from the Consent of the Governed . . .'.[31] The
first words of this sentence are: 'We hold these Truths to be
self-evident'. That these new 'Opinions in Fashion' are anything
but 'self-evident' ought to be clear enough. Their derivation,
after all, involves the application of the methodological principle
of resolution. The use of that principle, for Locke as for Descartes,
goes together with the belief that there are simple ideas, concepts
which are knowable in isolation from any other concepts. And
that this fundamental doctrine about the possibility of our knowing single items in total isolation is a highly questionable one I
have pointed out more than once before.

[31] That more than just the *ideas* of the *Second Treatise* entered into the composition of the *Declaration of Independence* becomes evident when we compare
two sentences from the *Declaration* (taken from the same paragraph as the
statement I have just quoted) and place them side by side with phrases from the
Second Treatise. The *Declaration* states that 'Prudence, indeed, will dictate that
Governments long established should not be changed for light and transient
Causes: and accordingly all Experience hath shewn, that *Mankind are more
disposed to suffer* . . .'. Locke wrote that 'the alteration of the Government' is not
likely to arise from mere 'mischief' on the citizens' part, for '*the People* . . . *are
more disposed to suffer, than right themselves* by Resistance . . .' (§ 230). The
Declaration continues: '. . . Mankind are more disposed to suffer, while Evils are
sufferable, *than to right themselves by abolishing the Forms to which they are
accustomed.*' And Locke wrote: 'People are not so easily got out of *their old
Forms* . . .. They are hardly to be prevailed with to amend the acknowledg'd
Faults, in *the Frame they have been accustom'd to*' (§ 223). The *Declaration*'s
next sentence is: '*But when a long Train of Abuses and Usurpations, pursuing
invariably the same Object, evinces a Design* to reduce them under absolute Des-
potism, it is their Right, it is their Duty, to throw off such Government, and to
provide new Guards for their future Security.' In the *Second Treatise* we read:
'*But if a long train of Abuses,* Prevarications, and Artifices, *all tending the same
way, make the design visible* to the People, and they . . . see whither they are
going . . . they should then rouze themselves, and endeavour to put the rule
into such hands, which may secure to them the ends for which Government was
at first erected . . .' (§ 225). (The italics in all these passages are mine. In his
notes to these passages from Locke, Laslett draws attention to these similarities.)

VIII

METHOD IN LOCKE'S THEOLOGICAL WORKS

Many of the *Essay's* central doctrines also find their application in Locke's theological works. Of particular interest, again, is the powerful presence in these works of certain parts of the *Essay's* doctrines on general knowledge. For we shall find Locke adopting as *hermeneutical* principles (as principles which are to be applied if we are to obtain an understanding of the contents of the Scriptures) the very methods required in the *Essay* for obtaining general knowledge.

I do not wish at all to suggest that on Locke's view the Scriptures present us with a body of general knowledge. As we shall see, Locke ascribes to the Scriptures a large number of characteristics which he also ascribes to general knowledge. But Locke's point is that unless one applies the *Essay's* principles for the attaining of general knowledge, one cannot come to an understanding of anything written in the Bible.

As in the previous chapter, I shall focus on the role of the methodological principle of resolution. Here I hope to show how the application of this methodological principle determines what Locke takes to be some of the most important characteristics of the Scriptures. Other doctrines presented in the *Essay* will be introduced only to the extent that they help elucidate this aspect of method in Locke's theological works.

As representatives of Locke's theological work I shall take the four *Letters Concerning Toleration, The Reasonableness of Christianity* with its first and second *Vindication,* and *A Paraphrase and Notes on the Epistles of St. Paul.*[1] (In the text and subsequent footnotes I shall refer to these works as T, R, and P, respectively.) I call these works 'theological' because in all of them Locke, to varying degrees, concerns himself with questions like: 'What ought one to believe to become a Christian?' and 'How does one come to know-

[1] The quotations from these works are from the readily available edition of Locke's *Works* of 1823 (reprinted by Scientia Verlag Aalen, 1963), in which *Toleration* is Vol. VI, *Reasonableness* Vol. VII, and *Paraphrase,* Vol. VIII.

ledge of God and God's will for man's life?'. Mine is, no doubt, a somewhat loose use of the word 'theological', but it will suffice for the purposes of this chapter. There are of course passages in some of Locke's other works which could be similarly called 'theological'. However, the points I want to make in this chapter can be amply documented from the three sets of works I have mentioned.

A further indication of the scope of this chapter may be useful here. In the preceding chapter I did not make it my task to examine the viability of Locke's political theory, but merely to discuss his mode of argumentation. Thus, it is not my intention here to make judgements about the correctness or incorrectness of Locke's interpretation of Scriptural texts, but rather to lay bare the principles of method which guide him in his interpretation.

Which of the *Essay's* methodological principles are present? What is the manner in which they function in the theological works? These questions can best be answered if we ask another: 'How, according to Locke, is man able to come to an understanding of Scripture?'. This question about methodology will be central to the present chapter.

Because such a question is central I shall be concerned only incidentally with the epistemological autonomy which characterizes the knower of Scripture.[2] Instead, I shall concentrate on the nature of what is known, on the characteristics of Scripture which Locke takes to make it possible that this 'object' can come to be known. Whereas in political theory Locke is primarily concerned with the individual and his rights and duties, in theology Locke is concerned above all with the individual and his knowledge of a particular 'object'. In political theory, rights and duties are rights and duties of the individual, and they are explained ultimately in terms of the nature of the individual. In theology, knowledge is not explained merely in terms of the nature of the individual's reasoning, but also in terms of the nature of a unique 'object' which confronts the individual, namely, the word of God revealed in Scripture. Of course the individual is involved in an essential way, for Scripture is brought before the bar of each individual's reason. To pose the question 'How can man come to an understanding of Scripture?'

---

[2] For a discussion of individual epistemological autonomy in the context of religious knowledge, see John Dunn's 'The Politics of Locke in England and America in the eighteenth century', in John W. Yolton, ed., *John Locke, Problems and Perspectives*, pp. 45–80, esp. pp. 52–6.

one must first ask: 'What does Locke take to be the nature of that which is brought before the bar of reason?'. But we must also ask: 'What does Locke take to be the nature of the judge, of the process of reasoning?'. For it will be seen that the nature of that which is brought before the bar of reason is determined in part by reason's procedure, by how reason goes about its business in obtaining knowledge of Scripture.

More particularly, it will be argued that, for Locke, there are four principles which are to be brought into play if we are to come to an understanding of Scripture. Two of these, the empiricist principle and the principle of resolution, are enunciated in the *Essay* and have been shown to be of importance in the argument of the *Second Treatise*. The terms 'empiricist principle' and 'principle of resolution' have the same meaning in this chapter, as they had in the preceding ones. Thus the first points to the tenet that all knowledge begins with experience. The second leads us to the doctrine that a necessary pre-condition for the advancement of knowledge is the determination of concepts by means of initially decomposing the complexity experienced, then achieving a careful composition and hence a determination of complex ideas out of the original materials. The principle of resolution, to be precise, is specifically connected with just one part of this doctrine's scope. That is, with the decomposition of the complexity experienced.

The *application* of the principle of resolution is slightly different in the present chapter from what it was in the preceding one. This is because, although in both of them there is decomposition of the complexity obtained in experience, in the previous chapter this complexity often consisted in the mixed modes obtained through 'custom' and 'common conversation', mixed modes which were therefore obscure because indetermined. In the present chapter the complexity consists in the mixed modes of Scripture. Although these mixed modes may initially appear obscure to the reader of the Bible, they are nevertheless taken by Locke to be determined. It is because of the fact that these ideas are held to be determined from the start that a somewhat different application of the principle of resolution is called for in this chapter.

This different application calls for the introduction of two further principles. These I shall call the *principle of coherence* and the *principle of comparison*. Both of these are operative in the attempt to come to an understanding of the Scriptures because of certain unique characteristics which the Scriptures are held by Locke to possess. An indication of the nature and function of these principles will be provided in a subsequent part of this chapter.

How, according to Locke, is man able to come to an understanding of Scripture? A clear answer can best be given if the question is subdivided into the following four: (i) Is reasoning for Locke an adequate means for coming to an understanding of God's will for man's life and therefore also of Scripture? (ii) What are some of the characteristics of Scripture which he takes to allow man to attain an understanding of it? (iii) How ought one to proceed in coming to an understanding of Scripture? (iv) What characteristics of Scripture does this methodological procedure imply? I shall deal with these questions, in the order in which they have been raised, in the four succeeding sections of this chapter. Consideration of the third and fourth of them will show that Locke's methodological principles help to determine what he takes to be the nature of Scripture, and that the empiricist principle, as well as the principle of resolution, are as indispensable in theology as they are in the construction of a political theory.

1. The adequacy of reason

The *XXXIX Articles of the Church of England,* a creed well know to Locke and his contemporaries,[3] contains a statement which is categorically opposed to Locke's view of man. The offending segment, quoted by Locke in full, is article XIII:

Works done before the grace of Christ, and the Inspiration of his Spirit, are not pleasing to God; forasmuch as they spring not of faith in Jesus Christ; neither do they make men meet to receive grace, or (as the school-authors say) deserve grace of congruity; yea rather, for that they are not done as God has willed and commanded them to be done, we doubt not but they have the nature of sin. (T397)

Some defenders of this creed (like Jonas Proast, Locke's fierce opponent in the toleration debate) held at the same time 'That

---

[3] This creed, as its preamble states, was 'agreed upon by the Archbishops and Bishops of both Provinces, and the whole Clergy, in the Convocation holden at London in the year 1562 for the avoiding of Diversities of Opinion and for the establishing of consent touching true religion'. It was 'republished' after the Restoration, with an Introduction by Charles II.

God denies his grace to none who seriously ask it'. Locke objects,

But how . . . will this stand with your thirteenth article? For if you mean by seriously, so as will make his seeking acceptable to God; that cannot be, because he is supposed yet to want grace, which alone can make it acceptable: and if his asking has the nature of sin, as in the article you do not doubt but that it has, can you expect that sinning should procure the grace of God? (T398)

This confusion of ideas bears witness to the fact that it is not 'the law of nature' which has 'delivered into his hands the XXXIX Articles' (T428). Not all a man does has 'the nature of sin'. Man, for Locke, can come to God without the help of special grace. This is because 'As men, we have God for our King, and are under the law of reason . . .' (R229). Since God made man 'a rational creature' man can be expected to live by 'that rule which was suitable to his nature', by 'the law of reason, or, as it is called, of nature'. Since 'God . . . commands what reason does', man can be expected to discover God's will for his life if he makes use of his natural faculties (R11).

It is, first, important to obtain a clear answer to the following questions. Is it Locke's position that human reason is able to provide a system of 'morality' which, if practised, allows man to lead a life pleasing to God? If the answer to this question is an affirmative one, further questions arise, namely: why then did God give man a *special* revelation in the Scriptures? And is man able to understand this special revelation through unaided reason? These questions ought to be answered at the outset. For if in Locke's later works there is genuine scepticism with respect to the efficacy of reason this would call for emendation of a good deal of what he wrote in the *Essay*, Book 4, chapters 17, 18, and 19 ('Of Reason', 'Of Faith and Reason', and 'Of Enthusiasm'). This in turn would call for an interpretation of the theological works different from the one I am about to present. Such a different interpretation would be called for especially if it turned out to be the case that man cannot come to know God's will without special revelation (an act of grace) and, more seriously, if man cannot attain knowledge of such a relevation without a special enlightenment from the Holy Spirit (a further act of grace). Laslett has asserted that in his later works Locke was 'led . . . into his attempt to supplement his rationalism and empiricism with revelation . . . because of the patent insufficiency of reason'.[4] In opposition to Laslett I shall show that Locke consistently maintains that there is no natural inability related to man's power of understanding which makes it impossible for him to know God and God's will for his life, whether through special revelation or apart from such a revelation.

That reason unassisted by revelation can come to knowledge of a way of life pleasing to God Locke makes clear regularly in the *Paraphrase*. 'The invisible things of God lie within the reach and discovery of Men's reasoning and understanding.' When men 'hold the truth in unrighteousness' (Romans 1:18) this means that 'they are not wholly without the truth, but yet do not follow what they have of it, but live contrary to the truth they do know, or neglect to know what they might' (P257–8). And when St. Paul writes about the Gentiles who 'keep the righteousness of the law' (Romans 2:26) he refers to Gentiles who 'keep the moral rectitudes of the law', where 'rectitude', says Locke, is used by St. Paul 'for all those precepts of the law, which contain in them any part of the natural and eternal rule of rectitude, which is made known to men, by the light of reason'. Thus 'the moral rule to all mankind' is 'laid within the discovery of their reason' (P267–8; see also P262, note *y*).

Without a special revelation, without grace, men could know the will of God for their lives. Without such a revelation they could know as well whether or not their actions conformed to the will of God. 'Mankind, without the positive law of God, knew, by the light of nature, that they transgressed the rule of their nature, reason, which dictated to them what they ought to do' (P294). And without such a special revelation 'God . . . by the light of reason, revealed to all mankind, who would make use of that light, that he was good and merciful', so that no one could 'miss to find also the way to reconciliation and forgiveness, when he had failed of his duty' (R133). Thus Locke takes it as beyond question 'That there were some among the heathen as innocent in their lives, and as far from enmity to God, as some among the Jews'; indeed, 'that many of them were . . . worshippers of the true God, if we could doubt it, is manifest out of the Acts of the Apostles' (P288). 'Worshippers of the true God' are such as know God's will and conform their lives to it.

---

[4] Laslett, in the Introduction to *Two Treatises of Government*, p. 101. In support of his position Laslett quotes a passage from the *Reasonableness*. I shall deal with this passage in what follows.

How then must we take a statement like the following, part of which is quoted by Laslett?

> . . . natural religion, in its full extent, was nowhere, that I know, taken care of, by the force of natural reason. It should seem, by the little that has hitherto been done in it, that it is too hard a task for unassisted reason to establish morality in all its parts, upon its true foundation, with a clear and convincing light. . . . Experience shows, that the knowledge of morality, by mere natural light, (how agreeable soever it be to it) makes but a slow progress, and little advance in the world. And the reason of it is not hard to be found in man's necessities, passions, vices, and mistaken interests; which turn their thoughts another way. . . . [Thus] it is plain, in fact, that human reason unassisted failed men in its great and proper business of morality. It never from un-questionable principles, by clear deductions, made out an entire body of 'the law of nature'. (R139–40.)

Laslett quotes only part of these statements, namely, that incor-porated in the last two sentences. Once this part is placed in its context, it becomes clear that what man lacks is not sufficient intellectual capacity, but reason assisted by a will impervious to 'necessities, passions, vices, and mistaken interests'.

If Locke had any sympathy for any part of the *XXXIX Articles*, it would be article X. Under the heading 'Of Free-Will' this article states:

> The condition of Man after the fall of Adam is such, that he cannot turn and prepare himself, by his own natural strength and good works, to faith, and calling upon God: Wherefore we have no power to do good works pleasant and acceptable to God, without the grace of God by Christ preventing us, that we may have a good will, and working with us, when we have that good will.

Even with this article Locke would not be in full sympathy. There would be some sympathy for the implicit separation of will and intellect; and for the location of the inability to please God in the corruption of man's will. But the sympathy would be limited. For man's will is not wholly corrupt, and the will of some has withstood the onslaughts of corruption very well indeed. It is, for Locke, true that:

> Though the works of nature, in every part of them, sufficiently evidence a Deity; yet the world made so little use of their reason, that they saw him not, where, even by the impressions of himself, he was easy to be

found. Sense and lust blinded their minds in some, and a careless inadvertency in others, and fearful apprehensions in most. . . .

However, not everyone of 'the world' was blinded by lust or carelessness or fear. For 'The rational and thinking part of mankind . . . when they sought after him, they found the one supreme, invisible God' (R135). Thus, 'because they might come to the knowledge of the true God, by the visible works of the creation . . . the Gentiles were without excuse, for turning from the true God to idolatry'. They were fully responsible for their 'revolt', and therefore fully responsible for their ensuing lack of understanding: it was a deliberate 'worship of false gods, whereby their hearts were darkened, so that they were without God in the world' (P250, 256).

It is therefore not a recognition of 'the patent insufficiency of reason' which, in his later works, led Locke to 'supplement his rationalism and empiricism with revelation'. The situation may be summed up as follows. Some, a small minority of men, were men of unperverted will and with leisure to use their reason to the utmost; they discovered God's will and ordered their lives in accordance with it. Others, though knowing some of God's will, rebelled and were given over to an 'unsearching mind'. And the 'illiterate bulk of mankind', having neither the leisure nor sufficiently developed tools to discover God's will, fell prey to the corrupting influence of those who, in rebellion, created their own gods. For 'fearful apprehensions in most . . . gave them up into the hands of their priests . . . [who] every where, to secure their empire . . . excluded reason from having any thing to do in religion' (R135).

It is especially for the sake of the illiterate bulk of mankind that the incarnation took place. For 'one coming from heaven in the power of God, in full and clear evidence and demonstration of miracles, giving plain and direct rules of morality' will be 'likelier to enlighten the bulk of mankind, and set them right in their duties, and bring them to do them' than any sage could 'by reasoning with them from general notions and principles of human reason' (R146). The incarnation introduces the notion of 'grace'. An indication of the role of the concept of grace in Locke's theological works will help to clarify the picture needed for the argument of the remainder of this chapter.

In the Old Testament God revealed 'things above reason', specifically, gave 'prophecies' and 'types' of the Messiah who was to come. These intelligible prophecies and types were sufficient grounds for both the discerning Jew and Gentile to recognize Jesus as sent from God. But these grounds were revealed grounds, and this revelation was a gift from God, was grace.[5]

'Knowledge of the Gospel', Locke writes, 'was not attainable by our natural parts, however they were improved by arts and philosophy, but wholly owing to revelation'. This is because the grounds for belief in the Gospel are grounds given by God, grounds which would not have been available to man unless God had given them. There were, therefore, 'two sorts of arguments, wherewith the apostle confirmed the Gospel'. 'The one was the revelations made concerning our Saviour' in the Old Testament, 'the other, miracles and miraculous gifts accompanying the first preachers of the Gospel'. Thus the faith of the early New Testament believers was 'built wholly on Divine revelation and miracles, whereby all human abilities were shut out' (P86). Faith, given that the grounds for it were the 'gift of God', is in this sense founded on 'grace' (P414). The believer of Locke's day had the same grounds for his faith, except that the miracles of Christ and his apostles were now a matter of well-attested record. Thus 'Faith is the gift of God. And we are not to use any other means to procure this gift to any one, but what God himself has prescribed' (T519). These means are: the diligent examination of both the grounds and of what was said by those of whom these grounds were given. For once the grounds had been examined and found to be well attested,

there needs no more, but to read the inspired books, to be instructed: all the duties of morality lie there clear, and plain, and easy to be understood. . . . The most elevated understandings cannot but submit to the authority of this doctrine as divine; which . . . hath not only the attestation of miracles, but reason to confirm it: since they delivered no precepts but such, as though reason of itself had not clearly made out, yet it could not but assent to, when thus discovered . . . (R147)

[5] There is a further use of 'grace' in Locke's works. It becomes relevant in the following context: whether, before the coming of Christ, the heathen discovered God's will in the law of nature through the natural light; or whether after Christ had come the Jew and Gentile knew God's will through Christ's teachings; in neither case were they able fully to conform their lives to God's will. Yet their attempt to conform was taken by God as sufficient to merit eternal bliss. The gift of heaven on the grounds of such partial success was a gift of grace. In view of my concerns in this chapter, we need take no further notice of this additional use of 'grace'.

Man therefore needs no special further help to come to an understanding of the Scriptures. This Locke maintains consistently. The only passage I know of which might throw doubt on this interpretation is in the *Paraphrase* when Locke writes that although St. Paul:

owns the doctrine of the Gospel, dictated by the Spirit of God, to be contained in the Scriptures of the Old Testament, and builds upon revelation, yet he everywhere teaches that it remained a secret there, not understood, till they were led into the hidden, evangelical meaning of those passages, by the coming of Jesus Christ, and by the assistance of the Spirit, in the times of the Messiah, and then published to the world by the preachers of the Gospel. (P85)

Even here, it seems reasonable to suppose that 'assistance of the Spirit' does not refer to the presence of an element which is added to or replaces reason. The 'assistance of the Spirit' merely refers to the additional information given in the words of Jesus and his apostles, additional information which dispelled the Old Testament mysteries, which were mysteries because the Old Testament merely *alluded* to the full 'evangelical meaning' of the New Testament. Once, through the words of Jesus and his apostles (that is, through this additional information—'assistance'—provided by the Spirit of God) the full doctrine had been presented, reason was fully capable of grasping its meaning.

If some through laziness or prejudice remained aloof from Christianity, the means to procure the gift of faith for them is: 'discoursing with men seriously and friendly about matters in religion'. Such discoursing, if it leads them to a diligent and unprejudiced examination, will make them 'knowing and sincere converts' (T433; see also T11). For 'there is enough recorded abundantly to convince any rational man, any one not wilfully blind' of the fact that Jesus is the Messiah; and acceptance of that fundamental proposition makes a man a Christian (R324).

The theological works thus uphold the doctrine of the *Essay*. There, Locke writes that 'Revelation is natural Reason enlarged by a new set of Discoveries communicated by GOD immediately, which Reason vouches the Truth of, by the Testimony and Proofs it gives, that they come from GOD' (4.19.4). The most fundamental 'discovery communicated by GOD' is that 'Jesus is the Messiah'. This proposition becomes acceptable to reason once it has found that Jesus 'answers' the Old Testament 'types' and 'prophecies', once it has found that Jesus was indeed sent from God through its examination of the record of the miracles Jesus performed. Miracles themselves, being 'above reason', are not in conflict with any of the clear dictates of reason. Hence, for Locke, there is no conflict between reason and faith. For 'Faith is nothing but a firm Assent of the Mind: which if it be regulated . . . cannot be afforded to any thing, but upon good Reason; and so cannot be opposite to it' (4.17.24). This relation between reason and faith is reiterated regularly in the theological works. One is not obliged to believe, in fact, one cannot believe, what one cannot understand (R355; T410). Even the teachings of Jesus, though he came with clear divine authority, are to be believed only 'as soon as he understands what it was he taught', and 'in the sense he understands it to be taught' (R408). That one can in fact believe these teachings is because the '. . . law of morality Jesus Christ hath given us in the New Testament' is 'conformable to that of reason' (R143).

Reason remains autonomous. It is each individual's reason which remains autonomous. Each must use his natural light to understand for himself. Since it is reason which makes each man properly human (R133), it is the individual which remains autonomous, also the individual as 'believer'. 'If I must believe for myself, it is unavoidable that I must understand for myself' (P22); 'persuasion, belief, or assurance of the true religion' always remains one's own (T562). And when, as a Christian, one conforms one's life to the will of God, it is a conformity to the law of reason. It is a conformity to a law which, whether attained through examination of 'the invisible things of God' which 'lie within the reach and discovery of man's reason', or through examination of the 'visible' revelation of God in Scripture, is obtained through a purely natural human faculty.

Man is able to understand Scripture through his natural power of reason. What, then, must he do to come to an understanding of Scripture? This question has two parts. The first concerns what he must do to himself, to the subject; the second is about what he must do with Scripture, the object to be understood. The second of these questions will be taken up in the third section of this chapter.

If 'men's necessities, passions, vices, and mistaken interests' turned 'their thoughts another way' so that 'morality' made 'little advance in the world' (R140), these same factors will prevent man from coming to understand Scripture. Hence Locke argues that whoever approaches Scripture must be free from preoccupations with daily pressing needs, must be calm and dispassionate, must lead a virtuous life, and must be disinterested or free from theological and philosophical preconceptions. It is the first of these requirements which is responsible for Locke's directing himself primarily to the leisured class of his society. For although the illiterate bulk of mankind is able to understand the basic principle of Christianity—'Jesus is the Messiah'—and thus can become a Christian, the constant pressures of daily life virtually prevent them from further examination. Even for becoming a Christian, for coming to an understanding of the basic proposition of the Christian religion, they are largely dependent on exhortation and arguments presented by those whose task it is to take care of their souls. Since there is a leisured class in the England of Locke's day, the first condition is met. Perhaps the chief vice of the man of leisure is laziness. Locke regularly admonishes against this vice of laziness. The examination of Scripture must be 'diligent' (R4); they must not 'stick through laziness' (T433); they ought not to be satisfied with 'one or two hasty readings; it must be repeated again and again, with a close attention' (P14). At least as important is disinterestedness, for it is the mistaken interests of philosophical or theological partisanship which leads to the all but dispassionate wranglings of the various factions.

To be disinterested, unbiased, or impartial, is for Locke to be free from blind adherence to church creeds, from rigid acceptance of systems of divinity, and from dogmatic attachment to any school of philosophy. Those who want to understand Scripture must free themselves from these because the first two act like the third: 'every one's philosophy regulates every one's interpretation of the word of God'. This 'regulation' consists in 'affixing ... to the terms of the sacred Scripture' notions which have been developed in the creeds, theological systems, and philosophies. Creeds are 'partial views, and adapted to what the occasion of that time, and the present circumstances they were then in, were thought to require' (P20). Contemporary creeds, and contemporary theological systems (which in the minds of their progenitors and their adherents, readily assume the status of creeds) are equally partial views. To the extent that they are partial the interpretation of Scripture will

be partial if we approach it through them. 'Partial', in this context,
means having words or phrases which though they occur in both
Scripture and the theological or philosophical system, refer to a
(set of) idea(s) in these systems different from the idea(s) referred
to by them in Scripture. Some prime examples of such words and
phrases are 'sin' (1.3.19), 'Adam's fall' (R4 ff.), 'death' (R6–7),
'soul', 'spirit', 'body' (P21). The writers of Scripture 'conformed'
'their expressions . . . to the ideas . . . which they had received
from revelation. . . . We shall, therefore, in vain go about to
interpret their words by the notions of our philosophy, and the
doctrines of men delivered in our schools' (P21). Scripture must
be understood through 'the plain direct meaning' of its 'words and
phrases: such as they may be supposed to have had in the mouths
of the speakers, who used them according to the language of that
time and country wherein they lived'. Since 'each one has been
bred up in' the confines of theological or philosophical positions
which gave a 'learned, artificial, and forced' (R5) meaning to
Scripture, to become impartial is a difficult task; much leisure and
diligence are required.[6]

We are all men, liable to errors, and infected with them; but have this
sure way to preserve ourselves, every one, from danger by them, if,
laying aside sloth, carelessness, prejudice, party, and reverence of men,
we betake ourselves, in earnest, to study the way of salvation, in those
holy writings, wherein God has revealed it from heaven . . . (P23)

To prepare oneself for the understanding of Scripture one must,
in fact, as far as philosophy and theology are concerned, become a
tabula rasa. We must, from Scripture's words, 'paint' its 'very
ideas and thoughts in our minds' (P21).

The outcome of this dual process will be twofold. First, a study
of the Old Testament will acquaint one with the prophecies about
and types of the promised Messiah, and a study of the Gospels will

---

[6] To overcome 'partiality' seems, then, to be equivalent to being able to
discern which opinions are held strictly because of the cultural epoch in which
one happens to live. Each historical period has its own 'Opinions in Fashion',
and one must be able to discern which are and which are not dictated by reason,
which are and which are not articulations of the 'law of nature'. Therefore
Abrams is quite right when, in a context different from that of theology, he
writes that for Locke '. . . men are rational to the extent that they master partiality'.
See Philip Abrams, *John Locke: Two Tracts on Government* (Cambridge, 1967),
p. 96 ff.

give a clear indication of the characteristics of Jesus. Comparison of the Old Testament promises and New Testament actuality will 'prove' Jesus 'to be the person promised, by a correspondence of his birth, life, sufferings, death, and resurrection to all those prophecies and types of him' (R353). An unbiased comparison will 'plainly' show that Jesus is the deliverer promised by God, and agreement with that proposition is sufficient to make one a Christian. Rejection of that proposition, after such an examination, is conscious and explicit rebellion against both God and reason. For although the statement 'Jesus is the Messiah' is neither a self-evident truth nor deduced from self-evident truths, it is a proposition obtained through a comparison of well-attested sources. The probability of its truth is sufficiently high for any rational being to be able to stake his eternal salvation on it.

Second, the law of nature rather than a theological or philosophical system tells man he ought to obey God and every one whose commission is attested to be from heaven. That Jesus has his commission from heaven is acknowledged in accepting the proposition that he is the Messiah. That the disciples and apostles have their commission from heaven as well is clear from the fact that they are commissioned by Jesus and that their preaching, like that of Jesus, is accompanied by miracles. Thus the words of Jesus, and the words of his disciples and apostles, become the words of God. It is through them that man is told how to order his life as a subject of the Kingdom of God. It is incumbent on the subject to act in accordance with the laws of the kingdom. Hence it is the Christian's duty, so far as his circumstances allow him, to come to as clear an understanding of the contents of the New Testament as he possibly can. That such an understanding is attainable is, in an important way, related to the fact that the writers of the New Testament were commissioned from heaven. This leads to the next subject for consideration.

2. Characteristics of Scripture

The answer to the question: 'What, according to Locke, is it about Scripture that allows man to attain a full understanding of it?' has a considerable number of distinct major elements in it. Of these, the following should be listed at this time:

(a) The authors of the various epistles were men inspired and

230 METHOD IN LOCKE'S THEOLOGICAL WORKS

hence devoid of partiality; their writings were disinterested, without hidden designs or secular interests. The authors of the four Gospels and the Acts, given the authority which the apostles had over them, were equally devoid of self-interest or party spirit, and hence reported events objectively. Scripture therefore is fully trustworthy; nothing but the truth is related in it. (b) Since Scripture's authors were competent men, their writings present the truth in orderly, masterfully managed arguments. (c) Scripture's truths are completely adequately expressed in propositions which contain determined ideas only. (d) In Scripture there is consistency in the use of words which stand for these ideas: the same word or phrase, or its synonym, is always applied to the same determined idea. (e) All the ideas signified by the words of Scripture are composed out of simple ideas which are commonly accessible in the experience of a corporeal rational being. This entails that these words can indeed excite in the reader's mind the ideas of which they are signs, and that therefore the way is open to attain an understanding of the propositions composed out of these words. (f) The notions of Scripture are mixed modes and, *qua* mixed modes, their nominal and real essences coincide. Thus, once a complete definition has been given of the particular notions which make up a certain proposition, the person who understands this definition (and sees how the notions are connected) can come to a complete understanding of the proposition in question. Such a definition consists in a complete enumeration of all the simple ideas which make up each of the proposition's notions, and since all these ideas are available in common sensible experience, any man can come to a complete understanding of Scripture's propositions. (g) Scripture is a uniform discourse of dependent reasonings. This implies that, in the attempt to understand Scripture, man must be guided by the criterion of logical coherence. An interpretation of any proposition which makes that proposition logically isolated with respect to whatever propositions form its context, is a misinterpretation. The correct interpretation of any given proposition will show this proposition to be either a premiss or a conclusion in a discourse of dependent reasonings.[7]

[7] At least some of the characteristics which Locke ascribes to the Scriptures are characteristics which today are ascribed to them by the leaders of the 'fundamentalist' movement. One may speculate and say that Locke believed the Scriptures to possess these characteristics for reasons similar to those which lead contemporary fundamentalists to ascribe them to the Scriptures. And

All of these characteristics are to be kept in mind when we attempt to answer the question: 'How, according to Locke, can man obtain knowledge of the contents of the Bible?' Except for the characteristic mentioned in (g) no more need be said about any of the others in order to be able to follow the argument in the next sections of this chapter. Elaboration on (g) is relevant at this point because it will make explicit an additional methodological principle which, according to Locke, needs to be implemented if one wants to attain an understanding of the Scriptures. This additional hermeneutical tool I shall call the *principle of coherence*.

Since Locke's theological works are not as familiar to twentieth-century readers as are the *Essay* and the *Second Treatise*, I shall provide an Appendix to this chapter. In this Appendix I shall elaborate on the characteristics mentioned in (a) to (f). This elaboration will reveal that what I have now claimed to be Locke's view

---

perhaps such a statement is not all that speculative. As we shall see, for Locke the Scriptures *must* possess these characteristics *if*, by means of the application of his philosophical and methodological principles, we are to be able to obtain knowledge of the contents of the Scriptures. Is it perhaps the case that contemporary fundamentalism has adopted part or all of Locke's methodological stance, and that this explains the similarity in their views on the nature of the Scriptures? In this context it is of interest to note that, in today's world, we find Locke's political principles acted out most consistently by those committed to an individualistic and capitalistic view of politics and economics. It may be no accident that some of the most successful politicians and businessmen who are committed to this kind of view in politics and economics are also among the staunchest defenders of the inerrancy of the Scriptures in terms of the view that the Scriptures present us with a body of indubitable truths presented in propositional form. And it may be no accident that some of the leading theologians of the fundamentalist movement are staunch supporters of free-enterprise capitalism. These facts are perhaps not surprising because it is the same methodological stance which gives rise to the politics of individualism, to the economics of inalienable and individual rights to the products of one's labour, and to the theology which takes the Scriptures to be a body of truths in propositional form. As James Barr has written: 'In modern revelational theologies, it is a stock argument against fundamentalism to say that it depends on a propositional view of revelation. . . . It is wrong to attribute a propositional view of revelation to fundamentalism as a whole. Such a view is found only in a limited stratum of the fundamentalist movement, the more intellectual leadership no doubt, but also a stratum which has its roots in the old Protestant scholasticism.' (James Barr, *Old and New in Interpretation*, London, 1966, p. 201.) Locke's *Paraphrase* may be fairly classified under the rubric of 'old Protestant scholasticism', or at least under that of 'old liberal Protestant scholasticism'. Locke's theology could, then, be one place in which at least the 'intellectual leadership' of the fundamentalism of the English-speaking world 'has its roots'.

of the nature of the Scriptures is in fact the view which emerges from a careful reading of his theological works.

The characteristic stated in (g) is that Scripture is a 'discourse of dependent reasonings'. Reason, 'our last Judge and Guide in every Thing', must judge whether a proposition for which revelation-status is claimed is indeed 'revealed from God'. Reason 'must . . . examine their Truth by something extrinsical to the Perswasions themselves' (4.19.14). Once we have this 'extrinsical' criterion it will also help us to 'proceed rationally' 'through all the dark passages of Scripture'. In the very first sentence of the *Reasonableness* Locke gives a clue to the nature of the criterion: 'The little satisfaction and consistency that is to be found in most of the systems of divinity I have met with, made me betake myself to the sole reading of the Scriptures . . . for the understanding of the Christian Religion' (R2). Does a 'system of divinity', or a 'religion', give the 'satisfaction' of understanding if we find systematic consistency or coherence in it? This question is answered in the affirmative in many places in both the *Reasonableness* and the *Paraphrase*.

We must, Locke writes, not focus our attention on 'scattered sentences in Scripture-language'; instead, we must 'look into the drift of the discourse, observe the coherence and connexion of the parts, and see how it is consistent with itself and other parts of Scripture' (R152). If we cannot take 'several texts, and make them consist together', to 'interpret one by the other', we shall not understand any of their propositions, and shall have to 'suspend . . . opinion' (R157). In one's reading of an epistle one must 'suppose that the epistle has but one business', but one 'drift and design', which is expressed through 'coherent reasonings, that carried a thread of argument and consistency all through them' (P14–15). And if, in commentaries on the writings of one of Scripture's authors, 'any sense is given to his words that disjoints his discourse, or deviates from his argument, and looks like a wandering thought', one can only conclude that the commentators are presenting a misinterpretation of the passage in question (P330). This is as close as Locke comes to an explicit formulation of 'consistency' or logical coherence as the criterion extrinsic to propositions which will determine whether or not these propositions belong to the body of revealed truths.

All the canonical books are accepted by Locke as revelation. This means that the coherence criterion, within the parameters of the canonical books, is not needed to determine which of its propositions do, and which do not, contain revealed truths. Instead, within the parameters of the canon, the coherence criterion functions as a principle of interpretation. Any interpretation of a proposition which deprived this proposition of logical coherence within the context of the discourse in which it appears—even though such an interpretation may present that proposition as quite intelligible on its own—is a misinterpretation.

This role of the coherence criterion is manifest in what Locke says both about the overall 'argument' of a book of Scripture, and of the details of the 'argument'. A Pauline epistle is a 'uniform discourse of dependent reasonings' (P7). Also, 'he that will read' these epistles 'as he ought, must observe . . . the coherence and connexion of the parts' (R152). 'St. Paul's argument' is 'coherent and easy to be understood, if it stood together as it should, and were not chopped in pieces, by a division into chapters' (P108). Even the letter to the Ephesians, written 'all as it were in a rapture, and in a style far above the plain, didactical way' (P392) is a 'discourse' which displays 'order', 'connexion', and 'coherence' (P410). When a set of texts (like 2 Corinthians 12:14 to 13:1) is coherent as a set but seems to disrupt the coherence of the epistle, it 'must be looked on as an incident discourse, that fell in occasionally, though tending to the same purpose with the rest' (P239). And when, in the New Testament, a text is quoted from the Old Testament which, in its Old Testament context, has a meaning which would disrupt the coherence of the New Testament argument if its Old Testament meaning were to be retained, the Old Testament meaning is to be disregarded. For 'it will be an ill rule for interpreting St. Paul', given that he is 'a close reasoner, that argues to the point', if we were to 'tie up his use of any text he brings out of the Old Testament, to that which is taken to be the meaning of it there' (P348).

This emphasis on coherence does not, of course, do away with the intelligibility of the various individual propositions contained in Scripture. It is true that 'the thread of St. Paul's discourse . . . is impossible to be understood without seeing the train of it', for 'without that view, it would be like a rope of gold-dust, all the parts would be excellent, and of value, but would seem heaped together, without order or connexion' (P409-10). Still, the parts are gold dust and remain of value; the propositions are truths, consisting of notions correctly related. But which truth a proposition contains is to be discovered through finding out which simple ideas are incorporated in each of the proposition's determined notions. Whether one has been succesful in discovering the relevant simple ideas and in combining them to form the relevant mixed modes, can be ascertained through seeing whether the various propositions, and the various mixed modes related in them, logically relate to one another.

3. Procedure for understanding Scripture

With respect to knowledge of physical objects Locke writes: 'Herein . . . is founded the reality of our Knowledge concerning Substances, that all our complex Ideas of them must be such, and such only, as are made up of such simple ones as have been discovered to co-exist in Nature', for 'Whatever simple Ideas have been found to co-exist in any Substance, these we may with confidence join together again, and so make abstract Ideas of Substances' (4.4.12). The foundation of the 'reality' of our knowledge of Scripture can be put in words which form a near-parallel to this statement. All the complex ideas which we make the meaning of the words which we read in the Bible must be such, and such only, as are made up of the simple or simpler ones we have actually discovered to coexist in Scripture. For whatever simple or simpler ideas we have found to coexist in Scripture, these we may with confidence join together again, and so recompose the mixed modes which are contained in the propositions of Scripture. The 'reality' of our knowledge, in both cases, is founded on something given in experience. The empiricist principle is therefore operative in both. In case of knowledge of physical objects, we must, through repeated exposure to them, discover which properties coexist in nature. In the case of Scripture we must discover which ideas coexist in it by means of a study of its propositions accessible to us through the printed words in the Bible. Thus, to be able to 'paint', from the Bible's printed words, Scripture's 'very ideas and thoughts in our minds' (P21), we need to expose ourselves repeatedly to these words: only 'by a frequent perusal of it, you are forced to see . . .' (P14); and 'the knowledge of Christianity . . . in the way I sought it, in its source, required . . . the more than once reading over the Evangelists and Acts, besides other parts of Scripture' (R179).

Repeated exposure to the 'object' is called for both in the attempt to gain knowledge of the physical world, and in the attempt to come to understand the subject-matter of any treatise of a considerable degree of complexity. But apart from this initial similarity, there is a profound salient difference in the case of one of these treatises, namely, Scripture. The outcome of exposure to physical objects does not lead to a full understanding of them, for their 'formal Constitution' or essence does not 'lay open to our Senses' (3.11.22). For a different reason, a similar statement can be made about the study of books other than the Bible. For whereas none of their authors can claim infallibility, some of their propositions will contain vague terms. To the extent that these terms are genuinely vague, they are unintelligible. Some of these authors' complex ideas will be indetermined. Moreover, it is human to fall into the trap of 'partiality'; hence 'partiality' can be expected in all of these works. None of these works can therefore be used to 'paint' their 'very ideas and thoughts in our minds'. Their complex ideas cannot be taken as the archetypes or models we keep in mind when, from the simple or simpler ideas we have discovered, we ourselves reconstruct these complex ideas and thus construct our own archetypes to coincide with those present in such a work's propositions. A treatise like Sir Robert Filmer's *Patriarcha* can serve merely as a point of departure for our own construction of, often if not generally, quite different complex ideas. Scripture's complex ideas are, however, determinate. Hence the end-product of recomposition of the relevant complex ideas in this instance are to be identical to the ones from which we started, the ones given in Scripture. Nevertheless, since it is a particular individual who (re)composes these complex ideas, there is the guarantee of coincidence of their real and nominal essences. Understanding of what Locke calls 'traditional revelation' is, then, the activity of thinking after them the thoughts God gave to the prophets and apostles. Because they were thoughts given by God, there is necessarily determinacy. Because it is also each individual who thinks these thoughts, their 'formal Constitution' does fully 'lay open to' his mind's inspection.[8]

Apart from the empiricist principle there are three distinct principles which need to be brought into play if one wants to attain an understanding of Scripture. Two of these, the principle

---

[8] On the possibility of making one's complex ideas 'conform to' the 'archetype' which is in someone else's mind, see, for example, the *Essay's* 3.6.44–5.

of resolution and the principle of coherence, are necessary to come to an understanding of any part of Scripture. The third, the principle of comparison, is necessary to come to an understanding of whatever complex idea cannot be made determined by means of a study of that idea's immediate context.

The principle of resolution is to be applied in all cases because resolution is always a necessary pre-condition for obtaining determined complex ideas. This principle presupposes the empiricist principle both because resolution is of what is given in the sensible experience of Scripture through reading of the Bible; and because determination of complex ideas is, ultimately, in terms of the single simple ideas which are obtained through resolution of the complexity of experience of commonly accessible sensible objects.

Since each person can only obtain the complex ideas of Scripture through his own activity of resolution and recomposition of its mixed modes, the principle of resolution plays a necessary role in coming to an understanding of Scripture. Locke's quarrel with the 'sticklers for orthodoxy' is founded especially on the denial of this principle in their practice: 'For we see generally that numbers of them exactly jump in a whole large collection of doctrines, consisting of abundance of particulars; as if their notions were, by one common stamp, printed on their minds, even to the last lineament' (R377).

Full application of the principle of resolution involves the division of a discourse into its component propositions, division of these propositions into their component complex ideas, and further division of whichever of these complex ideas appear obscure into their constituent simple or simpler ideas. Locke's practice in the *Paraphrase* indicates that not all three of these steps of resolution need always be taken. Sometimes a discourse is clear from the start, because the determined complex ideas which constitute its propositions, as well as the relation among these ideas and among these propositions, are understood as soon as the discourse is read. Sometimes, the meaning of a word which stands for a certain complex idea can be ascertained through the substitution of a synonym (as, e.g., in P289, note *e*). If there is no understanding of all the terms from the start, or if substitution of a synonym is not possible or not helpful, it usually seems to be sufficient to resolve the discourse into its propositions and divide the complex ideas which appear obscure into their simpler, though not into their simplest constituent ideas.

Since resolution is of ideas which appear to the reader as obscure or indetermined ideas, this means that the kind and (or) number of the simple or simpler constituent ideas is unknown. The question: 'Which are the relevant simple or simpler ideas which make up this concept?' may be answered in one of two ways. (a) Through application of the principle of coherence by means of the attempt to discover from the immediate context which simple or simpler constituent ideas are called for to make the proposition which contains the obscure complex idea(s) logically consistent within its immediate context. (b) If this does not lead to determination, there follows the application of the principle of comparison: one attempts to discover the relevant simple or simpler ideas from other, but related passages in the same and (or) in other discourses. This application of the principle of comparison is in turn to be followed by the use of the principle of coherence: the introduction of the thus determined idea ought to make for logical coherence if this idea is indeed the one used by the author. I shall deal with the second of these first.

Locke believes that the 'subject treated of' in Scripture is 'wholly new', that its 'doctrines' are 'perfectly removed from the notions that mankind were acquainted with', so that 'most of the important terms in it have quite another signification from what they have in other discourses' (P5). This brings into play the principle of comparison. Locke holds that without the use of this principle many of the doctrines of Scripture cannot be known with certainty. Of those doctrines which Locke believes he knows with certainty he writes: 'I took . . . my sense of those texts . . . from the Scripture itself, giving light to its own meaning, by one place compared with another' (R172); and: although 'We are all men, liable to errors, and infected with them', we 'have this sure way to preserve ourselves . . . if . . . we betake ourselves, in earnest, to the study of . . . those holy writings . . . comparing spiritual things with spiritual things' (P23). By means of the use of the comparison principle even the doctrine contained in St. Paul's epistle to the Ephesians, though he there wrote 'as it were in a rapture, and in a style far above the plain, didactical way', 'may be so clearly seen, and so perfectly comprehended, that there can hardly be a doubt left about it'. But this perfect comprehension is attainable only by the person who places this epistle firmly in the context of those written to the Colossians and Philippians, 'to any one who will examine them diligently, and carefully compare them together' (P392–3).

The comparison principle is so evidently right to Locke that he is quite ready to introduce it as part of a paraphrase. I Corinthians 3:2 ('I have fed you with milk, and not with meat; for hitherto ye were not able to bear it, neither yet now are ye able') he renders as: 'I could not apply myself to you, as to spiritual men, that could compare spiritual things with spiritual, one part of Scripture with another, and thereby understand the truths revealed by the Spirit of God . . .' (P94).

The principle of comparison functions in the context of the coherence principle. The coherence principle is always to be applied in the attempt to come to an understanding of Scripture. For given that Scripture is a set of discourses of dependent reasonings, the test of whether a complex idea has indeed, in the reader's mind, become a determined idea consists in seeing whether or not it makes the proposition in which it occurs a premiss or a conclusion or part of such a premiss or conclusion of a logically valid argument.[9]

Often the coherence principle alone directs us to the meaning of words and phrases which initially appear obscure. This principle is implemented whenever Locke refers us to the immediate context of such a word or phrase for its signification. For if the immediate context itself is 'plain' one often need not go beyond it to make 'comparisons' with more remote parts of Scripture. The immediate context then makes the 'sense of the words . . . necessary and visible' (e.g. P57, note *b*), or 'very easy and intelligible' (e.g. P166, note *u*), or 'plain' (e.g. P97, note *o*; P297, note *l*).[10] Sometimes

---

[9] Locke writes of the syllogism as 'the true touchstone of right arguing' (R385).

[10] Locke is very fond of the word 'plain'. Not counting words used synonymously, like 'manifest' and 'visible', it occurs over fifty times in the *Reasonableness* and over one hundred times in the *Paraphrase*. Comparison of the various passages in which it is used shows it to have the same technical meaning there as it has in the *Essay*'s phrase 'historical, plain method': its use gives notice of the fact that the interpretation or doctrine presented is taken not to be speculative, but is one easily *observed* in Scripture by anyone not blinded by prejudice. Some interesting occurrences of 'plain' are: in the *Reasonableness*, pp. 5, 13, 48, 50, 313, 356; in the *Paraphrase*, pp. 48, 54, 58, 65, 90, 97, 110, 117, 197, 202, 273, 281, 324, 332, 340, 352, 357, 366, 401, 421. One of the most interesting statements incorporating the word 'plain' in the *Reasonableness* is 'But when I had gone through the whole [of Scripture] and saw what a plain, simple, reasonable thing Christianity was . . .' (R188). In the *Paraphrase* this word helps make clear what Locke takes to be the meaning attached to 1 Corinthians 1:21, where 'the foolishness of preaching' becomes 'the plain, and, (as the world esteems it) foolish doctrine of the Gospel' (P82).

initial incoherence of a passage makes one suspect the presence of a mistranslation, as in Romans 5:18 where, once we substitute 'one offence' for 'the offence of one', the 'discourse, which at first sight seems somewhat obscure and perplexed', becomes one of 'harmony, beauty, and fulness' (P297).

The principles of coherence and comparison function jointly when even after several readings a passage appears obscure and hence incoherent. The meaning of the obscure words or phrases is then found by 'comparison'; the thus discovered meaning is given to the initially obscure words or phrases and the passage is tested for coherence. Several clear examples of this procedure can be found in the *Paraphrase*. One of these is Locke's commentary on 2 Corinthians 3:18 (P201–2). The context, 2 Corinthians 3:12 ff., suggests a comparison with certain passages from Exodus. Once the comparison has been made the phrases 'with open face, beholding, as in a glass, the glory of the Lord', obtain 'an easy sense', which they 'must signify here'. They 'must signify' this because once the meaning from Exodus is introduced into the Corinthian passage, the latter becomes coherent.

Sometimes, although the normal meaning of a word or phrase is quite easy to grasp, it makes the passage in which it occurs difficult to understand or even incoherent. One then studies the passage and its immediate context to see which doctrine is suggested. Once one gets some clues to the doctrine suggested, one compares this passage with places in Scripture where this particular doctrine is more explicitly stated, in order to find out to which part of the doctrine the words or phrases in question give expression. If one can compare the obscure passage with several places in Scripture, it should be possible to fix quite adequately the meaning of the words or phrases which gave rise to the obscurity. The meaning thus determined is then substituted for the normal meaning of the words or phrases in question and if such substitution makes the passage coherent, the substituted meaning is accepted as the one intended by the author. One place where this process may be observed very clearly is in Locke's commentary on Ephesians 1:10. There, the literal meaning of a Greek word, according to Locke, 'cannot possibly be the meaning of this word here'. Locke then writes that 'we must search for the meaning which St. Paul gives it here in the doctrine of the Gospel, and not in the propriety of the Greek'. An extensive comparison then follows with passages in over half a dozen other books of the New Testament, and this comparison determines the meaning of the word (P400–1).

4. Methodology and the nature of Scripture

The most important conclusions to be drawn at this point are that, for Locke, reason's procedure in its attempt to come to an understanding of Scripture involves as a necessary step the process of resolution, and that this process of resolution presupposes that the object to be resolved ultimately is made up of discrete, epistemically atomic units. The correctness of the second of these conclusions is corroborated by the fact that, for Locke, his principle of comparison can function as a principle of interpretation. Moreover, this conclusion in no way conflicts with the use of his principle of coherence as a principle of interpretation.

The use of Locke's principle of comparison itself presupposes that what is to be compared are discrete, epistemically atomic items or, more usually, clusters of such discrete, epistemically atomic items. For the possibility of obtaining the meaning of words and phrases through comparison presupposes that such words or phrases stand for ideas which have an unvarying, constant composition; that their meaning is not context-dependent in the sense that different contexts would make for different meanings i.e. different sets of ideas.[11] This can be easily seen once it is recognized that the principle of comparison involves finding out the meaning of a word or phrase which stands for a complex idea which is known to be determinate but of which the precise composition is not known, through comparison with an equivalent word or phrase which stands for a complex idea which is known to be determinate and of which the precise composition is known. Knowledge of any complex idea as determined presupposes knowledge of invariable simple, epistemically atomic ideas.

In several ways the use of Locke's principle of comparison is analogous to a scientist's use of experiment. If, in classical chemis-

---

[11] That different contexts do not alter the nature or number of the ideas contained in the 'notions' of Scripture is a condition which also holds for all abstract ideas in all general knowledge. About mathematics, for example, we read: 'If then the Perception that the same Ideas will eternally have the same Habitudes and Relations be not a sufficient ground of Knowledge, there could be no knowledge of general Propositions in Mathematicks, for no mathematical Demonstration would be any other than particular' (4.1.9).

try, a chemist is confronted with a reaction between compounds and is puzzled because he does not know what, precisely, is taking place, the first task is to determine the nature of whichever of the reacting compounds is unknown to him. If we suppose that there are two compounds in the reaction, and that the nature of one of these is unknown, its nature can be discovered by introducing that compound into a context where it can react with other compounds. The unknown compound will cause one reaction in a base and, in the same base, will always cause the same reaction; and it will react differently in different bases. It will behave differently in an acid, and differently in different acids. If the composition of the acids and bases is known, observation of the unknown compound's different modes of behaviour in its different contexts gives various clues to the composition of the compound. After a number of experiments, the scientist will be able to determine the nature of the compound, that is, he will know enough about the compound to write down its chemical composition or to name it accurately.[12] The use of Locke's principle of comparison is analogous to this scientist's use of experiment in that, for example, for both the scientist and the interpreter of Scripture there is the presupposition of a constant unvariable nature of the compound—in the one case the constant presence of certain elements in a definite proportion, in the other case the constant presence of a certain number of simple ideas in a definite relation.

Once the scientist has determined the compound's chemical composition, the reaction originally observed is no longer puzzling. He can now confirm his findings by reintroducing the compound into its original context and finding the mystery dispelled. This final experiment is analogous to Locke's use of the principle of coherence after first having implemented the principle of comparison. Thus, speaking of Scripture as ultimately made up of discrete, epistemically atomic, items does not conflict with the use of Locke's principle of coherence, but the application of this principle itself presupposes the existence of such atomic items. The latter point can be made in a different way, taking as point of departure Locke's own words.

As 'preface' to the *Paraphrase* Locke wrote "An Essay for the

---

[12] Of course, 'to write down its chemical composition or to name it accurately' would, for Locke, give us no more than a nominal definition. But this point of difference in no way invalidates the comparison I am making.

Understanding of St. Paul's Epistles, by consulting St. Paul himself." In this (P7 ff.) he argues that one of the major causes 'that keep us from an easy and assured discovery of St. Paul's sense' is the standard division of the epistles into chapters and verses. These 'partitions' make the epistles into 'parcels' and 'scraps' and make it difficult to see their inner 'connexion and consistency'. The result is 'Scripture crumbled into verses, which quickly turn into independent aphorisms'. This standard partitioning is one of the chief causes of the proliferation of 'sects', for one 'need but be furnished with verses of sacred Scripture, containing words and expressions that are but flexible (as all general obscure and doubtful ones are), and his system, that has appropriated them to the orthodoxy of his church, makes them immediately strong and irrefragable arguments for his opinion'. In the middle of this discussion Locke writes:

I crave leave to set down a saying of the learned and judicious Mr. Seldon: 'In interpreting the Scripture', says he, 'many do as if a man should see one have ten pounds, which he reckoned by 1, 2, 3, 4, 5, 6, 7, 8, 9, 10, meaning four was but four units, and five five units, etc. and that he had in all but ten pounds: the other that sees him, takes not the figures together as he doth, but picks here and there; and thereupon reports that he had five pounds in one bag, and six pounds in another bag, and nine pounds in another bag, etc. when as, in truth, he has but ten pounds in all. So we pick out a text here and there, to make it serve our turn; whereas if we take it altogether, and consider what went before, and what followed after, we should find it meant no such thing.'

At least something very like the principle of coherence is implied in this passage, for one will not grasp the correct meaning of 'six pounds' unless 'we take it altogether, and consider what went before, and what followed after'. On the other hand, neither can one understand the meaning of 'six pounds' unless one understands what is meant by 'one' or 'unity', the single simple (atomic) idea needed to generate all the simple modes of arithmetic.

    The relevance of this example to the understanding of Scripture is clear. Because each text or proposition of an epistle is like a number in a series of numbers, it cannot be understood simply in terms of the words which it contains; one gets at its real meaning only in the context of the total discourse or in the context of a number of such discourses. Application of the coherence principle is therefore essential. On the other hand, because a text is like a number in a series of numbers, the meaning of each text is to be found in the words related in that text, and the meaning of these words is to be found (with or without the use of the principle of comparison) in the ideas they signify; the meaning of these complex ideas, in turn, is to be ascertained in terms of the single simple ideas out of which they are composed. The latter activities are applications of the principle of resolution.

A necessary condition for understanding a text is, therefore, resolution of what is complex into what is simple and, in the end, epistemically atomic. The coherence principle plays its role only after out of the simple ideas a complex idea has been reconstituted.

The question which has guided the discussion throughout this chapter is: how, according to Locke, is man able to come to an understanding of Scripture? This question called for an answer to two further questions, namely, what does Locke take to be the nature of the object (Scripture) which reason attempts to understand? and what is the nature of the process of reasoning, of the manner in which the object comes to be understood? In Chapter VI it has been argued that the principle of resolution together with the principle of composition express the essence of reasoning. These principles are methodological principles. Their application to whatever is to be understood presupposes that the object is susceptible to the application of these methodological principles. This entails that the object is presupposed to have certain characteristics, particularly, characteristics which make it susceptible to resolution into epistemically atomic items. The application of these principles therefore results in a determination of the object to be known.

Locke accepts Scripture as a set of discourses which contain nothing but truths. These discourses consist of logically related propositions containing determined ideas composed of simple ideas obtainable through common experience. Since Scripture is taken to be information given by God for the benefit of man, it contains nothing but truths, and nothing but truths accessible to man. Acceptance of these two elements as characteristics of Scripture leads Locke to believe that man can understand Scripture through his natural process of reasoning. Such reasoning necessarily involves resolution. Resolution presupposes an object resolvable into simple ideas. Determinate mixed modes are such objects .Therefore Locke holds that the 'truths of Scripture' are presented to man in the form of propositions which contain determinate mixed modes. This aspect of the nature of Scripture is one it is presupposed to possess because of what Locke takes to be part of the essence of reasoning. Scripture is supposed to possess this characteristic because it is presupposed that it can be understood by means of the application of the methodological principle of resolution, because it is presupposed that it is susceptible to resolution into epistemically atomic items. These epistemically atomic items are Locke's simple ideas.

Simple ideas are abstract concepts which are held to be knowable in isolation from any other concepts. The basic question about the possibility of such knowledge is as relevant to Locke's hermeneutics and to his views on the nature of the Scriptures, as it was to his political theory presented in the *Second Treatise*, or to the epistemological aspects of the *Essay*. This basic question is therefore as relevant to any of Locke's major writings as it is to those of Descartes.

APPENDIX

In this Appendix I shall show that Locke does in fact ascribe to Scripture each of the characteristics which I enumerated under (a) to (f) at the beginning of the second section of this chapter. Given Locke's emphasis, and given the material he provided in terms of paraphrases of and notes on the epistles of St. Paul, 'Scripture' now practically refers only to the writings of the New Testament, and particularly to the Pauline epistles.

(a) Christ, in sending St. Paul as a preacher, 'did not so much as convey his apostolic power to him by the ministry or intervention of any man'; instead, St. Paul's 'commission and instructions were all entirely from God, and Christ himself, by immediate revelation' (P29; see also P15). His 'expressions were confirmed to the ideas and notions . . . received from revelation, or were consequent from it' (P21). Therefore, and since he 'made no use of any human science', of 'philosophical speculations', or of 'ornaments of human learning' (P85), his speaking and writing is devoid of partiality. His was a 'clear, plain, disinterested preaching of the Gospel', a preaching 'without any hidden design, or the least mixture of any concealed, secular interest' (202–3).

Not all the writings of the New Testament are thus inspired. Some, like St. Luke's Gospel, merely report Jesus's words and deeds, and some, like St. Luke's Acts, merely report the sayings and doings of various apostles. Yet,

The credit and authority our Saviour and his apostles had over the minds of men, by the miracles they did, tempted them not to mix (as we find in that of all the sects and philosophers, and other religions) any conceits, any wrong rules, any thing tending to their own by-interest, or that of a party, in their morality. No tang of prepossession, or fancy; no footsteps of pride, or vanity; no touch of ostentation or ambition; appears to have a hand in it. It is all pure, all sincere; nothing too much, nothing wanting; but such a complete rule of life, as the wisest men must acknowledge tends entirely to the good of mankind, and that all would be happy, if all would practice it. (R147)

Whether it is Scripture from the pens of those directly inspired, or from the pens of those who were close associates of Jesus or his apostles, it is, in its entirety, fully trustworthy. It is all infallibly true information from God, which provides man with the materials necessary for a complete rule of life pleasing to God.

(b) Infallibly true writings have, however, not escaped the charge of being difficult to understand. Even St. Peter wrote about the Pauline epistles that they contained 'some things . . . hard to understand, which the ignorant and unstable twist to their own destruction' (2 Peter 3:16). But Locke maintains that wherever, in St. Paul's 'commentators and interpreters, any sense is given to his words that disjoints his discourse, or deviates from his argument, and looks like a wandering thought', it is the commentator's 'impertinence' (P330). St. Paul may not be easy to understand for the partial or over-hasty interpreter, but he is in no way obscure to 'Whosoever hath with care looked into St. Paul's writings' (P348). This Locke maintains throughout his commentary on the Pauline epistles. St. Paul wrote with 'method and order', with 'clearness of conception', with 'pertinency in discourse' (P15); he exhibits 'a very skilful management of the argumentative part' of his epistles (P61); he supports the points he makes with 'very good arguments' (P80); he 'does not . . . contradict his own reasoning' (P154), but 'steadily and skilfully he pursues his design' (310). When St. Paul 'gave his thoughts utterance upon any point . . . it is plain, it was a matter he was perfectly master of: he fully possessed the entire revelation he had received from God; had thoroughly digested it; all the parts were formed together in his mind, into one well-contracted harmonious body' (P19). Thus even the most difficult books of Scripture contain nothing but truth expounded by means of competent argumentation.

(c) In the preceding chapter we have seen that in the *Essay*'s 'Epistle to the Reader' Locke writes that 'The greatest part of the Questions and Controversies that perplex Mankind', are the result of 'the doubtful and uncertain uses of Words, or (which is the same) indetermined Ideas, which they are made to stand for'. A condition which must be met if one's discourse is to be clear is that the ideas in it be 'determined'.

And 'If men had such determined Ideas in their enquiries and discourses, they would both discern how far their own enquiries and discourses went, and avoid the greatest part of the Disputes and Wranglings they have with others.'

The major reason why in discourses on religion there is 'the greatest difficulty' is that the doctrines contained in Scripture are 'so perfectly remote from the notions that mankind were acquainted with, that most of the important terms in it have quite another signification from what they have in other discourses' (P5). Men are not at all agreed on the signification of the mixed modes central to such discourses. Words like 'faith', 'grace', 'religion', 'church', have 'for the most part but a very loose and undetermined, and consequently obscure and confused signification' (3.9.9).

This charge, left unsubstantiated in the *Essay*, is given ample grounds when Locke examines the arguments of Proast and Edwards, his protagonists in *Toleration* and *Reasonableness*, respectively. Time and again, Locke points out that Proast speaks 'indefinitely' and seldom leaves himself 'accountable for any propositions of a clear, determined sense' (T193); that he uses 'fair words, of indefinite signification, to say that which amounts to nothing' (T306; see also T423 and T545). And Locke challenges Edwards to present his 'evangelical truths' 'reduced to certain propositions' in the form of a 'creed in clear and distinct propositions' (e.g. R223).

Locke's injunction to commentators on and interpreters of Scripture is to 'consider things, and not words. For the party of God and souls needs not any help from obscurity or uncertainty of general and equivocal terms, but may be spoke out clearly and distinctly' (T541-2). Considering 'things' is, according to Locke, precisely what the New Testament authors did. It has already been pointed out that their 'ideas and notions' were received from revelation or were consequent from it. To speak of an idea received directly from revelation as indetermined would place the cause of such indeterminacy in God; and given that 'indeterminacy' comes about through carelessness or lack of knowledge, this is a contradiction in terms. Furthermore, when the apostles, in their writings, drew consequences from the immediately revealed ideas, they still wrote 'nothing but truths'; and this presupposes that their ideas were determinate also in the consequences they drew from the truths revealed to them.

One fundamental difference between a commentary on Scripture and Scripture itself is, then, that the latter is to be trusted absolutely and in all respects; not only were there nothing but truths in the minds of those who wrote it, but these truths were given a completely adequate expression in propositions which contain nothing but determined ideas. This characteristic of Scripture places it in a class by itself, and must be seen to be of prime importance as an element in the answer to the question of how man can come to an understanding of Scripture.

(d) Should a discourse have nothing but determined ideas it cannot give rise to 'disputes and wranglings' (*Essay*, 'Epistle', p. 14; see also T423), if only the following conditions are met: that there be consistency in the use of the words that stand for these ideas, and that the discourse be read without partiality and with the necessary care. Scripture, according to Locke, meets the first of these conditions.

Understanding of Scripture is to be attained through understanding the propositions contained in Scripture, and understanding of propositions is through the understanding of the words joined together in these propositions. When reason judges whether a proposition is indeed one belonging to the body of revealed propositions, it must first judge of the 'signification of the Words, wherein it is delivered' (4.18.8). In the *Essay* it sometimes looks as if Locke ascribes to the language of Scripture the same weaknesses which are inherent in the language of all human writing. Especially relevant is 3.9.22–3;

. . . ancient Writings, which though of great concernment to us to be understood, are liable to the unavoidable difficulties of Speech, which, (if we except the Names of simple Ideas, and some very obvious Things) is not capable, without a constant defining the terms, of conveying the sense and intention of the Speaker, without any manner of doubt and uncertainty, to the Hearer. . . . The Volumes of Interpreters, and Commentators on the Old and New Testament, are but too manifest proofs of this. Though every thing said in the Text be infallibly true, yet the Reader may be, nay cannot chuse but be very fallible in the understanding of it. Nor is it to be wondred, that the Will of God, when clothed in Words, should be liable to that doubt and uncertainty, which unavoidably attends that sort of Conveyance. . . . revealed Truths, which are conveyed to us by Books and Languages, are liable to the common and natural obscurities and difficulties incident to Words . . .

It is especially the last two sentences quoted that seem to place the cause of a fallible understanding of Scripture in Scripture. However, consideration of their context changes this picture. For 'every thing said in the Text' is 'infallibly true'. It would call for a strange interpretation of 'saying' and of 'Text' to make this statement refer to sets of related ideas which had not yet been given names (even though Locke, of course, believes it quite possible to have such unnamed sets of ideas). Furthermore, 'without a constant defining of Terms' there remains doubt and uncertainty whether the reader has fully grasped the writer's meaning. This does not so much intimate that 'the Terms' are not susceptible of definition, but rather, since the reader's uncertainty remains, that the reader is not capable of constantly making the relevant definitions. The 'common and natural obscurities and difficulties incident to Words' is, thus, in this case, on the reader's side. This allows room for the assertion that 'every thing said in the Text' is 'infallibly true'.

Is it likely that Locke intends us to read these passages as stating that all writings and interpretations, except the writings of the authors of Scripture, are fallible because of natural obscurities and difficulties incident to words? An affirmative answer is supported by statements he makes about his own writings as compared with the Scriptures. For example: 'I am far from pretending infallibility, in the sense I have anywhere given in my paraphrase, or notes: that would be to erect myself into an apostle; a presumption of the highest nature in any one, that cannot confirm what he says by miracles' (P22). When therefore Locke writes about St. Paul that 'his thoughts were all of a piece in all his epistles, his notions were at all times uniform, and constantly the same, though his expressions very various. In them he seems to take great liberty', there is no accusation of carelessness in the latter part of this statement. To use 'very various' expressions for constant notions is a help to the reader. It means that St. Paul regularly uses synonyms to assist the reader to grasp his meaning. The sentences following the material just quoted support this interpretation:

This at least is certain, that no one seems less tied up to a form of words. If then, having . . . got into the sense of the several epistles, we will but compare what he says, in the places where he treats of the same subject, we can hardly be mistaken in his sense, nor doubt what it was that he believed and taught. (P19)

The qualification of 'hardly' remains; but that is due to the reader rather than to what is read. St. Paul, for Locke, is as much a master of language as he is of argumentation.

It is this consistency in the use of words and phrases, a consistency manifesting itself in the constant application of the same word or phrase, or their synonyms, to the same determined ideas which allows for the kind of comparison of various parts of Scripture which leads to the interpretation of the words of Scripture by the notions which were in the writers' minds.

(e) To understand Scripture is to understand the propositions in it. But:

a man cannot possibly give his assent to any affirmation or negation, unless he understands the terms as they are joined in that proposition, and has a conception of the thing affirmed or denied, and also a conception of the thing, concerning which it is affirmed or denied, as they are there put together. (R239–40)

Words or names are 'external sensible Signs' of 'invisible Ideas' (3.2.1). One ought only to name that which one knows; in that case

'Words are the Marks of . . . the Ideas of the Speaker' (3.2.2). Speaking or writing presupposes that the words one uses are 'Marks of the Ideas in the Mind also of other Men. . . . For else they should talk in vain, and could not be understood' (3.2.4). Speech therefore presupposes that a word 'excite in the Hearer, the same Idea which it stands for in the Mind of the Speaker' (3.9.4). Hence words are unintelligible to the hearer if they stand for ideas which the hearer does not possess. It is impossible to remove such unintelligiblity if these words stand for 'any simple Ideas, which another has not organs or Faculties to attain' (3.9.5), or if the hearer is denied exposure to the objects from which the speaker obtained his simple ideas. In such a case communication is an absolute impossibility.

Names of complex ideas can be defined. Their definition consists in enumerating all the simple ideas which make up the complex idea. Such definition presupposes 'that none of the terms of the Definition stand for any such simple Ideas, which he to whom the Explication is made, has never yet had in his thoughts' (3.4.12).

Since simple ideas can be obtained only from the impressions which objects make on our minds (2.22.2), 'Words being Sounds, can produce in us no other simple Ideas, than of those very Sounds; nor excite any in us, but by that voluntary connexion, which is known to be between them, and those simple Ideas, which common Use has made them Signs of' (3.4.11). Therefore, 'The Names of simple Ideas are not capable of any definitions' in the way the names of complex ideas are. This is because 'the several Terms of a Definition, signifying several Ideas, they can altogether by no means represent an Idea, which has no Composition at all' (3.4.4,7). When the name of a simple idea is not understood there are only the following ways of 'exciting' the idea in the hearer's mind: (a) the use of a synonymous word; (b) 'naming the Subject, wherein that simple Idea is to be found' (e.g. 'Feuillemorte . . . is the Colour of wither'd Leaves falling in Autumn'); (c) 'by presenting to his Senses that Subject, which may produce it in his Mind, and make him actually have the Idea, that Word stands for' (3.11.14).

All speaking or writing that can be understood by the hearer or reader presupposes 'common sensible ideas' (3.1.5), shared experience or at least commonly accessible objects of experience. It presupposes the use of only such complex ideas as were constructed out of simple(r) ideas accessible in normal experience to any rational corporeal being.

Therefore no man, not even a man:

inspired by GOD, can by any Revelation communicate to others any new simple Ideas which they had not before from Sensation or Reflexion. For whatsoever Impressions he himself may have from the immediate hand of GOD, this Revelation, if it be of new simple Ideas, cannot be conveyed to another, either by Words, or any other signs. (4.18.3)

There are several indications both in the *Essay* and in the theological works that Locke believed the Scriptures contained no such new simple ideas; that, therefore, in terms of idea-content, all the propositions in the Scriptures can be fully understood. First, there are his frequent remarks about the capacity of the ordinary person, the person not contaminated by the scholars' commentaries, to understand the texts of Scripture without difficulty (e.g. 3.10.12). Second, Locke often states that obscurity, even incomprehensibility, of Scripture passages is the result of scholars' affection. For example, he believes that promoters of sects in both philosophy and religion often introduce words 'less clear and distinct in their signification, than naturally they need be', 'affecting something singular, and out of the way of common apprehensions' (3.10.1,2). Third, Locke writes that 'the doctrine proposed in the Reasonableness of Christianity' was 'borrowed . . . only from the writers of the four Gospels and the Acts' (R420). Since this 'doctrine' contains a statement both of how a man becomes a Christian, and of how a Christian ought to live in obedience to the revealed word of God in Scripture; and since, in the *Reasonableness*, Locke takes himself not to be 'affecting something singular, and out of the way of common apprehensions'; he can therefore conclude that at least those parts of Scripture from which this doctrine was 'borrowed' contain only such complex ideas as were formed out of simple ideas available to any rational being through common experience. Fourth, in order to come to an understanding of the most difficult part of Scripture, of the Pauline epistles, the reader must, says Locke, 'represent to himself the notions St. Paul . . . had in his mind' when he wrote these epistles. We can succeed in understanding St. Paul when 'from his words' we 'paint his very ideas and thoughts in our minds' (P21). Again, this makes sense only if it is presupposed that all the simple ideas incorporated in St. Paul's notions are commonly attainable.

(f) Although there are no new simple ideas in Scripture, yet 'the New Testament is a book written in a language peculiar to itself'. This is because 'the subject treated of' in it is 'wholly new', and 'the doctrines contained in it' are 'perfectly remote from the notions that mankind were acquainted with' so that 'most of the important terms in it have quite another signification from what they have in other discourses' (P5).

Locke often speaks of Scripture's 'notions', or of the 'notions' in St. Paul's mind. The use of the term 'notion' implies an important doctrine. Locke writes that '. . . in mixed Modes, at least the most considerable parts of them, which are moral Beings, we consider the original Patterns, as being in the Mind', and it is for this reason that 'these Essences of the Species of mixed Modes, are by a more particular Name called Notions; as by a peculiar Right, appertaining to the Understanding' (3.5.12; also, see 2.22.2). The 'original pattern' in the mind is that peculiar combination of simple ideas which the mind has put together arbitrarily to form the new unity. The simple ideas were in the mind, the mind put them together, and the result of this activity is the unified (new) mode (2.22.5). Modes, or notions, are then 'the Creatures of the Understanding, rather than the Works of Nature'; and 'their Names lead our Thoughts to the Mind, and no farther', that is, 'our Thoughts terminate in the abstract Ideas . . . and . . . not farther' (3.5.12). Given that, in simple ideas, the real and nominal essences coincide, and given that the mind itself makes its own modes so that also their names signify real essences, it follows that once a complete definition is given of modes or notions, there is nothing which has escaped the knowledge of the person who understands the definition (cf. *Essay*, Book 3, Chapters 4, 5).

Scripture is considered by Locke to be a 'moral' discourse of a peculiar nature. It is peculiar because it differs from all other writings in that the writers' 'expressions were conformed to the ideas and notions which they had received from revelation, or were consequent from it' (P21). The notions of Scripture are therefore the work of God's understanding, or are 'consequent from' it. God's notions are necessarily determined notions. And since God has put together simple ideas commonly obtainable by man there is, in principle, nothing in the doctrines of Scripture which is not accessible to the human mind. Although Scripture is written in a language peculiar to itself, careful decomposition and recomposition of its mixed modes will lead to full understanding of the 'doctrine . . . taught by the apostles', of the doctrine 'that tends wholly to the setting up of the kingdom of Jesus Christ in this world, and the salvation of men's souls' (P21). For the careful reader the names of Scripture's mixed modes lead him, through the minds of the apostles, to the mind of God. Thus, through tradition (the notions of the apostles written down and preserved as the canonical books) every man has access to revelation (to the mind of God). For that reason Locke can call Scripture 'traditional revelation'.

EPILOGUE

In the seventeenth century influential thinkers began to take up a common methodological stance with respect to any matter on which they believed man could attain knowledge. This stance I have discussed in terms of the method of resolution and composition. 'Resolution' and 'composition' name the methodological principles of which Descartes writes in the *Discourse on Method*. He refers to the first of these when he writes that one must 'divide up each of the difficulties . . . into as many parts as possible'. Resolution is, thus, the process of division of complexity into parts. It is a process which is to end in the obtaining of the relevant simpler or simplest items which form the starting-points for construction of intelligible complexity. This construction is to be guided by the principle of composition. Descartes refers to this principle in the injunction that one must 'carry on' one's 'reflections in due order, commencing with objects that were the most simple and easy to understand, in order to rise little by little, or by degrees, to knowledge of the most complex'. Through an examination of important works by Descartes and Locke it has become clear that at least these two thinkers shared this stance. I have shown that this methodology is bound up with a specific view of reason and of man. I have also explained how this method of approach structures their theory about subject-matter, and how it presupposes a particular nature of the object to be known or how it imposes such a nature on the object. Now that we have before us the picture I wanted to present, I should like to use these last pages to touch up some of its details. I shall also draw a few additional lines to create a clearer perspective.

1

I have argued, with respect to both Descartes and Locke, that the method of resolution and composition imposes a certain nature on the object to be known—on, for example, the object of the geometrician's interest as illustrated in Descartes' work, or on that of the political theorist in the writings of Locke. But it is also important to stress that it is not the *entire* nature of the object which is thus determined by methodological considerations. It is some, not all of the more prominent characteristics which come to be assigned to the object as the result of the methodology through which the object is approached. This point can be illustrated in terms of parts of the argument in any one of the last six chapters. Thus it can be illustrated equally well with respect to Descartes in terms of geometry or metaphysics, and with respect to Locke in terms of politics or theology. Since we have dealt with Locke's theology in the immediately preceding pages, I shall use that topic to illustrate my claim.

I have argued that Scripture, the object of the theologian's interest, is presupposed to possess certain characteristics because of what Locke takes to be part of the nature of reasoning. For he assumes that the application of the methodological principle of resolution is a necessary step in the process of coming to an understanding of the Bible's contents. Some of the features which Locke ascribes to Scripture are ones which were also ascribed to it prior to Locke's time. That the authors of the various books of the Bible were men 'inspired from God', men without 'secular interests' *qua* authors of Scripture and therefore men who 'wrote nothing but the truth', are tenets which were generally held throughout the history of Christianity up to Locke's time. Unless one were to argue that Locke's hermeneutical principles were also those of the early and medieval church—a conclusion for which it would be difficult to find plausible support—it cannot be said that the view of Scripture as revealed truth is one ascribed to this object for purely methodological reasons. Of course, a characteristic like this is one which Locke needs if the application of his hermeneutical principles is to lead to an understanding of God's will for the conduct of man's life. For unless the authors of Scripture were 'inspired' and 'disinterested' one cannot both pattern one's archetypes on those which these authors had in mind, and at the same time claim with any degree of assurance that one has obtained knowledge of *God's* will for the conduct of man's life. If these authors were not 'inspired', or if they were as 'partial' in their writings as anyone else, the best one could claim would be that one had obtained knowledge of what these authors believed (or hoped or, perhaps for selfish reasons, wanted others to believe) to be God's will. Some of the other characteristics which Locke ascribes to Scripture are, however, clearly imposed on it because of what he took to be involved in reasoning, because of what he took to be right methodic procedure.

I have illustrated this theme in terms of the two assumptions that all the ideas which are signified by the words of Scripture are composed out of simple ideas; that these are commonly accessible in the experience of a corporeal rational being, since simple ideas are knowable apart from any particular context.

2

It is of interest to note that, in the *Essay Concerning Human Understanding,* Locke claims to be an 'Under-Labourer'. With respect to *some* of their works this label fits both Descartes and Locke. But in other works, the activity of both goes well beyond what is implied by this label; for both are also Master-Builders. The claim about being an 'Under-Labourer' we find in the 'Epistle' which Locke prefaced to the *Essay:*

> But every one must not hope to be a Boyle, or a Sydenham; and in an Age that produces such Masters, as the Great--Huygenius, and the incomparable Mr. Newton, with some others of that Strain; 'tis Ambition enough to be employed as an Under-Labourer in clearing Ground a little, and removing some of the Rubbish, that lies in the way to Knowledge . . .

From the *Essay's* contents we know what being an 'Under-Labourer' entails. It involves making clear that one should not presume to have innate knowledge; that one should not get entangled in the medieval web of talk about 'substantial forms' and 'final causality'. Doctrines like these constitute some of the 'Rubbish' which Locke believed needed removal. But there is another side to this coin. If we cannot be 'arm-chair scientists' in any parts of realms like medicine and physics, then we are limited in them to careful observation of what we find constantly conjoined in our experience, and we must be content with probability rather than with absolute certainty. This statement embodies positive injunctions, one of which is a prescription of procedure for gaining what approaches *practical* certainty in sciences concerned with 'substances'. Soon Locke turns out to be more than an 'Under-Labourer'. For he not only presents procedural rules for sciences like medicine and physics; he also provides the methodological principles for political theory and a hermeneutics for theology. And in these latter areas he was hardly satisfied to be an 'Under-Labourer'. To the extent that he was an 'Under-Labourer' in areas like these, he 'cleared Ground', for example, for his own work in theology through 'removing some of the Rubbish' by means of the argument presented in the *Essay's* chapter 'Of Enthusiasm'. And, as we just saw, this coin's other side provides prescriptions for correct procedure in both theology and political theory. These prescriptions, scattered throughout the last three Books of the *Essay*, I have discussed in terms of what I have called the empiricist principle, the principle of resolution, and the principle of composition.

In the previous chapter we have seen to what extent Locke was not just an 'Under-Labourer' in his theological writings. And in Chapter VII we saw that he was no mere 'Under-Labourer' in political theory either. In both of these fields he developed his own position through applying to the respective sorts of subject-matter the methodological principles enunciated in the *Essay* for the development of general knowledge. Thus, in the *Second Treatise,* it is through the application of the method of resolution and composition that Locke attempts to provide an alternative to the position presented in the opening paragraph of that work, to the position '. . . that all Government in the World is the product only of Force and Violence, and that Men live together by no other Rules but that of Beasts, where the strongest carries it, and so lay a Foundation for perpetual Disorder and Mischief, Tumult, Sedition and Rebellion'. Application of this method leads to an articulation of a political theory founded on reason. Once men act on the precepts of this theory, they have mastered the threat of tyranny of the strongest. If a government created by means of a contract among people who act rationally were to become 'degenerate' through usurpation of power, the people may revolt. In that case revolution is not an act of 'Mischief, Tumult, Sedition and Rebellion'; instead, it is an 'Appeal . . . to Heaven' (§ 242). God is not on the side of force, but on the side of reason.

3

Reflection on works in which Locke clearly presents himself as a Master-Builder easily leads one to a recognition of important relations between these works. The most illuminating example of such a relation is this: the same methodological stance underlies the argument both of the *Second Treatise* and of the theological

works. One could speak of a 'methodological symmetry" among
these works. That such a symmetry exists needs no proof beyond
that which may be gleaned from the two preceding chapters. Other
examples of important relations, in terms of the specific contents
of these works, can be brought easily to mind. For instance: some
of the most crucial doctrines of the *Second Treatise* are supported
by conclusions reached in the theological works. The *Second
Treatise* states that revolution is legitimate when a government
ceases to act in terms of the principles of 'Right Reason'. Revolution is legitimate because God commands that government be
founded on and act in terms of these principles. For the Scriptures
tell us that God's will for man is that he act in accordance with the
dictates of 'Right Reason'. Christianity itself is a 'plain, simple,
reasonable thing' (R188). A government which rules through the
might of the strongest rather than through the right of reason is a
government which acts against the will of God as revealed in the
Scriptures. It is, thus, clear that there is a far greater coherence
among Locke's works than commentators have often granted:
methodological principles presented in the *Essay* structure the
positions we find in the *Second Treatise* and in the theological
works; doctrines presented in the theological works support conclusions reached in the *Second Treatise*.

4

The methodological symmetry which exists in the works of Locke
derives from his view of the nature of reasoning. In the opening
pages of this study I drew attention to Maurice Cranston's words
in which he evaluates Locke as one who 'changed' man's 'ways of
thinking'. This is an evaluation as applicable to Descartes as it is
to Locke. Indeed, as I have shown, it may be said to be more
applicable to Descartes than it is to Locke, for in many ways Locke
did little more than adapt Cartesian methodological principles to
an 'empiricist' outlook.

In the *Discourse on Method* Descartes writes that 'reason is a
universal instrument which can serve for all contingencies' (HR1,
116; AT6, 57). He believes that through its consistent application
we can 'render ourselves the masters and possessors of nature'
(HR1, 119; AT6, 62). In a later work the crucial step towards such
mastery is said to consist in 'a perfect knowledge of all things that

man can know, both for the conduct of his life and the invention of all the arts' (HR1, 203–4; AT9-2, 2). Through the consistent application of the method of resolution and composition we are to attain the happy state of a life lived in harmony with God's will and with the desires of fellow men, a life free from bodily suffering and untrammelled by great physical exertion expended in providing for daily bodily needs. Can we call Descartes an 'Under-Labourer' at all? He certainly never spoke of himself in terms as humble as these! But I think we can and should. Descartes's work in that role consists in making explicit the workings of reason, in providing an explicit statement of the method of resolution and composition. Once this task was accomplished in the *Rules for the Direction of the Mind* and in the early parts of the *Discourse on Method*, he proceeded to a rigorous application of these principles in the areas of metaphysics, mathematics, medicine, and physics. In the first of these, he sought to provide the foundations for the latter three; in medicine and physics, he attempted to make real the mastery over nature. For political reasons Descartes considered it the better part of wisdom to refrain from applying his method systematically to theological issues; death prevented him from extending it to the realm of 'morals'. But before the end of the century in which Descartes presented his method, it was applied by Locke in politics as the key to provide a theory which was to open the door to temporal security, and in theology to reveal the way to eternal bliss. Thus Descartes's ideal of 'mastery' seemed well on its way towards realization: in his own works the application of the method promised alleviation of bodily suffering and mitigation of man's daily burden through power over nature; in those of Locke, it provided a blueprint for the temporal enjoyment of life, liberty, and estate, and opened the way to a life lived in temporal and eternal harmony with God. Through the application of the method of resolution and composition man was promised the overcoming of suffering, drudgery, tyranny, and the fear of hell.

5

We have seen that for Descartes the efficacy of resolution and composition is founded on his view of reason as a faculty which gives man absolutely trustworthy information. One might say that, in a sense, the problem of the trustworthiness of reason has come full circle as we move from Descartes to Locke. For Descartes, there was the need to attempt to show that the results obtained through reason are absolutely trustworthy, the need to show that proceeding by resolution and composition is the way we must travel if we are to gain knowledge which can be considered unshakeable. There was the need to show that reason is autonomous, that neither devil nor God is able to mislead man when he scrupulously applies the method of resolution and composition. The question whether reason might possibly be fallible never arises for Locke in the *Essay*. And in the *Paraphrase* we are presented with a picture of a God who, when he reveals to man the way to live in accordance with his will, presents this way in such a manner that man cannot come to knowledge of it unless he applies the principles of this methodology to revelation. Thus, for man in his creaturely and temporal context, the principles of this methodology are held to be absolute: God must use them if he wants to be understood by man.

<h1 style="text-align:center">6</h1>

The reductionism implicit in the application of the principle of resolution has been seen to be accompanied by the belief that the end results of such a reduction are clear and distinct 'atomic' items. The reductionism of this methodology goes well beyond the proper and necessary activity of *making distinctions* as a step in the attempt to gain knowledge. But one's possessing the capacity to make distinctions does not necessarily entail that one has the further ability for *absolutely separating* from its context that which has been so distinguished, and then for intellectually grasping the full meaning of such a contextless item. Neither does the activity of making distinctions presuppose that whatever it is one attempts to understand is of such a nature that a reductionistic analysis is a legitimate step in the process which leads to an understanding of it. For Descartes, only an item which can be fully grasped by the intellect is a 'clear' item; and only an item which can be grasped entirely in separation from any specific context may become one which he calls 'distinct'. The final paragraphs of the *Essay's* 'Epistle to the Reader' make clear that Locke's use of 'determined' or 'determinate' is like Descartes's use of 'clear and distinct'. The use of this terminology alone therefore already indicates that both Descartes and

Locke take man to possess the power of separating items entirely from their context and then obtaining knowledge of such items in isolation. It further shows that they both assume that whenever one attempts to understand something—unless such an item is already of an 'atomic' nature, as is any simple idea in the framework of epistemology, or as is the concept of an *individual* in the framework of political theory—it will prove to be of such a nature that a reductionistic analysis leads to knowledge of it. As we have seen, the foundations of all of what they take to be certain and systematic are, for both Descartes and Locke, to be found in the intuitive grasp of items which are 'clear and distinct' or 'determinate'.

7

Many contemporary philosophers and scientists have rejected the notion that anything can be known strictly in terms of itself. This growing conviction about the impossibility of knowledge of anything *per se* has not led to a situation in which the methodological stance of the reductionism which we have seen to accompany this doctrine has been fully overcome. One need only mention the position of 'individualism' in politics and economics to be reminded of the fact that this stance is certainly not totally absent from the contemporary scene. Perhaps Ryle did not overstate the case all that much in the words to which I drew attention at the beginning of this study. It may indeed not be 'much of an exaggeration to say that one cannot pick up a sermon, a novel, a pamphlet or a treatise and be in any doubt, after reading a few lines, whether it was published before or after the publication of Locke's *Essay Concerning Human Understanding*'. Ryle may well be right in his implication that these words of his are as germane to many sermons, novels, pamphlets and treatises written in the twentieth century, as to many of those written in the eighteenth or nineteenth. To what extent some treatises of the seventeenth century were structured by the method of resolution and composition has been the subject of this study in terms of an analysis of the major writings of Descartes and Locke. This analysis has at the same time revealed the important presuppositions which are implicit in this methodological stance. To the extent that these (in Cranston's words) 'changed ways of thinking' continue to be manifested in contemporary thought and practice they, like any other 'way of thinking', need to be submitted to a thorough critique. As a preliminary but necessary step to such a critique, one must understand the nature of these 'ways of thinking', and one must be able to discern the presuppositions on which they rest. Because they cover in detail the first important articulations and implementations of these 'ways of thinking', my studies in this book are meant to be contributions towards the gaining of such an understanding and towards the deepening of such a critique.

BIBLIOGRAPHICAL NOTE

Since there exist excellent and comprehensive bibliographies on both Descartes and Locke, I shall in my own bibliography list only such works as have been cited in the text. For further references, I refer the reader to the following works.

Christophersen, H. O., *A Bibliographical Introduction to the Study of John Locke*, Oslo, 1930.

Doney, W., *Descartes, A Collection of Critical Essays*, New York, 1967.

—— 'Some Recent Work on Descartes: A Bibliography', *Philosophy Research Archives*, Vol. II, 1976.

Hall, R. and Woolhouse, R. S., 'Forty Years of Work on John Locke', *Philosophical Quarterly*, July and Oct. 1970.

—— 'More Addenda to the Locke Bibliography', *Locke Newsletter*, 1970.

Sebba, G., *Bibliographia Cartesiana: A Critical Guide to the Descartes Literature 1800–1960*, The Hague, 1964.

BIBLIOGRAPHY

(including only works cited in the text)

PRIMARY SOURCES

Descartes

Adam, C. and Tannery, P., *Œuvres de Descartes*, Paris, 1965–75.

Anscombe, E. and Geach, P. T., *Descartes, Philosophical Writings*, London, 1954.

Cottingham, J., *Descartes' Conversation with Burman*, Oxford, 1976.

Haldane, E. S. and Ross, G. R. T., *The Philosophical Works of Descartes*, Vols. I and II, Cambridge, 1911.

Kenny, A. J. P., *Descartes, Philosophical Letters*, Oxford, 1970.

Olscamp, P. J., *Discourse on Method, Optics, Geometry, and Meteorology*, New York, 1965.

Locke

Works of John Locke, London, 1823; reprinted by Scientia Verlag Aalen, 1963.

Laslett, P., *John Locke, Two Treatises of Government*, revised edn., Cambridge, 1963.

Nidditch, P. H., *John Locke, An Essay concerning Human Understanding*, Oxford, 1975.

von Leyden, W., ed., *John Locke, Essays on the Law of Nature*, Oxford, 1954.

SECONDARY SOURCES

Aaron, Richard I., *John Locke* (3rd edn.), Oxford, 1971.

Abrams, P., *John Locke: Two Tracts on Government*, Cambridge, 1967.

Alquié, F., *La Découverte métaphysique de l'homme chez Descartes*, Paris, 1950.

Aristotle, *Politics*, translated by Benjamin Jowett, published in Richard McKeon's *The Basic Works of Aristotle*, New York, 1941.

Axtell, James L., *The Educational Writings of John Locke*, Cambridge, 1968.

Barr, James, *Old and New in Interpretation*, London, 1966.

Beck, L. J., *The Method of Descartes*, Oxford, 1952.

Bennett, Jonathan, *Locke, Berkeley, Hume, Central Themes*, Oxford, 1971.

Boutroux, P., *L'Imagination et les mathématiques selon Descartes*, Paris, 1900.

Buchdahl, G., 'Descartes' Anticipation of a "Logic of Scientific Discovery"', *Scientific Change*, ed. A. C. Crombie, London, 1963.

Caton, H., *The Origins of Subjectivity*, New Haven and London, 1973.

Collins, J., *Descartes' Philosophy of Nature*, A.P.Q. Monograph No. 5, Oxford, 1971.

Cranston, M., *John Locke, A Biography*, London, 1957.

Crombie, A. C., *Robert Grosseteste and the Origins of Experimental Science*, Oxford, 1953.

Curley, E. M., *Descartes against the Skeptics*, Oxford, 1978.

Doney, W., 'The Cartesian Circle', *Journal of the History of Ideas*, Vol. XVI, 1955, pp. 324–38.

—— ed., *Descartes, A Collection of Critical Essays*, Garden City, N.Y., 1967.

Dunn, John, 'The Politics of Locke in England and America in the eighteenth century', in John W. Yolton, *John Locke, Problems and Perspectives*, pp. 45–80.

Frankfurt, H. G., 'Memory and the Cartesian Circle', *Philosophical Review*, Vol. LXXI, 1962, pp. 504–11.

—— 'Descartes' Validation of Reason', in W. Doney, ed., *Descartes, A Collection of Critical Essays*, pp. 209–26; first published in *American Philosophical Quarterly*, Vol. II, No. 2, 1965.

—— *Demons, Dreamers, and Madmen*, New York, 1970.

Gauthier, D., 'Reason and Maximization', *Canadian Journal of Philosophy*, Vol. IV, No. 3, 1975.

Gewirth, A., 'Experience and the Non-Mathematical in the Cartesian Method', *Journal of the History of Ideas*, Vol. 2, 1941, pp. 183–210.
—— 'The Cartesian Circle Reconsidered', *The Journal of Philosophy*, Vol. LXVII, No. 19, 1970, pp. 668–85.
Gouhier, H., *Essais sur Descartes*, Paris, 1949.
Grotius, H., *De Jure Belli ac Pacis Libri Tres*, 1625.
Habermas, J., *Technick und Wissenschaft als Ideologie*, Frankfurt am Main, 1968.
Hamlyn, D. W., *The Theory of Knowledge*, London, 1970.
Hartshorne, C. and Weiss, P., eds., *Collected Papers of Charles Sanders Peirce*, Cambridge, Mass., 1934.
Hintikka, J. and Remes, U., *The Method of Analysis, Boston Studies in the Philosophy of Science*, Vol. XXV; Synthese Library, Vol. 75; Dordrecht and Boston, 1974.
Horkheimer, M. and Adorno, T. W., *Dialectik der Aufklärung: Philosophische Fragmente*, Frankfurt am Main, 1947.
Kelley, P., 'Locke and Filmer; was Laslett so wrong after all?' *The Locke Newsletter*, No. 8, 1977, pp. 77–91.
Kemp Smith, N., *Studies in the Cartesian Philosophy*, New York, 1962 (first published in 1902).
Kenny, A. J. P., *Descartes, A Study of his Philosophy*, New York, 1968.
—— 'The Cartesian Circle and the Eternal Truths', *The Journal of Philosophy*, Vol. LXVII, No. 19, 1970, pp. 685–700.
Klapwijk, J., *Dialektiek der Verlichting*, Amsterdam, 1976.
Klein, J., *Greek Mathematical Thought and the Origin of Algebra*, Cambridge, Mass. and London, 1968.
Koyré, A., 'Introduction' to *Descartes' Philosophical Writings*, E. Anscombe and P. T. Geach, London, 1954.
Laslett, Peter, Introduction and Notes to *John Locke, Two Treatises of Government*, revised edn., Cambridge, 1963.
McKeon, R., *Selections from Medieval Philosophers*, Vol. I, Modern Students Library, Scribner's.
Mackie, J. L., *Problems from Locke*, Oxford, 1976.
Macpherson, C. B., 'The Social Bearing of Locke's Political Theory', *The Western Political Quarterly*, Vol. VII, 1954; reprinted in Martin and Armstrong, *Locke and Berkeley, A Collection of Critical Essays*.
McRae, R., *The Problem of the Unity of the Sciences: Bacon to Kant*, Toronto, 1961.
Malcolm, N., *Knowledge and Certainty*, Englewood Cliffs, N.J., 1963.
Mandelbaum, M., *Philosophy, Science, and Sense Perception: Historical and Critical Studies*, Baltimore, 1964.
Marcuse, H., *One Dimensional Man: Studies in the Ideology of Advanced Industrial Society*, London, 1964.

Martin, C. B. and Armstrong, D. M., *Locke and Berkeley, A Collection of Critical Essays*, New York, 1968.

Morris, J., 'Cartesian Certainty', *Australasian Journal of Philosophy*, Vol. 47, No. 2, 1969, pp. 161–8.

Nakhnikian, G., 'The Cartesian Circle Revisited', *American Philosophical Quarterly*, Vol. 4, No. 3, 1967, pp. 251–5.

Nichols, J., *The Works of James Arminius*, Vol. II, Buffalo, 1853.

Polin, Raymond, 'John Locke's conception of freedom', in John W. Yolton, *John Locke, Problems and Perspectives*.

Popkin, Richard H., *The History of Scepticism from Erasmus to Descartes*, New York, 1964.

Randall, J. H., 'The Development of Scientific Method in the School of Padua', *Journal of the History of Ideas*, Vol. I, No. 2, 1940, pp. 177–206. (This article is reprinted in *Renaissance Essays*, eds. Paul O. Kristeller and Philip P. Wiener, New York, 1968, pp. 217–51.)

—— *The Career of Philosophy*, Vol. I, New York, 1962.

Ring, M., 'Descartes' Intentions', *Canadian Journal of Philosophy*, Vol. III, 1973–4, pp. 27–49.

Russell, B., *The Concept of Mind*, London, 1921.

—— *Human Knowledge. Its Scope and Limits*, New York, 1948.

Ryle, G., 'John Locke', *Critica*, Vol. I, No. 2, 1967.

Schouls, P. A., 'Communication, Argumentation, and Presupposition in Philosophy', *Philosophy and Rhetoric*, Vol. II, No. 4, 1969, pp. 183–99.

—— 'Cartesian Certainty and the "Natural Light"', *Australasian Journal of Philosophy*, Vol. 48, No. 1, 1970, pp. 116–19.

—— 'Review of Curley, Williams, and Wilson', *Philosophical Books*, Vol. 20, No. 2, May 1979.

Smith, D. E. and Latham, M. L., *The Geometry of René Descartes*, Dover edn., 1954 (first published in 1925).

Stout, A. K., 'The Basis of Knowledge in Descartes', *Mind*, N.S., Vol. XXXVIII, Nos. 151 and 152, 1929, pp. 330–42, 458–72; reprinted in W. Doney, ed., *Descartes, A Collection of Critical Essays*, pp. 169–91

Strauss, Leo, *The Political Philosophy of Hobbes*, Oxford, 1936

Tipton, I. C., *Locke on Human Understanding*, Oxford, 1977.

von Leyden, W., *Seventeenth-Century Metaphysics*, London, 1968.

Watkins, J. W. N., *Hobbe's System of Ideas*, London, 1965.

Williams, B., 'The Certainty of the Cogito', in W. Doney, ed., *Descartes, A Collection of Critical Essays*, pp. 88–107. (This paper first appeared in French in *Cahiers de Royaumont, Philosophie No. IV: La philosophie analytique*, Paris, 1962, pp. 40–57.)

—— *Descartes: The Project of Pure Enquiry*, Hassocks, Sussex, 1978.

Wilson, Margaret Dauler, *Descartes*, London, 1978.

Wittgenstein, L., *Philosophical Investigations*, Oxford, 1953.

Yolton, J. W., *John Locke and the Way of Ideas*, Oxford, 1956.

—— ed., *John Locke, Problems and Perspectives*, Cambridge, 1969.

—— *Locke and the Compass of Human Understanding*, Cambridge, 1970.

—— 'Philosophy of Science from Descartes to Kant', *History of Science*, Vol. 10, 1971.

—— *The Locke Reader*, Cambridge, 1977.

SUBJECT INDEX

INDEX OF PERSONS

Randall, John Herman, Jr., 5, 10, 15
Regius, H., 32
Ring, Merrill, 90n., 94n.
Russell, Bertrand, 101n.
Ryle, Gilbert, 3, 21, 259

Sanchez, François, 91
Sextus, Empiricus, 91
Shaftesbury, First Earl of, 214
Smith, D. E., 66n., 72
Stout, A. K., 56n., 90n., 114n.
St. Thomas, 9n.

Tipton, I. C., 150n.

von Leyden, W., 22n., 204n.

Watkins, J. W. N., 4n.
Williams, Bernard, 1n., 34n., 145n.
Wilson, Margaret Dauler, 1n.
Wittgenstein, L., 37n.

Yolton, J. W., 19, 22n., 150f., 161n.

Zabarella, Giacomo, 5f., 10f., 15